THE WHITELAW MEMOIRS

The Whitelaw Memoirs

William Whitelaw

HEADLINE

Copyright © 1989 William Whitelaw

First published in 1989
by Aurum Press Ltd

First published in paperback in 1990
by HEADLINE BOOK PUBLISHING PLC

10 9 8 7 6 5 4 3 2 1

Illustrations kindly supplied by the following sources: BBC
Enterprises Ltd, 19; Courtland Press Bureau, 4; Cumbrian
Newspapers Ltd, 10, 21, 24; Rowell Friers, 14; Gale & Polden
Ltd, 5; D. A. Grant, 3; Home Office (R. W. Speirs), 15;
Pacemaker Press, 17, 22; Syndication International Ltd, 12;
University of St Andrews Library, 7; Ian Wright, 8. Other
photographs are taken from the author's archives. While every
effort has been made to contact copyright holders, anyone who
has been inadvertently omitted should apply to the publishers,
who will be pleased to credit them in full in any subsequent
editions.

ISBN 0 7472 3348 9

Typeset in 10/12¼ pt English Times
by Colset Private Limited, Singapore

Printed and bound in Great Britain by
Collins, Glasgow

HEADLINE BOOK PUBLISHING PLC
Headline House
79 Great Titchfield Street
London W1P 7FN

To Celia

Acknowledgments

In writing this personal account of my life, I have realized how many people have helped and supported me on my way. Many of them are mentioned individually in the text, and others collectively. I want to thank them all.

In particular, I must express my real gratitude to those who have helped me in the production of this book. Tom Arnold persuaded me to write it and thereafter gave me constant help and encouragement, together with all those involved at Aurum Press. Martin Gilbert has given me much valued advice. Nick True did extensive research work and reminded me of many important details. My secretary, Liz Huckle, typed the whole book and in the process interpreted my dictation and my handwriting – a major task in itself. David Howell, Harry Tuzo, Robert Ford and Philip Woodfield read the manuscript of my time in Northern Ireland, with which they were associated, and gave me considerable assistance on various details. Brian Cubbon, who was so closely associated with my work at the Home Office, also gave me invaluable help on that part of the book.

Contents

Early Days

My earliest memories are rather sad. As a child of three I learnt that my father had died as a result of his wounds in the 1914–18 war, just a year after I was born. I cannot remember exactly how I found out, but I do recollect going to bed that night and crying. But, like most young children, I had a short memory and I soon put this tragedy behind me.

I was right to do so, because my mother, a remarkable lady, did her utmost to make up for the loss; she never married again and devoted herself to my upbringing. I never realized quite what I owed her until she died, nearly sixty years later, exactly ten years to the day before my resignation from the Government in January 1988.

If, in my childhood, I suffered from the lack of a full family background – for I had no brothers or sisters either – I enjoyed other substantial advantages. My grandfather, also William Whitelaw, was generous and kind to me and I came to regard him as a hero, feeling proud whenever I was told that I closely resembled him in many ways. He and my grandmother must have found me a sad reminder of their own family tragedy, for they had lost not only my father but three sons as a result of service in the First World War and I was their only grandchild. I did not

1

see much of my grandfather as a child, because he was fully occupied during the 1920s and 1930s as Chairman of the London and North-Eastern Railway, and my mother was naturally possessive of my childhood at Nairn in the far north of Scotland. Yet he had a most powerful influence on my life, for he provided generously for my upbringing and schooling. As a result, my mother was able to ensure for us both a secure, comfortable and relaxed home atmosphere, and for me a good education – advantages denied many children.

These circumstances – both the advantages and the disadvantages – had a profound effect on my character, attitude to life and relations with my fellow human-beings. On the one hand, I grew up rather a lonely, shy boy, surprising as that may seem to those who have known me in later years. I hated parties with other children, who found me easy to bully. Shyness as a child can cause unhappiness and, of course, breeds on itself. But the experience of it can be a positive advantage in later life, because it enables one to understand fellow sufferers and to be sensitive to their feelings, gaining one many friends and getting the best out of those with whom one works.

On the other hand, the obvious benefits of a well-kept home and shelter from some of the harsher challenges of life, such as I enjoyed, is often alleged to produce in later life what is called a patrician attitude. Some Tories, like me, are criticized for this supposed failing, which is said to lead to a moral softness, in contrast with the toughness of those who have had to fight their way in life. I regard this comparison as a gross over-simplification. Above all, I maintain that in politics, as in life, one must be true to one's self. I am not ashamed to be regarded as sympathetic to the anxieties of those whom life appears to be treating harshly.

Nor do I accept that such feelings are a sign of weakness, provided that they are accompanied by an inner toughness where necessary and justified.

This was the background against which I spent my first eight years at Nairn, in a house with beautiful views over the Moray Firth and the northern hills beyond. While I still feel nostalgic about that view and everything to do with Nairn, I have grown to hate and fear the sea. My family claims that I am liable to be seasick on even the shortest ferry crossing. As far as I am concerned, thank goodness for air travel.

My other memories of those early days are of lessons with an awe-inspiring lady who ran a small school at Nairn, and of an unhappy spell at the local boys' school where I was bullied and learnt little. Happier days were spent playing on the beach with contemporaries such as Ludovic Kennedy who came to Nairn for their summer holidays. I remember picnics on the neighbouring moors, motoring there in the 'dicky' of my mother's Calthorpe car, then considered rather dashing for a woman driver.

But Nairn's greatest influence on my life and character was that it was responsible for my introduction to the game of golf, which has given me much pleasure, enormous frustration and many friends.

My mother had one strongly held and wise view about life, which I must admit I did not always appreciate. It is no use, she said, being a big fish in a small pond. You must aim to be a large fish in a large pond. In furtherance of this theory, I was sent to school 500 miles away from Nairn in the south of England. Looking back now, I am profoundly grateful to her; but when I set off to preparatory school in Berkshire at the age of eight, I felt otherwise. Nor was I encouraged by my mother's obvious misery and apprehension at being parted from me. I was desperately homesick and formed a view which I have never had any reason to change: small boys are extremely nasty to each other. What is more, the lonelier the boy, the nastier the others will be to him. Gradually, though, I settled down. And I suppose I eventually became as nasty to other small boys as they had been to me, although I like to think not. Anyway, we were all united in our hatred of the headmaster, who appeared to enjoy beating us with a fives bat.

I did not shine at work, although I did well enough and, having a good eye, was quite successful at ball games, particularly cricket. Apparently the school had a good reputation and was recommended to my mother, but it was clearly going downhill while I was there. Not long afterwards it was closed down and the premises sold to another school, which has apparently prospered there ever since. I can only presume that my mother's choice turned out to be an unlucky one in the event. Certainly the scholastic standard must have been falling, because even though I was quite near the top of the school academically, my mother was told that I was unlikely to get into Winchester, her first choice of public school. In any case, her selection was unpopular with my grandfather who wanted me to follow my father to that fine Scottish school, Glenalmond. And so, hoping that I would fail to get into Winchester, he agreed to my sitting, the special examination. To his fury – and my mother's delight – I passed it successfully and set out once again on the long journey south.

It is possible to argue endlessly about the merits of the great public schools. But they have one characteristic in common: they command the loyalty of the vast majority of those who are educated at them. Certainly I feel that I owe a great deal to Winchester College. As a school it has an excellent reputation for its high standards of education, and the standards at the top ensure that whatever your basic ability you have to work and, even more important, learn how to work. That valuable lesson has enabled me over the years to withstand all the immense pressures which senior Cabinet Ministers have to bear.

I cannot claim that I shone at Winchester, either at work or at games, but I made steady progress at both. What is more, I began for the first time in my life to develop a little confidence in myself. I owed much of this to a remarkable housemaster, Major Robertson, always known as 'Bobber'. He had the largest feet I have ever seen and was in many ways an eccentric. He understood boys, though, and he took a special interest in each one of us. For example, he knew that I was passionately keen on golf and enjoyed cricket and other games, but was no athlete, had no ear for music and showed little interest in birdlife and butterflies. And so he was determined to redress the balance. He had to retire hurt in his efforts to make me a musician, but he did succeed in teaching me to appreciate and listen to good music, which I have found comforting ever since. I was not built to run and could never have won a race, but he made me try. And his delight was complete when I finished much higher up the field than he expected in a cross-country race and was then violently sick. As I sat on the ground looking white and miserable, he approached me, saying, 'Splendid performance! Gave everything you've got. Full marks for guts.' I felt proud, but I never ran again!

As for birdlife and butterflies, I could be seen on a summer afternoon in the Hampshire countryside with my bicycle, armed with a list of butterflies to catch and birds to observe and record. I suppose it did me some good. At least I have never forgotten an experience which I have never sought to repeat.

But this remarkable man's real legacy to those in his charge was that he cared for us in after life. All those who were in his house must have experienced those extraordinary letters, totally illegible and written all round every page. They pursued us wherever we went, right throughout the war and indeed thereafter until his death. In my case they continued long enough for him to give me his strong views on various political events at the start of my political career. If Major Robertson had lived longer I would certainly have received some stern and critical comments on my ministerial responsibilities. Many of them would undoubtedly have been justified, and I would have paid attention to all of them, such is the trust inspired by a really understanding schoolmaster.

The final comment on 'Bobber's' influence on me came on my Government resignation in a letter from Lord James of Rusholme, the highly distinguished educationalist who was an assistant master at Winchester when I was there and for a time my house tutor. In his letter he said simply, 'The Bobber would have been proud of you.' Shades of the cross-country race, I reflected. My political career had been a long race. I did not come first. I suspect I surprised many people who knew me by finishing as high as I did. I was stricken with illness in the end and, come to think of it, I had given it all that I had got.

Just as surprising to those who knew me in my school days was the climax to my life as a Wykehamist. On 12 May 1984 I was given the honour of being received *Ad Portas* by the school. I was very proud of this recognition as it is given to few Old Wykehamists. I was also delighted that my eldest grandson, Mark Cunliffe-Lister, was present as a member of the school, although I suspect he may have had to endure some leg-pulling and rude remarks about his grandfather.

The ceremony in itself is a frightening experience. The recipient, or perhaps more appropriately at that moment the victim, enters the courtyard accompanied by the Warden, in my case my old friend, Lord Aldington, and the headmaster. The school surrounds the distinguished old courtyard which dates back to the days of William of Wykeham. The senior college prefect then addresses the recipient, largely in Latin. You are expected to make some of your reply in Latin also. I had taken the precaution of enlisting the help of an excellent classical scholar in the Cabinet Office who translated for me and coached me in pronunciation. To some extent this confounded those in the audience who knew that at my best, some fifty years ago, I could hardly have been described as a Latin scholar. All seemed to pass off well, except that a high wind blowing round the courtyard made standing still quite an achievement.

I have one final reflection on Winchester College which I know applies to many old public schools whose history dates back hundreds of years. They have many fine old buildings but by modern standards they provide somewhat antiquated teaching accommodation. I remember showing some of the classrooms to some friends well acquainted with modern state schools. 'Surely,' they said, 'these are just for show. The boys can't be taught here.' I replied that this was just where the cleverest Winchester scholars were indeed taught. This only proves to me what I have always believed: good education depends far more on atmosphere and teaching than it does on the actual school buildings.

And so it was with some of the living accommodation in the houses at Winchester. Just before I was privileged to open the excellent modernized accommodation in my old house a few years ago, I showed my wife round the buildings as they were. She was horrified and asked what changes had been made since I was there. I replied, 'The earth closets of my day are now water closets.' My wife, who had been shielded from such experiences by having four daughters and no sons, was not impressed.

From Winchester my thoughts turned to university. Examinations were not as sophisticated when I was being educated as they are today. Nor was university entry nearly as competitive. Clearly, educational opportunities are now far more widespread and that must be good. But I admit to feeling secret relief that I did not have to undergo the pressures which my grandchildren have to endure today. In my time there was what can only be described as the rather peaceful examination called School Certificate, with credits in five or six subjects ensuring entry to a university. There was, however, a snag. One of the subjects had to be elementary mathematics, for which I had little natural ability. The eminent mathematician who taught me adopted a realistic attitude. 'I despair of teaching you how to solve even the simplest mathematical problems,' he said. 'But you have a good memory. You must learn all the formulae and at the examination answer those questions based on them first. Then you will probably pass even if your lack of natural ability for figures becomes all too obvious in the others.' I did so and passed with the necessary credit. When this splendid teacher saw the results he was delighted. 'Now,' he said, 'I shall never have to teach you mathematics again. You must give them up at once.' He didn't, and I did.

Armed with six or so credits in School Certificate, I was accepted by Trinity College, Cambridge, and went up in 1936. I would argue that the immediate pre-war years were not an easy time for undergraduates to get the best out of university life. By the time of the Munich Agreement in

1938, if not before, it was natural for our thoughts to be dominated by the feeling that we would have to fight a war in the near future. That old slogan 'Let us live for today for tomorrow we die' became increasingly attractive, and attention to work, examinations and degrees ever more irrelevant. One of my friends who had considerable academic ability succumbed totally to this mood, with a surprising result. He openly stated that he had given up work. When the final examination day came in the summer of 1939, he attended as required, stayed for the prescribed time but put in no paper. Imagine our surprise, and even more his (for obviously he did not study the results), when his name appeared in the Second Class Honours List. Presumably the examiners thought that his papers had been mislaid and gave him the rating which his tutor considered suitable. Such luck must be rare and such abstention is not to be recommended.

Fortunately, I was driven by two pressures. On the work side, my grandfather, who gave me a generous allowance, made it quite clear that I must obtain a degree. On the games side, I was utterly determined to get a golf blue. This dual purpose was made easier because university golf then, as now, was played in the winter with the university match in March, leaving the summer term for work leading up to the examinations. I adapted my schedule accordingly but it did not leave much time for lectures – golf made them difficult to attend in winter, and hours of desperate cramming from text books occupied all my working hours in summer. And so, as a grand gesture, I gave up lectures, which I have since regretted. I suppose, however, that I have been punished by having to listen to so many speeches for the rest of my life.

At least I gained my objectives. I read law, which I

disliked, for two years and got a Third, and history, which I enjoyed, for my last year and got a moderate Second. At the same time I got my golf blue in my second year, was Secretary of the Cambridge side in 1938–9 and was going to be Captain in 1940, if there had been no war. I thought my grandfather would be pleased by my results when I reported them to him. At first, however, I found him lukewarm. Soon he admitted the reason. He hoped, he said, that I would work hard enough to get a Third like him. 'You have rather overdone it,' he added with a delightful laugh. I remember being particularly thrilled by his characteristically human reaction and determined that I would try to do as well as him in life afterwards.

Because of these overriding preoccupations and a good deal of idle enjoyment and time spent at parties, I emerged from Cambridge one of the rare subsequent members of the House of Commons who had never been inside the Union or joined any political party. However, I did attend one political meeting when Winston Churchill came to Cambridge to address a rally after Oxford had voted not to fight for King and country. I was enlisted by some of my friends to stand in a group at the door with the purpose of letting in all who said they would vote for King and country and keeping out those who would not give such an assurance. We won – a result widely interpreted as a triumph for Churchill's oratory, although we felt that our tactics had not been given sufficient credit. Little did I know that this was to be the first political experience in the career of a later Whip and Chief Whip in the House of Commons.

The threat of war had persuaded me to join the university Officers' Training Corps and to pass the necessary certificates. At that time, some of my contemporaries were joining the Territorial Army, but I had friends who persuaded me instead to do an attachment with the Scots Guards based on my membership of the university corps. Having taken my degree in 1939, I therefore did an attachment that summer with a Scots Guards battalion at Windsor before war broke out. As a result, I was granted a commission in the Scots Guards soon after the war started in September, without having to undergo further officer training like many of my friends. So ended my education and began the traumatic experience of war service.

Baptism of Fire

I was twenty-one when the war started, a young and inexperienced undergraduate with a very restricted knowledge of life. By the end of the war I was a Major, second in command of a battalion, and had experience of all the pressures inseparable from responsibility for soldiers under one's command in all manner of circumstances. I was married with one child and was still only twenty-seven. We all had to grow up fast and we became old in experience well beyond our years. We were scarred by the horrors and brutalities of war which I suppose we all came to regard as normal. There can be no doubt that our wartime experiences had a profound effect on the lives of all those who took part, and that they are important in judging subsequent actions and, indeed, reactions. On the other hand, whatever our ranks, we all developed the special feelings of comradeship and loyalty to each other which come naturally from mutual experiences, happy and unhappy. What is more, we learnt the value of those selective memories which dwell on the good times and tactfully draw a veil over the days of misery, fear and despair.

I spent my early war days training at Pirbright in Surrey. On the principle that armies tend to train for the war that is past, rather than for the one to come, we became well versed in the minutiae of trench warfare. The older officers enjoyed it, with nostalgic memories of 1914–18. We younger officers regarded it as something of a waste of time, particularly after the German advance through Holland and Belgium and the evacuation at Dunkirk. Peacetime habits also ensured that drill occupied much of our time. Our drill squads must have been hilarious to watch, for our ages varied enormously. We younger ones regarded the thirty-year-olds training with us as very aged, and some of them indeed found an hour in quick time under a Drill Sergeant a considerable test of physical effort. None of us survived easily the period which coincided with everyone wearing a gas mask, whatever they were doing. I cannot recommend twenty minutes' drill, some of it at the double, wearing a gas mask.

My training over, I was sent to the old Croydon Airport as one of the officers on guard. Our guard consisted of a Captain, a retired officer from the 1914–18 war who had been recalled, and two of us Subalterns. The Captain was a splendid character with a large moustache whom we christened 'Blomberg' after the German Field Marshal. Most nights he went to parties in London and returned in a bad temper the next morning. He invariably reprimanded us for idleness and imposed some further duty on us as punishment. 'Mr Whitelaw,' he would say, 'you are very idle. You will go round the guard four times tonight.' It took about an hour and a half to walk round the perimeter and visit all the sentries, who of course enjoyed the joke.

Eventually the inevitable happened. 'Mr Whitelaw, I can tolerate your idleness no longer. You will go round the guard continuously throughout the night.' Dreading the endless walk, the Sergeant on guard had an idea. 'Sir, why don't we take your car?' – in fact one of the old-fashioned

Morris 8s of that time. So off we set and for a time all went well, much to the amusement of the sentries. Then, alas, it began to rain and by about 2 a.m. we bogged down the car at the far end of the airfield; Blomberg usually got back at 4 a.m. However, with the enthusiastic help of all available sentries, we got the Morris going again and returned to base just in time. Next morning, to universal amusement, Blomberg was heard to say, 'A good night's work, Mr Whitelaw.' I never told him the truth, but the members of that detachment never allowed me to forget it. Indeed, to this day I cannot drive past the open space where the Croydon Airfield was without a nostalgic laugh.

Thereafter, for no obvious reason, as my mechanical ability has always been limited, I was made a Transport Officer and eventually sent to the newly formed 3rd Battalion stationed near Loughton in Essex. There we stayed throughout the London blitz, with bombs steadily falling around us without causing too much damage. Then came the day when we were told that we were to be put into tanks and join the Guards Armoured Division. The decision to form such a division caused much derision in the Royal Armoured Corps. Large guardsmen would never be able to climb into the tanks and anyway would be mechanically incompetent, they said. As it happened, the Guards Tank Regiments all acquitted themselves with some distinction, and certainly our guardsmen drivers were most successful at keeping our tanks on the road. I continued my mechanical existence, for I was appointed, amazingly, Technical Adjutant. I was renowned for going round the repair lines with a small yellow stick, hitting the tank on the side and saying, 'Repairs going all right?' Luckily I had some excellent mechanics, who must have had the satisfaction of knowing that they could pull the wool over my eyes whenever they wanted.

Our early training was carried out from Codford Camp on Salisbury Plain. During that time my attention was dominated by getting engaged in December 1942 and married the following February. The immense happiness of my married and family life for the subsequent forty-five years merits separate treatment.

Militarily, the initial excitement of new training began to wear off and increasingly, as we moved to Thoresby Hall in Nottinghamshire and finally to Ashford in Kent, we longed for action. This anxiety was further increased as our brigade was split on reorganization from the Guards Armoured Division, and became the 6th Guards Tank Brigade amid rumours of our disbandment. Eventually, through the intervention of Winston Churchill himself, it is alleged, our brigade was retained with its Churchill tanks and lived on to distinguish itself in France and Germany in 1944. Until then we endured a period of waiting in which it was difficult to keep up morale. I have always thought that it is one of the strange aspects of war that away from the action one longs for the battle, and as soon as the horrors of the battle are experienced one secretly craves to leave the action again as soon as possible.

At last, in the middle of July 1944 – six weeks after D-Day – we were ordered to cross the Channel to Normandy. Our spirits were high, as we were going to take a real part in the war. But for the squadron, which by then I commanded, there was yet another setback. Our convoy encountered a severe storm in the Channel and our tanks in the ship's hold broke loose from their chains. Our efforts to secure them, once loose, while rolling about in the ship when we were being seasick, are not among the happiest experiences of my life. Nor did my morale rise when the ship's commander told me that we would have to heave to and become, in his words, 'a sitting duck for any U-boat'. Fortunately no U-boat appeared. We returned home, secured our tanks, crossed the Channel in perfectly calm weather and rejoined the battalion at Bayeux, who were overjoyed to see us, as they were convinced that our ship had been sunk.

Baptism of fire in war is inevitably a traumatic experience. No doubt for many people it may come in a short and minor incident, and so it may not be so deeply imprinted on their minds as it is in my case. For those, like me, who served in the 3rd Tank Battalion Scots Guards our first experience of war came in a major battle, and thus – to coin a phrase associated with a later period of my life – it was indeed a 'short, sharp shock'.

After about a week's preparation near Bayeux, we learnt that in co-operation with our old training friends, the 15th (Scottish) Division, we were to be used in the breakout from the Allied bridgehead. And so, on 30 July 1944, came our baptism of fire – the Battle of Caumont.

It is strange that in some particulars my memory of that day is as vivid as if it were yesterday. I shall therefore describe some of my reactions as they were at the time. If, in retrospect, they seem as naive to anyone reading this account as they do to me, I do not feel that I should fail to record them. On the contrary, if they show the reactions of a young man of twenty-six experiencing for the first time the full horror of war, they may have some interest. In any event, my state of mind at the time is important if the full effect of this one day on my whole attitude to life is to be understood.

I was commanding a squadron of fifteen tanks with five members in each crew. We had been training together for some years and all knew each other intimately. In fact, we were a harmonious family, although of course we came from widely differing backgrounds. That morning, when all our training was to be put to the test, we were strangely silent. It seemed no moment for jokes or leg-pulling. Nor, above all else, was it a moment when anyone wanted to show his emotions. For myself, I experienced for the first time in full measure that fundamental challenge of leadership: the need to keep calm and attempt to inspire confidence in those around you when you feel anything but confident yourself. We all seemed to experience a sense of relief as we mounted our tanks and moved forward to the start line.

Soon we reached the top of the Caumont ridge, which was the front line of the British troops, and saw the valley of the Normandy countryside across which we were to attack. It was part of what we called the *bocage* country. The fields were small, the hedgerows high and thick, with some trees in them. It was of course ideal defensive country and the German infantry was well dug in, with prepared positions in the hedgerows.

The enemy appreciation had been that tanks would not be able to cross such terrain. They had reckoned without that magnificent cross-country vehicle, the Churchill tank. We joined up with our own infantry, the Argyll and Sutherland Highlanders, and soon came under intense enemy mortar and small arms fire. Fortunately for us, tanks provide good protection against such fire and as we advanced we neutralized it with our own machine guns. We sprayed each hedgerow in turn before advancing across the intervening fields. Throughout this slow but steady advance the strangest sensation was that we never seemed to see any German troops, dead or alive. And yet afterwards we learnt that many had been killed and many more surrendered to the infantry accompanying us. I cannot explain this. I simply record it as a fact and an experience shared by others, including my own tank crew.

Gradually the enemy fire increased and the infantry line was brought to a halt. At this moment there was a loud bang as my tank landed over a particularly high hedgerow. My driver's single-word comment said it all – we had landed on a mine and our track had been broken in the blast. With my tank out of action, I summoned one of my Sergeants, left him and my own crew with the disabled tank and went on in his to maintain command. The story was told afterwards with great glee by both crews that I moved from one tank to another under fire with truly remarkable speed. Even in those days I was not renowned for my gymnastic prowess.

Almost immediately after this mishap our Commanding Officer, Colonel Dunbar, ordered me and the other leading squadron Commander, Alan Cathcart, to advance with all speed ahead of the infantry under the artillery barrage to a ridge called Les Loges which was our first objective. I remember it as rather an open stretch of ground with a wood on one side rising gently out of the thick hedgerows. As so often in life, apparent success can be rudely shattered, and so it was in this case. We had penetrated the enemy's defences and so our advance to the ridge was quick and uneventful. Once there, we were told to consolidate and maintain our position. Greater experience of war would have taught us that we were now in real danger, as we were isolated from the infantry and their anti-tank guns far behind in the hedgerows. We were therefore at great risk from an armoured counter-attack.

We were not, however, lulled into a totally false sense of security, as I remember issuing instructions to my troop Commanders to be protected behind the ridge and to guard our left flank. None of us, however, appreciated the risk from our left rear, which was to be brilliantly exploited by two German JAGD Panthers equipped with their dangerous 88-mm guns. Shortly before 6 p.m., I was summoned to an order group at the battalion headquarters nearby and travelled to it in a scout car. While there we listened to the BBC news describing the battle. Suddenly we heard heavy firing and loud bangs from my squadron area. I rushed back towards my tank and Sydney Cuthbert, our second-in-command and an outstanding character, went off to investigate in his tank. He had been a regular officer before the war and had been rapidly promoted. Being in a small scout car, I was able to keep comparatively out of sight on the edge of the wood.

All at once on my right I saw something so horrifying that my senses were completely dulled. The turret of Sydney Cuthbert's tank was lifted clean off as the vehicle burst into flames. At that moment it never occurred to me that for an armoured turret to be lifted off and deposited on the ground the tank must have suffered a direct hit from a heavy shell, nor did I realize then that a great friend and his crew must have been instantly killed. Sydney Cuthbert's death was a loss to the Army, as he clearly had a great career ahead of him. It was made all the more tragic for his family as his father had been killed in the Scots Guards during the 1914–18 war.

I cannot explain it, but in my naivety the whole event seemed almost natural. Nor can I understand how I managed to overcome my emotions when, on returning to my tank, I saw two of my other tanks in flames and heard my wireless operator saying, in a matter-of-fact-way, 'I can get no answer from the left troop commanders.'

Only then did we recover from what must have been a

state of shock to realize the full horror. I have often wondered how one is insulated from the real impact at such moments and enabled to carry on. In just five minutes I had lost three tanks and, most tragic of all, the lives of several members of my squadron, who were all my trusted friends and part of the happy family welded together by years of training. What a five minutes of life! The Scots Guards regimental historian, David Erskine, wrote in his book *The Scots Guards 1919–1955*, 'The battalion's first day of battle had been at once glorious, tragic and exceptional.'

There was the glory of a deep penetration of the enemy lines, the virtual destruction of an enemy division and the receipt of a host of congratulatory messages. But then and even now, all these years later, my abiding memory is of the tragedy. Then and now I would gladly have given up all the glory in return for the lives of my friends and colleagues. Nor could I ever quite get away from that awful 'if only' feeling. If only I had guarded the rear more effectively . . . But all that is part of life, and particularly of war. One must always look forward, never back. Yet as I have looked forward and lived through the succeeding years with the many traumatic experiences of a political career, I have never forgotten those five minutes – indeed, they signalled a great change in my attitude to life and to my fellow human-beings. As I reflect on them now I realize how much that experience – for better or worse – profoundly influenced my character and thus my reactions to different events throughout the rest of my life.

Following this fearsome baptism of fire, I was promoted second-in-command of the battalion and some months later was told that I had been awarded a Military Cross. Although obviously pleased at these developments, I could not help reflecting how much happier I would have been had I been able to exchange them for the lives of those killed in my old squadron. I also found myself haunted for a time by the feeling that my leadership had in some way contributed to these casualties.

However, as always in life, time is a good healer. I settled down to the role of closely supporting a Commanding Officer while not actually having a command position myself – something I became accustomed to later in my political life. During the winter of 1944 and early spring of 1945, like other British units, we advanced – sometimes in battle and at other times peacefully in reserve – through Belgium, Holland and into Germany. For a time German resistance was strong and the winter tedious. But as spring came and we crossed the Rhine, German resistance crumbled. My memories of those concluding days of the war are, first, of the sight of dispirited German troops and refugees. The scent of victory may be pleasant but the subsequent degeneration of the losers has a sobering effect. Second, I never forgot my visit to Belsen concentration camp. The countryside around it gave no clue to the horrors inside the compound, and I can readily believe that many Germans in the neighbourhood had little appreciation of what was happening. What can only be described as the total degradation of human life inside was a sight one would never quite forget.

Finally, I always imagined that the ultimate surrender of the enemy would be an exhilarating occasion. For me, in fact, it was not. I was ordered to take the surrender of Lütjenburg, a small town on the Baltic coast of Schleswig-Holstein, which was overflowing with refugees of all sorts. We were met by some smart German officers, beautifully turned out in field boots and breeches, putting to shame our rather dilapidated battle dress. The senior officer saluted and in perfect English declared, 'I surrender Lütjenburg to you and with it all responsibilities.' In typically British fashion, I thanked him rather lamely, not realizing until afterwards what he meant by 'responsibilities'. I had to find accommodation for our soldiers and this could only be done by forcibly evicting on to the streets huge numbers of desperate people. I knew a little German but, alas, '*Heraus*' was the only word necessary, and the reaction was not easy to bear. Yet one had to remember that we had won and our troops had to come first. At that moment there was little pleasure in victory.

However, that pleasure came in the weeks ahead and we settled down in reasonably comfortable accommodation with little to do except enjoy endless parties for those who were being demobilized early. By then I had been accepted as a regular soldier and was appointed a Staff Officer to the 1st Guards Brigade which was destined, before Hiroshima and the Japanese surrender, for an attack on the Japanese mainland. We certainly had little right to criticize the use of atomic bombs. However, by September 1945, we had a new role. We were to go to Palestine, where the British mandate was under terrorist assault from the Jews. And so I set off miserably, leaving my wife and baby girl again, for an extraordinary year in the Middle East.

We found ourselves in a situation which I can compare in some ways with my later experience of Northern Ireland. On the one hand, we were able to enjoy the fascination of the Holy Land, with all its biblical history; on the other hand, we had to undertake the duties of an army of occupation seeking to deal with insurrection and terrorism. Nor could I ever forget, when I was Secretary of State for Northern Ireland, how much as a soldier I had criticized the politicians in London during our actions in Palestine. Life plays strange tricks, for I do not imagine that my actions seemed any more sensible to soldiers in Northern Ireland in 1972-3 than those of Attlee and Ernest Bevin seemed to us in Palestine in 1945-6. For example, we were supposed to control and even prevent illegal immigration from Jews in Europe while, at the same time, they were being encouraged to enter by various rich Arabs, whose interests we were meant to be serving, selling them land for Jewish settlement. We were constantly ordered to search Jewish settlements for arms, when we knew that Jewish intelligence was so good that they were always waiting for us and that we would never find any arms. And it was not made any easier by the fact that we felt considerable sympathy for the Jews, whose herculean efforts in the heat of the day transformed barren land into fertile settlements. And I must admit that my feelings were endorsed when I revisited the area in 1978 – it was then the State of Israel – and saw the total transformation of that country.

In 1946, however, I began to have other preoccupations. My grandfather died and I inherited our family properties and responsibilities near Glasgow. I concluded that my duty to my family meant that I must leave the Army, and in any event I was greatly missing my wife and now two daughters. I therefore applied to resign my commission. After some delay, I gave up my command of the Scots Guards Company at the Guards Training Battalion in Pirbright, where I had started the war seven years before, and returned to civilian life.

As I reflect on those war years, I remember a saying which was often repeated to us when I first joined the regiment: 'Once a Scots Guardsman, always a Scots Guardsman'. Certainly, like all those who served with me, I have remained proud of the regiment to which I owed so much.

Many of my closest friends to this day are those with whom I served. Our regimental reunions of all ranks are highly enjoyable occasions which we do our best to attend. And when I was ill, just before I resigned from the Government at the end of 1987, I was touched by the many letters which I received from Scots Guardsmen who had served with me, many of whom I had not seen for years.

Perhaps the following simple story demonstrates both the value and the strength of the regimental loyalties. During the Falklands Campaign I was a member of the so-called War Cabinet. On the morning of what turned out to be the last day of the campaign, Lord Lewin, the Chief of Staff, was describing the situation to us. At the end he said, looking firmly at me, 'Much will depend on the Scots Guards Battalion. They have the major and very difficult task of capturing Tumbledown Hill, which dominates Port Stanley.' I remained silent and rather apprehensive, obviously fearing for their casualties because it was such a major task. Yet I realized that the success of the battle, and perhaps of the whole campaign, could depend upon my old regiment. I went back to my duties at the Home Office but found it hard to settle down to detailed discussions on internal questions. Eventually I could bear the suspense no longer. 'Do you think,' I said to my Private Secretary, 'you could ring up the Chief of Staff's office and ask how the battle is going?' Then I heard the splendid news that the Scots Guards had taken Tumbledown Hill and that our troops were entering Port Stanley. At that moment I was even more proud and excited by the Scots Guards' success than I was thrilled by the outcome of the entire campaign. Such is regimental loyalty; a feeling which should always be fostered and encouraged throughout our Armed Forces.

Fairways and Rough

Games provide an important outlet for our energies and essential recreation from the main tasks in life. Through them we may forge new friendships and face new challenges, which bring pleasure when overcome and disappointment when they are not met successfully. As a result, I believe the games we play do much to fashion our characters and are therefore an important element in our lives. That has been my experience with the game of golf, which has contributed to my life in all these ways.

And so it was, with feelings of nostalgia, that I went back to my old home of Nairn for the Golf Club Centenary there in September 1987. For that was where the game began for me some sixty-five years previously. With apologies to any of those present at that centenary dinner who may read this account, I feel I should repeat what I said then about my introduction to golf.

One day, when I was four years old, my mother, who was a keen player herself, as had been my late father, decreed that I was to learn golf. 'I shall take you to the professional, Mr Nelson,' she said. 'You will do what he tells you and you will always call him ''Mr Nelson'' or ''sir''.' And so, on the appointed day, a determined lady and a very apprehensive small boy set out on foot for the golf club.

On arrival I was introduced to Mr Nelson, a quiet, stern-looking man who showed little interest in me. 'You will have to learn the swing first,' he said, 'before you are fit to hit a ball.' And we proceeded on to the course where Mr Nelson collected some fir cones. I was told how to swing and instructed to hit the cones. For those, probably nearly all golf players, who have never had to hit fir cones, I can only describe them as unrewarding. There is little difference between a good and a bad shot; only air shots are different in their effect. The fir cone never flies very far, and seldom in the air. It can therefore be appreciated that several half-hour lessons with fir cones were neither encouraging for a four-year-old boy nor exciting as an introduction to a new game. Clearly, on the other hand, they were a peaceful occupation for Mr Nelson, who did not have to move or pick up the balls.

Not surprisingly, after several weeks of this I rebelled. I went home to my mother and said, in tears, 'I hate fir cones! I hate Mr Nelson! I hate golf! And I don't want to play any more!' My mother appeared very angry, for she did not like her plans being thwarted and obviously saw the danger.

The next time I reluctantly went for a lesson there was Mr Nelson armed with some white balls. 'I think,' he said to my mother, 'the boy is good enough to hit balls now. He has done well with the fir cones.' Their clearly pre-arranged plan seemed to me, in retrospect, my first example of the value of face-saving. The first ball flew splendidly in the air as I hit it and I became a golf addict for life. But, as the saying goes, 'It was a close-run thing.'

While growing up at Nairn I was on the golf course whenever the opportunity arose. I made a small course in our garden round the flower beds to play when kept at home. In the school holidays, particularly during the summer, I had other boys equally keen with whom to play and compete. Easily the best was the late David Blair, who could be considered in many respects the best natural golfer of our generation. He was to become a Walker Cup player of distinction and won numerous competitions. His brother, Chandos, later a distinguished soldier in the Seaforth Highlanders and a General, was also no mean player.

In those days it was quite common to play three rounds in a day, which may seem surprising to the slow players of the present time. I was lucky, too, since one of the few things I appreciated at my preparatory school in Berkshire was the golf course. At Winchester we were allowed to play golf at Hockley Golf Course nearby, provided it did not interfere with the traditional team games. This meant slipping away from my pursuit of butterflies and birdlife, as detailed by my housemaster, but it all added up during the year to a great deal of golf.

When I was fifteen I played in my first British Boys Championship at Carnoustie and won a match or two. Two years later at Royal Aberdeen I had great hopes in view of my previous comparative success. However, I was to learn my first good lesson. I was beaten in the first round by a boy who my mother had heard was no good; her intense displeasure was obvious for all to see. And it was not until I went to university that my golf career really started in earnest.

I did not play well during my first year at Cambridge in 1936-7 and got nowhere near the university side. However, some lessons in the summer of 1937 improved my game and I began to fulfil the promise of my earlier years. In July, I suddenly appeared on the national scene by leading the qualifiers in the first round in the Scottish Amateur

Championship at Barassie Golf Club in Ayrshire with a seventy-four. I was soon beaten in the match play stages but I had done enough to become a likely contender for the Cambridge side in the coming year. And so it proved, as I played in all the university matches that winter and was awarded my place in the university side in December 1937. My first major golfing ambition had been achieved.

In those days university golf at Oxford and Cambridge provided a great opportunity in the golfing world. Far fewer people played the game and therefore there were far fewer good players. Furthermore, Oxford and Cambridge provided the largest number of good university players for they had been the pioneers of university golf and few other universities had regular sides. And so, weekend after weekend during the winter months, we played against some of the best players on many of the best courses round London. In addition, at Cambridge we had the enormous advantage of playing during the week at Royal Worlington Golf Club, probably to this day the best nine-hole course in the country.

Our weekends were hectic affairs. We would leave at about 6 a.m. on a Saturday morning and motor in a bus or in players' cars to Hatfield, where we had breakfast in the Comet Hotel. We then motored on to courses such as Sunningdale or Woking, played eighteen holes foursomes in the morning, and eighteen holes singles in the afternoon. Then we motored back home to Cambridge. I can recollect countless occasions when we were fortunate to arrive back in our colleges in time and unscathed. Less important matches took place close to home on Sundays. Monday tended to be a day of rest from golf and from work or lectures. We were given marvellous hospitality at all the clubs and met not only great golf figures, such as Cyril Tolley, Roger Wethered and that great golf writer, Bernard

Darwin, but also other excellent players of our generation.

The university match in March 1938, held at that great golf links of golf's early days, Westward Ho in North Devon, was a memorable occasion for me. We had wonderful March weather with warm sunshine and, what was more, Cambridge won the match and I won my foursomes and singles. I had fulfilled my ambition of playing in the university match and indeed had played successfully. I went back to Westward Ho for the first time since then in November 1987 and played a round with my old friend, John Goodban, who had been in the Cambridge side with me in 1938. He has been President of the English Golf Union and a great figure in Devon golf. Some of the holes and carries seemed very long to us elderly gentlemen. But the rest, including the rushes, brought back many memories.

That same spring of 1938 I played for the first time in that most remarkable of golf competitions, the Halford Hewitt Cup at Deal and Sandwich, with teams ten a side from many public schools playing in two ball foursomes. Golf is such an individual game that playing in teams introduces a new element of strain. That splendid form of golf, two ball foursomes (all too seldom used today) increases tension, because playing alternative shots adds to the team element in each pair. It could become a most nerve-racking occasion for the pair on which the whole team result depended.

By this time also I had joined the Royal and Ancient Golf Club of St Andrews, of which I have now been privileged to be a member for fifty years. I was playing there in the Autumn Medal in September 1938 on the day the Munich Agreement was announced. My partner was Joe Fairlie, a good golfer from a great golfing family, a friend of Edgar Wallace and himself a writer of detective stories. When we set out on our round we thought there was destined to be a war. When we returned to the clubhouse we heard the news of Chamberlain's return from Munich. The fact that I had achieved quite a good score seemed at that moment irrelevant. I cannot remember my reaction to 'Peace in our time', but I did reflect that at any rate I should at least have another happy year at Cambridge as Secretary of the golf team. This turned out to be an accurate assessment.

My next Cambridge golf season was interrupted by an appendix operation at Christmas, but I was fit again to enjoy a memorable university match at Royal St Georges, Sandwich, a course I have loved ever since. Again Cambridge won. I won my foursomes and I halved a splendid match with my old friend Tom Harvey. We were both elected Captains for the following year, but such pleasure was not to be.

By 1949 my form had recovered sufficiently from the years without golf to achieve an ambition and to satisfy my mother by winning the Nairn Open Amateur Tournament. I also had the satisfaction of playing in the victorious Old Wykehamist side in 1948, in their only ever victory in the Halford Hewitt. In the following years, when we lived at Gartshore, I played with my friends at the lovely golf course of Prestwick, in addition to visits to the great Scottish clubs at St Andrews and the Honourable Company of Edinburgh Golfers at Muirfield. During that time I played without conspicuous success in four amateur championships in 1950, 1952, 1953 and 1954. At the same time I served on the Royal and Ancient Championship Committee in the days before the Open Golf Championship was transformed from its modest status into the tremendous occasion it is today. Of course television has played a major part, not least financially. But great credit for these modern championships, which are enjoyed by many millions of people on television and large numbers on the course itself, goes in particular to two Royal and Ancient Secretaries, the late Brigadier Brickman and Keith Mackenzie, and to Committee members such as my old friend, Gerald Micklem, who has done so much for golf over the years.

In 1952 I was appointed one of the selectors for the British Walker Cup team. I was a compromise choice and a bad one, for I was not a player of that standard myself. However, it was a fascinating job and we chose a reasonable team by the standards of that time. But the expansion of the game and consequent increase in amateurs of international standard demanded a broader and more professional approach to training and selecting sides. This has happened and British teams have improved dramatically as a result.

After my entry into Parliament I had much less time for golf and none at all for golf administration. I still went regularly, though, to the autumn meeting at St Andrews and kept up my contacts there. In 1969, when I was still Opposition Chief Whip, the Past Captains of the Royal and Ancient asked me if I was prepared to be nominated as Captain for the year 1969–70. This appointment is an honour and privilege for anyone connected with golf and I was proud to accept. The position of Captain of the Royal and Ancient Golf Club is really that of a ceremonial figurehead. The various committees working under their chairman run the club, as well as the British Championships under the club's control, and they also carry out worldwide responsibilities for the rules of the game. The Captain attends many functions as the representative of the club, both in Britain, the United States and, indeed, all over the world, and the prestige of the Royal and Ancient and of St

Andrews, as the home of golf, ensures him a great welcome wherever he goes. But before such privileges can be enjoyed there is a challenge to be met and overcome.

At the September meeting the Captain has to drive himself into office. This tradition stems from the award to the reigning Captain of the medal given to the club by Queen Adelaide. By custom, once nominated by the club, he is the only player entitled to play in the competition for the medal. Therefore once he has struck a ball on to the course he has won. What happens, the cunning will ask, if the Captain hits the ball out of bounds, which – as those who know St Andrews well can appreciate – is very easy, even if inexcusable? The answer is that no one knows, because no Captain has ever done so. Some hit very short tops but no one has yet hit out of bounds, although it is the dread of every succeeding Captain.

The occasion of the drive is extremely daunting. It takes place at 8 a.m., not a friendly hour at the best of times. The members of the club and the equally golf-conscious citizens of St Andrews assemble behind the tee and in front of the clubhouse. The incoming Captain is led down the steps by his predecessor with all the appearance of a victim for the slaughter. The caddies are out on the course, for by tradition the one who returns the ball is given a golden sovereign by the Captain. They station themselves near or far, right or left, in accordance with their assessment of a new Captain's play. A greenkeeper is stationed by a cannon ready to fire as soon as the ball is struck. Until his recent death the ball was teed up by Laurie Auchterlonie, a much-loved figure and the club professional. The scene is set. Will the Captain top it? Will he hit it out of bounds? Will he even miss the ball altogether? No doubt these thoughts are ghoulishly in the minds of the crowd. From my own experience they were certainly in the Captain's mind, and I am assured that even the most eminent players have their anxieties at this moment. Mine was not one of my best shots. It was low, rather to the left, but it did get into the air and went far enough not to be memorable as one of the historic misses. I never saw it for it was, as they say at St Andrews, a grey day with a sea harr. As a result I was clouded in the smoke from the cannon, added to the mist. All had gone well, but I was fortunate indeed – for two hours later, when I set out on the traditional eighteen holes medal with my predecessor Gerald Micklem, well encouraged by a champagne breakfast, I sliced my first tee shot far out of bounds.

This ordeal over, I settled down to the routine of dinners wearing the Captain's red coat, unfortunately indistinguishable from the Master of Ceremonies. This often prompted the question as to why Captains of ancient golf clubs wear red coats. The answer is simple, as many paintings of the early days of golf have shown. Surprising as it may seem, the original players always played in red coats. Each dinner meant a speech, which fortunately political practice made easier for me, and extensive hospitality, which no amount of practice can make good for you. I was lucky in one respect: my captaincy followed immediately after Tony Jacklin's victory in the British Open. This long-awaited British success by a worthy champion with great charm added greatly to many of the celebrations during my year in office.

Then, in April 1970, came an enormous treat. My wife and I went to the USA for the great Masters Tournament at Augusta, Georgia. Keith Mackenzie, Royal and Ancient Secretary, came with us and on the way to Augusta we visited that wonderful golf course, Pine Valley near Philadelphia and Washington. The course at Augusta is closely associated with that greatest golfer of the previous generation, known in Britain as Bobby Jones and by his fellow Americans as Bob Jones. He laid out the course there, which is as exciting and beautiful as it appears to the millions of television viewers all over the world who watch the Masters Tournament every year. It is a real privilege to be able to watch the tournament on the spot. When I was there it was run in what can only be described as a majestic manner by a tremendous character, Cliff Roberts, a close associate and friend of Bob Jones. He used his power ruthlessly in the best interests of the tournament. When it came to television coverage he laid down clear rules for the camera crews and enforced them by making it plain that any breach of his instructions would mean the end of coverage by the particular offending network. I did a short introductory television programme with him and the same command on that occasion was fascinating to watch. No interviewer would have dared to ask him the mildest awkward question; but of course that programme happened some eighteen years ago, before the days of television power at its most dominant.

After my visit to Augusta I received a charming letter from Bob Jones, which he signed himself. By that time illness prevented him from coming to the Masters Tournament, but he wrote to welcome me, as he had a great love for the Royal and Ancient and for St Andrews. Needless to say, for someone like me who, as a boy, remembered his remarkable achievements, this letter is a treasured golfing memento.

Soon after my return from the USA, we were involved in the June 1970 General Election. I therefore had to miss some of my duties, including the British Amateur Championship. But since it took place just after the Conservative victory, it was exciting for me to be able to take the new Prime Minister, Ted Heath, to the concluding stages of the British Open at St Andrews. I had been unable to get up there until the Friday of championship week because, as the new Leader of the House of Commons, I had to wind up the debate on the Thursday night. I still relish the happy memory of flying up to St Andrews with Ted Heath, whom I had served so closely as Chief Whip in the long years of Opposition, both in my capacity as Captain of the Royal and Ancient and as one of his senior Cabinet Ministers. It was, however, a championship with a tinge of sadness, for that was the occasion on which Doug Sanders missed a short putt on the last green and so tied with Jack Nicklaus instead of beating him. In those days a tie was settled by an eighteen-hole play-off the next day – an awful anticlimax for my championship year as Captain. But it had the consolation of enabling me to present the Cup to Jack Nicklaus, another dominating golf personality. Once again a golfing recollection to savour.

Since then I have enjoyed friendly golf, mostly at Penrith and Silloth on Solway Golf Clubs in Cumbria, but also at St Andrews and in Parliamentary Golfing Society matches. I had the pleasure of winning the Parliamentary Handicap after many failures and eventually, having tried for years, won two Royal and Ancient medals in successive years. Needless to say, by then they were not scratch medals, rather a medal called the Pine Valley Plate for those over fifty-five on handicap. Finally in 1986, after sixty-four years of golf, I did a hole in one at the Penrith August Meeting. I cannot pretend that it is a cheap amusement for the President of a club to do a hole in one at a crowded open meeting, but I did not grudge a penny – or perhaps I should say a pound – of it.

Now, as my golfing years draw inevitably towards their close, I can only report on the happiness the game has given me. No one who plays golf can ever forget the magic of the old course at St Andrews at its best, nor can anyone who has been lucky enough to be a member of the Royal and Ancient escape feelings of nostalgia when remembering the astonishing atmosphere in the big room in the clubhouse there on any crowded occasion. I also have simpler memories. I think of the feelings of gratitude when, at the more stressful moments of my political career, I have gone to play at Penrith and Silloth on Solway Golf Clubs, which are both in my old constituency. No one ever bothered me in the club about the political controversies of the moment, in which frequently I was deeply involved and of course longing to forget. They simply recognized that I had come to enjoy the game and treated me accordingly. I do not suppose the members realize how much I appreciated that, nor perhaps how honoured I felt at being asked to be President of both clubs. It was natural for them as golf players to think of me as simply another player. These are the real friendships which golf provides for its enthusiasts, addicts or slaves – whatever we are called.

A note in my possession provides the best illustration of all. When I was ill in Westminster Hospital in December 1987, I received a handwritten note from Sir Henry Cotton. I was delighted to get it but did not realize at the time that he was himself in hospital. A week later he died, alas just before his much-welcomed knighthood was announced in the New Year's Honours List. When I heard the sad news I picked up the note again. It read simply, 'Willie, Forward tees from now on. Henry.' At that moment this classic example of golfing friendship touched me deeply.

A Career in Politics

In the autumn of 1947, after leaving the Army, I returned to my family and our home at Gartshore, Kirkintilloch, about ten miles from the centre of Glasgow. This marked the real beginning of the married and family life which has been ever since the solid bedrock of my immensely happy and fortunate career.

I had first met my future wife, Celia Sprot, at her home, Riddell, in the Scottish Border country when I was just over eight years old. My mother had taken a house nearby for the winter months and was a friend of my future mother-in-law. I was soon asked to one of the children's tea parties at their home, which I dreaded. I remember that they were good at family card games, of which I had little experience, and I recall playing 'Racing Demon', at which I came last. I went home feeling miserable and rather frightened of the family in general, and of the apparently efficient young daughter in particular. It certainly was not love at first sight.

We met each other quite often, however, over the years leading up to the war and became friends. Then in 1942 when I was stationed at Codford Camp near Salisbury my mother told me that Celia Sprot, then an officer in the Auxiliary Territorial Service, was on a course at

Brockenhurst in the New Forest. I invited her to dinner in Salisbury. This time it clearly was love at what I suppose I should call renewed sight. We became engaged in a few weeks' time and married a few months later on 6 February 1943 in St Giles' Cathedral, Edinburgh. My chief memory of a wartime wedding is of our cake. Proper icing was not available during the war, so our fruit cake was placed in a paper container made to look like an iced wedding cake.

I soon found that I had acquired a perfect wife, and also one providing exactly the family background which I lacked. My father-in-law was a cavalry soldier and a countryman. He knew a great deal about agriculture and forestry and managed his property with meticulous care. Alas, he suffered from ill health and died only a few years after we were married. He had been extremely kind to me as his first son-in-law. My mother-in-law was a remarkable lady, a great character like my mother, although very different. She was a matriarch of the old school whose passion in life was her family. She lived to be over ninety and was adored by our children, with whom she played tennis and other games right up until the end of her life. It is a well-known saying that a man marrying should study his future mother-in-law, for girls are alleged to grow increasingly like their mothers. Certainly my wife is very like my mother-in-law in many respects, and I could not ask for anything better.

My wife's first interest has always been her family. She loves the country, her garden and country pursuits. She had no idea that she was marrying a politician and did not greatly care for the idea. But she thoroughly enjoyed constituency work, at which she excelled – particularly in a large agricultural area like mine, for she understood country people. She had, on the other hand, little interest in the London political social scene and was in no way a politically ambitious wife. Whenever she was required to help me, however (as, for instance, in the difficult circumstances of Northern Ireland), no one could have done more. Over the years she has been greatly preoccupied with our family of four daughters – and now twelve grandchildren, varying in age from twenty down to one year. When people commiserate with me for not having a son, my reply is simple and genuine. Remember the old saying 'A son is a son till he takes a wife, but a daughter is a daughter for the rest of your life.' I can assure anyone that this reference to daughters is totally correct. Ten days after I fell ill, the whole family – eight adults and twelve children – visited us at home. No one could have had a better tonic.

This then was the family which we were in the process of establishing when I returned to Gartshore from the Army. We were lucky in that this was eight years before I entered the House of Commons, so we spent the early years as a family together – a great advantage. During that time I learned about the management of property, agriculture and horticulture. I took part in the work of many local organizations which, incidentally, taught me much about the Scottish miners who lived in our neighbourhood. I also continued my interest in golf by serving on various committees at the Royal and Ancient Golf Club.

Our home at Gartshore was a large house of Scottish baronial architecture, of a kind common in the west of Scotland. It had been built very solidly indeed in 1887, replacing an old Scottish country house which belonged to the family from which my great-grandfather bought the property. In its sixty years it had outlived its day, being far too big and expensive to maintain, but it was comfortable and we decided to give it a try. Having never had any other settled home of our own, our family was extremely happy there. But my wife and I knew that sooner rather than later sheer expense, particularly of heating the house with an old-fashioned coal boiler, would force us to leave. And so, when I became Member of Parliament for Penrith and the Border in 1955, we decided to move to Cumbria. We tried to find another use for the house, and indeed offered it as a gift to the Glasgow Corporation to house the Burrell Collection, but it was too far out of Glasgow for them and as it was in the coal-mining area was considered unsuitable for the priceless tapestries. The Collection has now found a much better site at Pollok House. Eventually I concluded that the only solution was to pull the house down to the ground rather than let it decay. I am glad that I did so, because our family would have hated seeing our home as a ruin, and this appeared to be the only alternative.

Our two family properties at Gartshore and at Woodhall in Lanarkshire consisted of typical, comparatively small West of Scotland dairy farms, all close to industrial areas, towns and mining villages. They were bought by my great-grandfather, Alexander Whitelaw, who was Chairman of the great West of Scotland coal and steel firm, William Baird & Co., in the middle of the last century. He was also for a time Unionist Member of Parliament for the City of Glasgow and a leading figure in the development of Glasgow education. From what I have read of him, he certainly belied the contemporary image of the hard-faced Victorian coal-master. Perhaps some of his contemporaries considered him a 'Wet'. However, his family reputation was of a strict financial disciplinarian in the best Scottish tradition. My eldest great-uncle, also Alexander Whitelaw, inherited the properties at the age of twenty-one and, unwisely as it turned out, immediately built the large house. He married a niece of Disraeli's, but this did not seem to help him into Parliament for he stood on several occasions, always unsuccessfully. He had no children and the properties thus passed to my grandfather, who managed them on his retirement from the Chairmanship of the LNER in 1936. Before he went into railways, first as Chairman of the Highland Railway in Scotland, he had also been a Unionist Member of Parliament for Perth for a short time. Subsequently, he took a leading part in Unionist politics in Scotland and as a lay figure in the General Assembly of the Church of Scotland.

Since I took over the properties in 1946 much of the farmland has been developed for housing and industrial purposes. At the same time local coal mines, some situated on our land, have been closed. During the same period, I have handed over most of the remaining land to my daughters.

It was during the late 1940s that I embarked on a career in politics. My property and family affairs were managed by a great character, John Park, and his brother Willie. John was keen on politics and was a leading official of the Dunbartonshire Unionist Association, in the constituency in which we lived. This constituency was redistributed in 1948 and a new one called East Dunbartonshire was formed to include Clydebank, a Socialist stronghold represented by the redoubtable Davie Kirkwood, one of the famous pre-war Clydesiders. Certainly the new constituency included more salubrious Conservative country in Bearsden and Milngavie, but it was clearly not a winning prospect. On that basis, for I did not contemplate entering the House of Commons at that time, I thought it would be fun to gain political experience. Needless to say, I was selected for the best of all possible reasons – I was the only candidate.

My wife and I had little idea what was in store for us,

particularly as neither of us had any experience of politics. We had never been Young Conservatives. As I have already made clear, I had taken no part in politics at university. My only party political act previously had been to vote in 1945 for James Stuart, later Lord Stuart of Findhorn, in the Moray and Nairn constituency. He subsequently became not only my mentor – as Churchill's former Chief Whip – when I was made Opposition Chief Whip in 1964 but also a particular hero of mine. Many stories are told of his laid-back manner which disguised an acute political brain. Certainly James Stuart's political skills were worth studying, for he was an outstanding Chief Whip and a most successful Secretary of State for Scotland in the 1950s. I found his advice invaluable and all the easier to remember as it was delivered with splendid dry humour.

As political novices, we relied greatly on our constituency officers in East Dunbartonshire. We were strongly supported in the Bearsden and Milngavie areas, where many Scottish businessmen lived, and received enthusiastic backing in the Kirkintilloch district, which was outnumbered by Labour voters, particularly in the many mining villages. In the vast area of Clydebank, on the other hand, our organization relied on a tiny band of real enthusiasts who were totally overwhelmed, and indeed demoralized, by the vast Labour armies.

I had never made speeches of any kind and prepared everything meticulously from party literature at first. My supporters were always generous and I never learnt how insufferably boring I must have been. Of my first major speech to a Scottish Unionist conference at Perth, when I was asked to move a motion supporting the Conservative Industrial Charter, I remember only that I was desperately nervous and that everyone was very kind. I have made countless conference speeches since. I do not think I have ever been quite so nervous again and, equally, my audiences on several occasions have been noticeably less kind.

There is nothing like a general election campaign for improving one's public speaking. And the 1950 General Election was soon upon us. The campaign was vastly different from those of modern general elections. I suppose the campaigns of 1950 and 1951 were the last without the close attention of television. As a result public meetings were all-important. Even ordinary and insignificant candidates, as I was, spoke to packed meetings and the art of heckling was practised with great skill and much humour. I remember addressing a meeting of between 800 and 1,000 people in Clydebank Town Hall. I was supported by a distinguished parliamentarian of the day who, alas, had little experience of Clydeside audiences. Shortly after he started his speech, the inevitable man in muffler and cloth cap shouted out, 'Liar!'

'Who said that?' asked the distinguished speaker.

'I did and I'll say it again,' said the man in the cloth cap. 'Liar!'

To my horror my main speaker replied, 'If you say that again I will sit down and speak no more.'

Timing his intervention brilliantly, the heckler waited for about five minutes and then shouted, 'Liar!' again.

The great man sat down, turned to me and said, 'I shall now go, and leave this rabble to you. Goodbye.' I never saw him again and his ministerial career did not prosper, for which I was not sorry.

Still, facing 800 Clydesiders in those circumstances taught me a valuable lesson about public speaking and public meetings – one that I certainly could not have learnt from any amount of instruction. The audience, knowing – I suppose – that I was in a mess, was sympathetic towards me. I survived somehow, mainly by being conciliatory and speaking very fast, thereby making interruption more difficult. As I left the hall the man in muffler and cap who had started the trouble came up to me and said, 'Well done, laddie. You'll do fine.' I found that mood typical of those old-fashioned political meetings with genuine hecklers, so different from the senseless shouting and screaming which I have sometimes had to endure since. And it should be remembered that this happened in the heart of Red Clydeside. Nor was there anything rough about our meetings at the shipyard gates, or indeed about our visits to the huge tenement buildings.

My wife and I learnt much about human nature during that campaign. And I found that my wartime experience with soldiers from all these areas stood me in good stead. We also learnt a lot from our illustrious opponent, Davie Kirkwood, who treated us with a kindness and generosity which I have never forgotten. He taught me how to behave towards political opponents and I hope I have succeeded in following his example. And he gave me an elementary lesson in political propaganda. Candidates were asked to write an article for the local paper on our own party's attitude towards shipbuilding. I studied the Conservative manifesto and all the relevant pamphlets and produced what I felt was a good case. In his article, Davie Kirkwood paid no attention at all either to his own or any other party's proposals. He simply set out an account of what he had done for Clydeside shipbuilding over the years and added, 'That is the basis on which I ask you to support me in future.' Backed by his considerable reputation, it was a powerful piece and highly skilful.

In the end I lost by 4,576 votes – much better than I

expected at the start. After the count, though, I felt a sense of let-down. I discovered then that experience which I believe is undergone by all who fight elections. If you have little or no chance of winning you are buoyed up by the general excitement into believing that, incredibly, you may do so. If, on the other hand, which became my experience later, you are fighting a safe seat for your party which you really could not lose, you suffer increasing fears throughout the campaign that on this occasion you may actually do so. All this adds up to the nerve-racking nature of the electioneering process. Thank goodness our general elections are normally held at reasonable intervals. However, as the 1950 Election reduced dramatically the large Labour majority of 1945 and produced what amounted to a hung Parliament, there was clearly going to be another general election much sooner than normal. As a result, my constituency association – buoyed up by our result against Davie Kirkwood – begged me to stand again. 'Oh,' they said, 'you will win next time because he will have retired and you will be facing an unknown successor.' I did not wholly accept that argument, because I had learnt from studying election results of the limited personal value of candidates in terms of votes. Nevertheless, I agreed to stand.

Before the next election came I had my second experience of a major speech, however short. I was asked to second the vote of thanks to Winston Churchill at the Usher Hall, Edinburgh, after the end of the Scottish Unionist Conference in May 1950. Votes of thanks are like maiden speeches in Parliament: if you speak sufficiently shortly and do not actually fall down on your face, your audience will always be extremely kind. Such was my experience on this occasion.

By the autumn of 1951, the Attlee Government was in considerable difficulty with its small majority, and so it came as no surprise when a general election was announced for October. Davie Kirkwood had declared his retirement and a Welshman called Cyril Bence was chosen as his successor. He was a friendly man but a formidable candidate with his fiery Welsh eloquence. Our supporters hoped that the Scots would not take to his Welsh character, but as Celts they admired his fluency of speech. He was a good Socialist and that reinforced their support. My main memory of the campaign is of another crowded meeting in Clydebank. At that moment the Conservatives seemed to be winning, but the campaign against Churchill as a war-monger – 'Whose finger on the trigger?' as the *Daily Mirror* declared – had just started. Our campaign provided a good example of its effect. I remember the subject clearly, for it changed the tone of the meeting which until then seemed to be going well. A man asked, 'Is the candidate looking forward to another war so that he can return to the nice cushy job he had in the last one?'

The reaction of anyone who had fought in a war was bound to be one of incredulity and irritation. However, restraining myself, I replied (I hope in a dignified way), 'No one who has ever fought in a war could ever want to see another.' I remember being desperately disappointed by the reaction of the meeting. A few ex-servicemen clapped, the majority of the audience was silent, and the ardent Labour supporters appeared almost gleefully satisfied. Subsequently we learnt that exchanges of a similar sort were taking place at meetings all over the country. I have never had any doubt in my mind that the war-mongering charge against Churchill succeeded in substantially reducing the Conservative majority. I lost by 3,426 votes, this time considerably worse than I had hoped, although I did not start the campaign thinking that I could actually win. Afterwards

I was quite determined that I would not stand again for East Dunbartonshire, and my supporters understood.

I had become absorbed in politics, however, and really wanted to get into the House of Commons. I told our Scottish Unionist Headquarters that I would be prepared to stand for a winnable seat in Scotland. They told me that several seats were in prospect but, as often happens in the early years of a Parliament, no sitting Members announced their retirement. And so I waited until 1954 when a surprise offer came my way. One of my great Scots Guards friends, Charles Graham, now Sir Charles Graham and Lord Lieutenant of Cumbria, approached me about the possibility of becoming candidate for a Cumberland seat, Penrith and the Border, where the MP was retiring. My Whitelaw grandmother came from Brampton near Carlisle in the constituency, and my grandfather's sister had married her brother. I was therefore attracted to the proposition and agreed to put my name forward. In May 1954 I was selected as candidate much more simply than happens in the constituencies today. The Chairman, Colonel Fetherstonhaugh, later Sir Timothy Fetherstonhaugh, a determined figure and a powerful Chairman, had heard about me and decided that I was his man. He ensured that his selection committee shared his view.

And so I became the candidate for the vast rural constituency of Penrith and the Border, which was to be my political base throughout my career in the House of Commons. It included the delightful market town of Penrith, strategically placed – for coaching days, as for the motor car – at the junction of a road running east and west across the Pennines, of which there are few, and a road running north and south down to industrial Lancashire. It was not, and is not, a large town, but over the years it has had all the characteristics of a country town with a strong traditional and Conservative background. There were some other small towns in the constituency and a mass of villages; as well as all kinds of farms, some on the hills, others on the marginal land just off the hills, and lower down a good number of dairy farms on a variety of different land. There were tourist areas on the fringe of the Lake District and on the Solway coast, industrial areas in West Cumberland and residential villages around Carlisle.

I soon learnt that Cumberland people were reticent, and suspicious of strangers (to whom they referred as 'offcomers') and thus hard to get to know. When my wife and I first went into small village halls for functions, the assembled company usually waiting for their whist drive would turn round and stare at us in total silence – a disconcerting reception, to put it mildly. But in those early days whist drives were excellent political occasions. We went to several every week and gradually fewer people stared at us and more began to welcome us. Certainly this was a good way of getting to know people. To this day I am approached by those who say to me, 'Do you remember when we won so many tricks together?' or at other times reproachfully, 'Do you remember when you trumped my ace?' Today, cars and television have together changed the country and remote village life. New political methods have therefore to be used by candidates and Members. But in our day my wife and I found that whist provided us with a strong and secure political base, far better than any speech.

My predecessor as Member of Parliament, Sir Donald Scott, was most helpful to us and in the year before the 1955 Election we were able to get to know the constituency and establish ourselves to some extent. This in itself was no easy task in a large scattered area with something like 160 separate polling stations.

The 1955 Election campaign was a complete change from our experience in East Dunbartonshire. There was little opposition or excitement, simply endless small village meetings – up to five a night. Every village expected its meeting and in 1955 they were still quite well attended. It was only when television gained a hold on subsequent general elections that these village meetings gradually diminished in attendance, importance and value. Even in 1955 I remember particularly a meeting which made little, if any, impact. I entered the small village hall where I found about a dozen worthies, all men sitting silently with their caps on. When I came in, no one spoke or even moved a muscle. I made my speech, still no one moved. I asked for questions. Again no movement. I said good night and wished them well – no movement. I left the hall and they were still sitting silently just as I had found them on arrival. I often wondered whether they had been there for some other purpose and did not appreciate at all what I was there for. I never discovered, but I firmly removed that village from the meetings list for future elections.

The only other interest in an otherwise uneventful, if exhausting, campaign was one of my opponents, an eccentric local farmer who stood as a candidate in favour of cock-fighting and more pay for mole-catchers. What is more, he chose my Conservative colour: yellow in Cumberland, because of our association with the Lonsdale family over the years. Apparently, during the campaign he went round local pubs taking bets with his friends on the number of votes he would get. In fact, he achieved 368 – sufficient to bring him in a reasonable return. But he was far from satisfied and I remember him at the count shouting,

'Whitelaw has stolen all my yellow votes, bundles and bundles of them!' At the end of the count he became very belligerent and approached me saying, 'Now for the real fight.' He also tried to assault the returning officer. That was enough. He was led away by the police and I became a Member of Parliament with a comfortable majority.

I now faced the daunting prospect of entering Parliament for the first time as a Member. Like all new ventures it was an awe-inspiring experience, particularly as I knew few Members of Parliament. But I was enormously fortunate in an old friend who looked after me. Charlie MacAndrew, the Deputy Speaker, later Lord MacAndrew, was a great House of Commons figure and enormously respected. I had played golf with him at Prestwick and St Andrews and knew him well. He set out to ensure that I was properly educated in House of Commons procedures, which I found valuable later on when I became a Whip. I also knew Peter Thorneycroft, who is a relation of mine and was at that time President of the Board of Trade. In 1956 he asked me to be his Parliamentary Private Secretary and gave me my first opportunity to learn about the working of Government departments – a most useful experience for which I was extremely grateful. I made my maiden speech during a debate on what became known as Rab Butler's 'Pots and Pans' Budget on 25 October 1955. I spoke about the worrying effect of sudden changes in Government expenditure programmes, particularly in isolated country areas. At that time my constituency had many outlying farms still without electricity. My main recollection of the speech is, as always on such occasions, of the relief I felt when it was over.

*   *   *

Those of us who entered Parliament in 1955 were soon involved in the great Suez controversy. It was my first experience of a really emotional and turbulent House of Commons. Noise and shouting based on genuine anger and emotion are different, and far more understandable than the senseless barracking and shouting which, alas, are becoming a permanent feature of the House of Commons today. Both, however, can be unpleasant to experience.

There have been many accounts of the traumatic Suez controversy by those who were closely involved in it. I can only record the general feelings of a very new back-bencher who found himself swept up into furious arguments. Passionate views were held both by supporters and opponents of the operation. Frequently these caused splits, not only within political parties in Parliament and in the country, but even within individual families. This heightened the tension in Parliament, and of course particularly inside the Conservative Parliamentary Party, which had the major responsibility of supporting the Government. Many highly charged meetings of the 1922 Committee were held as a result.

At the start I felt simply, as I think many people did, that President Nasser could not be allowed to block the Suez Canal, a vital international waterway, apparently in contravention of basic international undertakings. But as the events unfolded, many complications clouded the basic issue. The Americans were in the middle of a presidential election and President Eisenhower, who was fighting it and thought to be a natural supporter of Britain, turned out to be furious at the British military action. There were arguments about collusion between Britain, France and Israel. International opinion became increasingly divided. Then, horror of horrors, we learnt that our invading force was not poised for an immediate landing at Suez and a quick victory, which would probably have taken international opinion by storm. Rather, it was an agonizing number of sailing days away in the Mediterranean. At this moment I found myself in sympathy with a group of Conservatives who felt increasingly that, against a background of United States dismay and sharply divided world opinion, the operation was unlikely to succeed in its objective of clearing the Suez Canal.

By the time our troops landed it seemed to be only too obvious that outside world pressures would bring the action to a halt before its objectives had been gained. And so it came as no surprise when the Americans withdrew financial support and basically forced our Government to stop its advancing troops. In fact, those who took the same view as I did were positively relieved that an action which was becoming increasingly embarrassing, because it was in conflict with majority world opinion, had ceased.

Reflecting on the matter later, it is easy to feel that this was a short-term view and that if only the British action had had sufficient support to enable our troops to reach the end of the canal, the Middle East problem would probably be much easier to solve today. But at the time international co-operation had not been assured before action was taken. There is, of course, still a strong view in the Conservative Party that, despite the withdrawal of international support, we should have gone on. I do not believe that that would have been possible. We can doubtless blame the Americans and other countries for their lack of foresight, but I feel we also had to take our share of the blame for lack of co-ordinated international planning.

As it was, we in the Conservative Party had succeeded in

voting for going in and then for coming out, not an honourable, or in any way logical, position. Curiously – thanks, I suppose, to our basic party unity at a difficult time, with Ted Heath as our Chief Whip and a magnificent example of leadership from Harold Macmillan thereafter – we recovered to win the 1959 Election.

I went with Peter Thorneycroft as his PPS when he became Chancellor of the Exchequer. I therefore had a ringside seat when he, Enoch Powell and Nigel Birch resigned from the Government in January 1958 on the Public Expenditure Programme. I was sad to see Peter Thorneycroft go because I had enormous admiration for him, but it must be accepted that his decision on a matter of principle has become increasingly justified over the years.

And so, early in my parliamentary career, I learnt something about the tensions surrounding a ministerial resignation. Indeed, even as a humble Parliamentary Private Secretary with no official position, I felt personally some of those pressures. I remain convinced to this day that Peter Thorneycroft, Enoch Powell and Nigel Birch were right in principle.

They were making a stand against their colleagues' demands for increased public expenditure, which they in the Treasury believed would be damaging to the economic strategy at that time if they were granted. Subsequent events have shown that strict control of public expenditure is essential for any Government, as departmental demands always substantially exceed what can wisely be made available.

Although I have had my disagreements with Enoch Powell since, I was deeply impressed by the single-minded logic and power of his arguments. Peter Thorneycroft demonstrated then, as so often since, the courage of his convictions and the strength with which he deploys his case.

From my humble position I had only one doubt at the time, which perhaps was prompted by my great admiration for Peter Thorneycroft. Did the disagreement justify the decision of the three Treasury Ministers actually to resign? In principle I thought it did and, for many people, that was sufficient justification in itself. But I did doubt the political wisdom of their position. I thought that the resignation would be highly damaging to the Government just at the moment when we were recovering from the Suez débâcle and when a general election was not far away.

In the event, Harold Macmillan managed, amazingly, to shrug off the whole incident as 'a little local difficulty', which clearly it was not. As a result, the political damage argument never arose, and thus justification of the decision as a matter of principle has become increasingly accepted.

At the beginning of 1959 Ted Heath asked me to become an Assistant Whip. I then joined the Government front-bench in a most junior capacity. Since then I have remained on the front-bench, either in Government or in Opposition, until I resigned in January 1988. For the first time in thirty years therefore I am now on the back-benches again, this time in the House of Lords.

I found the duties of a Whip fascinating. They certainly provide an excellent insight into the workings of the Parliamentary Party and its relationship with the Government. They also ensure an appreciation of human reactions and of the various personalities in one's own party. In addition I was lucky enough to work with great friends in the Whips' Office under Ted Heath until the 1959 Election, and with Martin Redmayne afterwards until I became Parliamentary Secretary at the Ministry of Labour in 1962.

My arrival at the Ministry of Labour, now called the Department of Employment, came about as a result of the controversial Government changes in Harold Macmillan's time, known as the 'night of the long knives', when he reshuffled his Government in July 1962. These changes subsequently came to be regarded as a great mistake. For me they provided a tremendous opportunity. I found a fascinating ministry under John Hare – later Lord Blakenham – whom I came to admire as a most skilful and sensitive Minister of Labour. He was an ideal Minister to serve under, as be brought his junior Minister in on all the discussions and once he had delegated work he left you to get on with it without interference. Subsequently, as a Minister myself, I have tried to follow that example and it must be the right way to run a Government department. It is, alas, more difficult today since Government departments are much larger and there are so many more Ministers involved with whom to keep in touch.

I had not long been Parliamentary Secretary before I found myself taking complicated legislation through Parliament. My first experience came with the Offices, Shops and Railway Premises Bill which sought to introduce conditions of work by laying down detailed arrangements for ventilation in offices, et cetera. I appreciated for the first time that while it is essential that Acts of Parliament remain in their present form and language for interpretation in the courts, they are extremely difficult for the layman to understand and explain while they are passing through Parliament.

My second Bill was easier to interpret and in many ways more interesting because it broke new ground. At that time there was a growing feeling that our apprentice training was inadequate and was harming our national industrial performance. The Industrial Training Bill was clearly a first step in the right direction and was generally welcomed as such. There have been many changes since then and some of the Bill's original provisions have been modified and even abandoned. But while many of the criticisms directed at particular aspects of the initial plans have been justified with the benefit of hindsight, John Blakenham certainly deserves credit for a much-needed initiative.

In addition to my parliamentary work, I made many visits all over the country to employment exchanges and to individual firms, for discussions on industrial relations and safety, health and welfare problems, for which I was made responsible. I thus became extremely interested in these matters, which vitally affect our industry and which at that time were the direct responsibility of the Ministry of Labour. When I returned to the Department of Employment as Secretary of State in 1973, not only the name of the department had been changed. Direct responsibility for the employment exchanges and for safety, health and welfare was being given to outside agencies.

As a junior Minister, I took no special part in the traumatic events of the leadership election in 1963 following Harold Macmillan's resignation. However, like all Conservative MPs, I was asked by the Whips who I wanted as Leader. I replied Rab Butler. I was then asked what I thought at the time was rather an extraordinary question – whether I would support Alec Douglas-Home if he was available. I replied that of course he would make an excellent Leader and Prime Minister, but that it was too much to ask anyone to renounce a peerage, fight a by-election and then come back to the House of Commons as Prime Minister. How wrong I was.

When Alec Douglas-Home took over as Prime Minister

from Harold Macmillan, Joe Godber was appointed Minister of Labour. I was fortunate, for I found him an excellent Minister to serve under and we had a happy relationship until the 1964 Election. During that time I led a small Ministry of Labour delegation to the Soviet Union. It had been invited there to study their employment practices. This was certainly a curious assignment for, as can well be imagined, our systems had little in common. However, it gave me the opportunity to visit the Soviet Union, an experience I was to repeat as the leader of the Inter-Parliamentary Union delegation in 1986.

It is difficult to compare the two visits for my personal circumstances were so different. In 1964 I was a junior Minister leading a small ministry team. In 1986 I was a very senior figure leading a parliamentary delegation on an exchange visit to the one made by Mikhail Gorbachev to Britain shortly before he became Soviet leader. There was one similarity – we went to exactly the same places: Moscow, Leningrad and Tbilisi in Georgia. I suspect that this is a favourite itinerary for Soviet visitors, but it is none the less agreeable for that. The business of the visit is conducted in Moscow which, apart from the magnificent Kremlin, is not an exciting city. The cultural side is splendidly provided for in the remarkable city of Leningrad with the Hermitage and its treasures, coupled with the beautifully preserved palaces outside the city. Lastly, the scenic and enjoyment side of the trip is reserved for Tbilisi with all its gaiety and generous Georgian hospitality.

Quite apart from the standing of the two visits, there was one difference of major significance, which in truth afforded some relief. Mikhail Gorbachev's campaign against alcohol ensured that in 1986 there was no drink at official functions and so the famous vodka toasts were no more. I describe this change as a relief, not because of any distaste for alcohol but rather out of a regard for one's health. A large number of toasts in vodka, proposed continuously throughout the meal, can be a major test of stamina.

My first experience of the Soviet Union gave me some understanding of the warmth of the Russian people's natural hospitality, which I found then – and still find – attractive. Their friendly attitude contrasts starkly with some of the harsher aspects of their regime. It is against that background that future developments under the changes being carried out by Mikhail Gorbachev could be significant.

Soon after this fascinating experience came the end of my time at the Ministry of Labour with the 1964 Election. This marked also the end of thirteen years of Conservative Government. Amid all the theories about the results of this election – with the narrow defeat of the Conservatives under Alec Douglas-Home by Labour under Harold Wilson – I have, for better or worse, one clear view. I am convinced that Alec Douglas-Home's achievement in leading us so nearly to victory after such a short time as Leader and against all the odds was remarkable. When he became Prime Minister the Party was in a demoralized state, particularly after the traumatic arguments about the leadership at the party conference at Blackpool when Harold Macmillan resigned. Two of the senior members of the Party, Iain Macleod and Enoch Powell, refused to serve under Alec Douglas-Home. Yet in one year he brought the Party to within a few seats of success by demonstrating the honest, straightforward leadership of which he was such a shining example.

Personally, in my own constituency, I learnt about the awkward position of a junior Minister in any Government, who is bound by collective responsibility and unable to speak in Parliament on matters affecting his constituency. In the months leading up to the election two railways were closed in my constituency: the Carlisle to Silloth line and the Penrith–Keswick–Workington line. Both were the subject of considerable' controversy. Worse still, when giving reasons for the closure of the Silloth line, Ernest Marples, then Minister of Transport, referred scornfully to the absurd number of petitions against closure compared with the small number of inhabitants in the area. This in any event was a weak approach, because Silloth reasonably prided itself as a holiday resort dependent on the railway, and many of the petitions against closure therefore came from holidaymakers. As a result of the closures I had a bad time during the election with several difficult meetings in the areas concerned. I was blamed twice over, first because the Government I supported was responsible for closing the railway, and second because I had failed to speak up in Parliament against the closures. I learnt further the emotional attachment which railways always have in any area. One farmer complained bitterly to me. In reply I asked him if he had travelled frequently on the line. 'A stupid question,' he replied. 'I have a car and I haven't travelled on the railway for many years. But,' he added, 'when I am in the fields close to the railway I rely on the train which passes at my dinner time to tell me when I should go home.' It would of course have been easy, but equally disastrous from an electioneering point of view, to suggest that he buy himself a watch.

Certainly I lost some support in the areas concerned, which was irritating because I had privately argued strongly against the closures. This underlines the difficult position of a junior Minister and the problems of conveying to the electorate the doctrine of the collective responsibility of a Government, particularly during an election. However, despite these difficulties and despite the fact that I have been consistently blamed for the closure of these railways almost ever since, I won my seat with a good majority in the constituency. It did not seem to be reduced much more than the Party average over the country as a whole.

Opposition Chief Whip, and Leader of the Commons

The harsh reality had to be faced. Although Labour had won the election by a much narrower margin than many expected, the Conservatives had lost power after thirteen years. For any party that is a traumatic experience, although easier to bear for a junior Minister, as I was. Yet I soon learnt some of the problems for, much to my surprise, Alec Douglas-Home asked me if I was prepared to be his Chief Whip. I had thought that in accordance with past practice I had left the Whips' world for good when I became a junior Minister. A problem had arisen, though, in the succession to Martin Redmayne who wanted to retire. The Deputy Chief Whip, Michael Hughes-Young, had lost his seat at the election and there was no other obvious candidate. I learnt subsequently that some leading members of the Party, and in particular Selwyn Lloyd, had favoured me for the job for some time. On the other hand, I did not believe that Martin Redmayne was keen on me for, although we had got on well personally, I had disagreed with him quite strongly when I was a junior Whip. Nevertheless, I was appointed to succeed him after a short handover period.

I was delighted at the prospect and, looking back today, I appreciate that being Chief Whip is a great parliamentary opportunity. Curiously, the Opposition Chief Whip is in some ways an even more interesting and important figure than the Government Chief Whip. The reason being that a Government Chief Whip is part of the great governmental machine and is surrounded by Ministers backed by large departments, while the Opposition Chief Whip is very much on his own. The whole conduct of parliamentary business has to be negotiated between the party Whips, officially known as the Usual Channels. In such negotiations a great deal depends on the Opposition Chief Whip. In consultation with the Leader of the Opposition and the Shadow Cabinet he has to make various deals with the Government. He has the complete responsibility thereafter for ensuring that such deals are honoured. The smooth working of Parliament depends to a considerable extent, first, on his judgment and, second, on the discipline he exerts in his own party. I hold the strong view that a party in Opposition will be successful only if it is disciplined. And a party in Opposition seeking to be the next Government must appreciate that as the Government it will be able to govern effectively only if its Parliamentary Party is founded on discipline. Third, Parliament as an institution is crucial to the success of our whole democratic system and a successful Parliament ultimately depends on good working relations between the parties.

Of course I understand that such views find little favour with the Press. That is hardly surprising, for newspapers thrive on controversy and if arguments are conducted between the parties, so much the better. A free Press is healthy for democracy because it is usually successful in uncovering the truth. But it still remains a fact that the more a party, through loyalty and discipline, manages to conduct its disagreements in private, the more successful its Government will be and, perhaps even more important, the more likely that party is to gain power and retain it. After all, if you believe in your party that must surely be the ultimate objective.

In fact I did not have time for such reflections when I became Opposition Chief Whip in 1964. I soon found that I had been thrown in at the deep end. It has always seemed to me that there is a strange difference between the Conservative and Labour Parties. The Labour Party at moments of difficulty usually indulges in fierce arguments about policies, whereas the Tories concern themselves with the personality of their Leader. Perhaps today the Labour Party is beginning to become involved in both at the same time – a development which cannot possibly do them any good.

In 1964 the wounds of the recent Tory leadership struggle were inevitably reopened by electoral defeat. Alec Douglas-Home was blamed by some, in my view totally unjustifiably. Nor did his obvious distaste for Opposition for its own sake improve his position. On the other hand, everyone admired him as a person, and a large body of opinion in the Parliamentary Party and the Party in the country was positively devoted to him and wanted him to remain.

Harold Wilson's strength at that time as a new Prime Minister fuelled the flames, for there were never two more contrasting personalities. The leadership critics in our Party wanted a rough, tough debater to knock the hell out of Harold Wilson. They did not accept that the strong position of a new Prime Minister makes this an almost impossible assignment. Nor did they realize that Harold Wilson was a powerful parliamentarian. Furthermore, the critics failed to appreciate how much Alec Douglas-Home was doing to make the Party fit for future battles. Major efforts were made at his instigation to increase the effectiveness of Conservative Central Office, to improve the quality of party agents and to bring new blood into the constituency associations and into the candidates list. For the first time Conservatives began to make systematic use of opinion polling.

Within nine days of the election defeat, Ted Heath was put in charge of a new policy-making process. His job was to get the Party into a position to fight an election with a fresh prospectus by the summer of 1965. Finally, because of the criticism both inside and outside the Party of what was described as the Magic Circle for electing a party Leader, an inquiry was launched into the best method of choosing one in the future. In February 1965 a new system was adopted under which the Leader would be elected by secret ballot among Members of Parliament before being presented to the National Union of the Conservative Party for endorsement.

It was clear that, despite the criticism, a large number of Conservative Members supported what Alec Douglas-Home was doing and were satisfied with his leadership. Furthermore, the Conservatives won more than 900 seats in the local government elections in May 1965. Harold Wilson, perhaps for that very reason, announced in June that there would be no election that year. In the circumstances that might have appeared to be a vindication of Alec Douglas-Home's efforts as a Leader in Opposition. Paradoxically this same decision stirred the leadership issue. Freed from fear of an imminent election, the critics in the Conservative Party could afford the risk of disunity which a leadership election might bring. They continued to harp on the need for a younger man and, indeed, the more successful Ted Heath was in his conduct of the Finance Bill Committee that summer, the more the critics felt that someone of his generation would be more suitable than Alec Douglas-Home as the Leader. This was accentuated by a feeling – which seems strange today – that there was a need for change simply for the sake of it. Anyone over sixty was to be subjected to instant derision as a member of the Old Guard.

Unfortunately these expressions of dissatisfaction were encouraged, as so often in politics, by an unlucky event from our party's point of view. Commander Donaldson, the Member of Parliament for Roxburgh and Selkirk, died soon after the general election and a by-election was pending in a difficult seat. It was also a seat with a strong Liberal challenge in the person of David Steel. Worse still, the constituency was in the Scottish Border country close to Alec Douglas-Home's home, so success or failure there inevitably became bound up with his prestige and position as Leader.

I was particularly apprehensive as the constituency, although across the Scottish border, was adjacent to my own. Furthermore, my wife's family lived there. Local information suggested that David Steel as a Liberal had made great inroads at the general election and that a bandwagon was rolling in his favour. A loss would, however, inevitably be represented by the critics, and so by the Press, as a vote of no confidence in Alec Douglas-Home's leadership. We lost the seat and so it proved. As the campaign against Alec Douglas-Home gathered force, my recollection is that the Parliamentary Party remained loyal on the whole. Nevertheless Members did report increasing anxiety in their constituencies along the lines I have already described.

As Chief Whip I had the task of assessing all these reports and of keeping my Leader informed. Looking back, I have often wondered if my reactions and advice would have been different if I had been more experienced in the task. I had little doubt that as a party we were in a bad position. At a time of his own choosing Harold Wilson would certainly call a general election, stating that he required a larger majority, but equally knowing that he would be taking advantage of our disarray. I reckoned that we would certainly lose that election quite substantially. Therefore if Alec Douglas-Home stayed on as Leader, his position after the election would be undermined. Alternatively, if he went and a new Leader was appointed who also lost, that would be a disastrous start for his leadership. What made it all the worse for me personally was that I was torn in my own mind between what I believed would be best for the Party and what would be best for Alec Douglas-Home. I felt that in the interests of the Party he should stay and fight the next election in the near future, as otherwise the new Leader would be handicapped by a probable electoral defeat. On the other hand, I did not want to see further criticism and unhappiness heaped on such a great man who deserved support from our party. In the end perhaps the outcome turned out for the best. By July the pressures for his resignation had become so great that Alec Douglas-Home decided that he would be right to resign. Ted Heath won the subsequent leadership election and, despite the inevitable loss in the 1966 General Election, was triumphantly successful in 1970. Alec Douglas-Home generously agreed to serve under him and became once again in 1970 a much admired and respected Foreign Secretary.

The actual resignation itself presented considerable risks for the Party. Despite the pressure for Alec Douglas-Home to go, a large and influential section of the Party remained fiercely loyal to him. He had to convince them that he was right to resign, otherwise our party disarray would have been complete.

We managed to keep the decision comparatively secret –

by today's standards amazingly so. Alec Douglas-Home was due to speak at a meeting of the 1922 Committee of Conservative Back-benchers before the summer recess on 22 July. He decided that he would announce his resignation then. Early in the day he touched me greatly by saying, 'Don't worry, I won't let you down.' He was certainly as good as his word, for his courage and bearing that day were worthy of the highest praise. At Question Time in the House of Commons he delighted our party with a devastating riposte which floored Harold Wilson. He broke the news to the 1922 Committee with such dignity and determination that his audience, many of whom were greatly shocked, simply had to accept it. I then accompanied him to a Press conference where the emotional feeling in his favour brought many of those there, hard-bitten reporters, close to tears. It was an experience I shall never forget.

Immediately the Party was launched into a leadership election under the new procedure, for we had to have a new Leader before Parliament rose for the long summer recess. This particular deadline has often made July both a traumatic and dangerous month in the parliamentary year. Subsequently in my career I have always dreaded it and all too frequently have had reason to do so. It was clear from the start that although Enoch Powell joined the election as the third candidate, the contest would be between Ted Heath and Reggie Maudling. My Whips and I were also convinced that it would be a close result. I was therefore determined that in this first test of the new procedure there must be no accusation of bias or, worse, of lobbying by the Whips. I told them that none of us must give any hint of how we would vote, not even to each other. I am glad to say that after the election no such accusations were made.

I learnt subsequently that my vote was entered by both camps on their lists, not an honourable position, but I suppose satisfactory in the circumstances. In truth, I voted for Ted Heath and told Reggie Maudling so immediately the result was announced. I hope I would have been equally frank with him if he had won. The Party had a difficult decision to make between two different personalities, both with excellent qualities. It was clear to me, watching from the sidelines, that Ted Heath's campaign was the more professionally run and was likely to give him the edge, but I never felt sure and was certain that the result would be close. Reggie Maudling, however, believed he was going to win and was bitterly disappointed by the result. Tragically, I don't think he was ever quite the same man again, which was sad for he had a remarkable talent. Outwardly, though, he took his defeat well and the Party settled down under Ted Heath's leadership with both Reggie Maudling and Alec Douglas-Home in the Shadow Cabinet.

Ted Heath invited me to continue as his Chief Whip and thus started an association which, from my point of view, was an extremely happy one. As a former Chief Whip, Ted Heath knew all about the job but he never interfered. Indeed, he gave me strong support and understanding even at the worst moments, for which I shall always remain grateful to him. His subsequent career after he was defeated as Prime Minister and lost the leadership of the Conservative Party has been sad for his friends to watch. But I suspect that all of us will retain happy memories of working with him.

Usually an Opposition Chief Whip escapes from his duties during parliamentary recesses. And so I hoped for a quiet time after the traumatic events of the change of leadership. But it was not to be. In September 1965 George Brown published what he described as the Government's National

Plan. He claimed that as it was a document issued on behalf of the nation, he should be allowed a television broadcast without any right of an Opposition reply which would have been normal in such cases. Iain Macleod was our economic spokesman and was furious when he heard the news. He argued vehemently that the National Plan was in effect a statement of the Labour Government's views and so the Conservative Opposition must be allowed a broadcast in reply. Ted Heath strongly supported him in his view and it fell to me as Chief Whip to sort out the controversy with the BBC. Those who remember Iain Macleod and George Brown will appreciate that neither was likely to give in.

I went to see Hugh Carleton Greene, then Director General of the BBC, and stated our case. I did not know him well. I was told that he naturally leant to the Left in politics and would almost certainly support George Brown and the Government. So I approached the large and formidable figure that he was with considerable trepidation. I had no need to do so, for I found him totally fair in his outlook and objective in our discussions. These took place against a background of fierce argument from both George Brown and Iain Macleod, each of whom was totally adamant. It would undoubtedly have been much easier for Hugh Carleton Greene to come down in favour of the Government, but eventually he decided that the BBC must allow the Opposition to state its case. I was delighted, since as a new Chief Whip I would have been subjected to much party criticism if my efforts had failed. George Brown was characteristically apoplectic at the decision and from then on Hugh Carleton Greene's relations with the Labour Party steadily deteriorated.

This incident, so early in my time as Chief Whip, dealing with these broadcasting problems, had a fundamental effect on my attitude to the whole problem of the relationship between the political parties and the broadcasting authorities. I had learnt, contrary to everything I had been told, that Hugh Carleton Greene on behalf of the BBC *would* stand up for the Opposition, the inevitable underdog, against Government demands. I appreciated his fairness on that occasion and the fearless attitude he took against what was undoubtedly strong Government pressure. Subsequently he often ruled against my representations on behalf of the Conservative Party, but I always retained a great admiration for him and firmly stood up for him against his critics, many in my own party.

This affair also profoundly affected my attitude to the handling of party matters in broadcasting. Since then I have had considerable experience in this field, both in Opposition and later as Home Secretary – the responsible Minister in Government. I have never changed my views, although I appreciate that they are not always widely shared. Of course the problems that arise seem totally different from a Government and an Opposition standpoint, as I have frequently found. Therefore I believe very strongly that the decisions must not be taken by the politicians closely concerned. An impartial judgment has to be made. That raises the question as to who should make such judgments, because sometimes they give rise to extreme political controversy.

I stand by the system which we in this country have devised and which has stood the test of time. The Government of the day chooses the Governors of the BBC to whom the Director General is responsible. The Governors are expected to be chosen on the basis of a reasonable political balance on the board. Similarly, for independent television the Government chooses the Chairman and members of the

IBA board. Both boards have the unenviable job on occasions of arousing considerable political controversy in deciding the rival claims. These are often presented against the backdrop of endless Press comment and indeed pressures of public opinion generally. I do not deny that on occasions I have been doubtful about the boards' judgments. But the alternative is surely for the Government of the day to make the decision in its position of being accountable to Parliament. This would inevitably lead to some governmental and parliamentary control of programmes. I would regard this as a most dangerous development in our system of parliamentary democracy.

When Parliament reassembled in the autumn of 1965 the Party was to discover that changing a Leader does not automatically solve any problems. It is a strange fact of British politics that often the frontiers of diverging attitudes, particularly on emotional issues, come down not between the main parties but rather inside one or the other. Thus African problems, immigration and racial difficulties divide the Conservative Party, whereas defence and public ownership cause similar problems in the Labour Party. It was therefore inevitable that Ian Smith's illegal unilateral declaration of independence in Rhodesia on 11 November 1965 would stir deep emotions in the country and would cause conflict inside the Conservative Parliamentary Party. Immediately the declaration was made, Harold Wilson as Prime Minister announced the withdrawal of British aid and a range of economic sanctions against Rhodesia. The House debated the issue on 12 November. Ted Heath deplored the act of UDI on constitutional grounds and this standpoint was broadly acceptable within the Party. The Conservative front-bench gave general support to the

Government's policy, but even then Patrick Wall warned that the right wing of the Conservative Party could not support 'punitive' sanctions against Rhodesia. In the Upper House, Lord Salisbury, with his substantial influence, defended Ian Smith and expressed sympathy for our 'kith and kin' in Rhodesia. Naturally there were many on the left of the Party who believed equally passionately that UDI was not only illegal but evil. These feelings were aired at a stormy meeting of the Parliamentary Party in the Commons on 16 November.

At a Monday Club meeting in the House on 22 November, on the eve of a second Commons debate, a number of back-benchers made clear their sympathy for Ian Smith. They pledged total opposition to an oil embargo and called on the Party leadership to reflect that view. In the Whips' Office we were all too conscious of the extent of feeling on both sides of the Party. The Shadow Cabinet tried to reflect most reasonable opinion by issuing a considered statement which supported economic sanctions but stopped short of acceptance of the oil embargo. The statement read, 'The proposal to break off all economic relations with Rhodesia contained in Paragraphs 8 & 9 of the Security Council Resolution goes far beyond the action recommended to Parliament as necessary and would have the effect of alienating loyal elements in Rhodesia, thereby defeating the purpose of our policy.' In the debate the following day Ted Heath backed Government action to date but challenged Harold Wilson to spell out his view on oil sanctions. At that stage Wilson did not do so.

Further economic sanctions were announced by the Prime Minister on 1 December. Limited military support for Zambia was also proposed; the Prime Minister stated that Britain could not 'stand idly by' if Zambian copper production was threatened by Rhodesia. Oil sanctions were not, however, mentioned. At this point, while we had misgivings about the extent and implications of any possible military commitment, the views of the two front-benches were not far apart. When Alec Douglas-Home on 13 December set out four principles for returning Rhodesia to constitutional, and eventually to majority, rule these were readily accepted by the Government. They in fact became the basis of the Six Principles on which Harold Wilson later made his stand.

So far, inside the Conservative Parliamentary Party, an uneasy truce had been preserved. But it was clear to me that trouble was just around the corner and that oil sanctions would trigger it off. And so it was with dismay that I heard the news on 17 December. Harold Wilson had bowed to strong pressure internationally and in his own party and had introduced an oil embargo. The measures were debated in the House of Commons on 20 and 21 December with the Conservative Party in a high state of emotion.

Opinions were sharply divided. Those on the left of the Party basically supported the Government and wanted a total economic blockade. This, however, was wholly unacceptable to those on the right, who were in essence against any sanctions and vehemently opposed oil sanctions in particular. In the main debate Ted Heath skilfully kept the Party together on the basis of a compromise motion rejecting the use of force. But the real crunch came on the oil sanctions order itself. All day I had worked desperately hard attending meetings of the opposing groups and arguing with individuals, my purpose being to obtain agreement on the Party as a whole abstaining on the order. We would therefore not be approving it but we would not be seeking actively to frustrate its passage. This was not in itself a particularly honourable or logical position, but it was the only means of preserving party unity under the leadership.

In the end, as the vote approached, I thought I might have succeeded. I obtained promises from both groups that they would stay out of the lobbies provided that all Members of the Party did so as well. That was good as far as it went, but I knew the risks. As all those with experience of whipping will know, such delicate arrangements are totally at the mercy of what we call the 'rogue elephants'. These are the Members who have not been involved in the internal party discussions and have managed to avoid their Whips, either by design or through absence from Parliament. They arrive at the last moment and, acting sometimes on a sudden impulse, walk into a lobby and vote. On this occasion there was undoubtedly some deliberate intent among those who adopted this course. Anyway, the rival groups were absolved from their bargain with me. The result was a total disaster for a Chief Whip: thirty-one Conservatives voted with the Government on the order; fifty others voted against the oil sanctions. The bulk of the Party and the front-bench abstained. Few Chief Whips achieve three-way splits of such an order and I can confirm that it is not a pleasant experience.

I left to catch my sleeper train home to Cumbria for Christmas in a state of misery, certainly lacking any spirit of goodwill towards my parliamentary colleagues. I blamed myself for the failure and reflected sadly that a Chief Whip's lot is frequently not a happy one. Little did I then know how often in my subsequent career I would be involved in similar emotional controversies with the Conservative Parliamentary Party. Worse still, coming when it did, this party split was particularly damaging for Ted Heath's leadership. It also gave Harold Wilson an opportunity to call an election in order to gain a bigger majority when the Opposition in Parliament and the country were weakened by internal strife.

On 27 January 1966 the Labour Party won a decisive victory in a by-election in Hull North. The swing of 4.5 per cent to Labour was the highest of the Parliament by that stage. Harold Wilson watched the polls for a few more weeks before announcing on 28 February the inevitable general election. No one seriously believed that Labour could lose. The campaign was as predictable as it was decisive. Labour returned with a majority of ninety-seven and the freedom to manage the country as they wished for the next five years.

From my own constituency point of view this was the most difficult general election I had to fight in my entire career. Once again, as Chief Whip, I had been silent in Parliament and so did not appear active in constituency matters. However, careful attention to correspondence on individual cases does build up a good reputation and I hope that I had managed to achieve that. I had an additional disadvantage in this election, though. My agent, Tommy Handy, who had introduced me to the constituency in 1954 and had been a tower of strength to me ever since, retired after the 1964 Election. He was a first-class agent of the old school, much loved in the area and greatly assisted by his wife. It was a sad loss as far as we were concerned. Fortunately the constituency obtained a worthy successor in Norman Dent, who remained my agent for the rest of my career. Again it would be impossible to express adequately my thanks to him and his wife. But in 1966 he was taking on a mammoth task in a vast country area which was unfamiliar to him.

In any case this was not a propitious moment to fight an election when public opinion was running strongly against the Conservative Party. It is, however, at such moments that a Member of Parliament learns the importance of becoming personally established in his constituency. Since we had moved to our home there, Ennim near Penrith, my wife and I had become closely involved in many activities not directly associated with party politics. In addition, I had bought a farm next door to my home and started to farm there in 1957. Of course I had not the time to be directly involved with the details, but the interest kept me in touch with farming problems in an agricultural constituency. Furthermore, I was lucky enough to obtain the services of an outstanding farm manager from a local farming family, Laurie Shuttleworth. He and his splendid family have been most happily associated with us ever since. Some time later he and his sons became partners with me in an enterprise called Mount Pleasant Farms which, thanks to their skill, established an excellent reputation for Charollais cattle. Now the farm is theirs and I am sure that the Shuttleworth family will farm it successfully for many years to come.

During the election campaign I spent some time as Chief Whip away from the constituency helping elsewhere – a requirement which increased greatly in subsequent elections. My wife therefore played a major role. Indeed, I began to discover that the more I was away and the more responsibilities she assumed, the better my majority became. Balancing all these factors, I think we had reason to be satisfied with a comfortable, if reduced, majority. But I returned to Parliament knowing that the task of an Opposition Chief Whip in maintaining party morale against a Government with a large majority was bound to be difficult.

This was also the moment of greatest difficulty for Ted Heath, as a new Leader, and I realized the responsibility that I owed to him.

Soon, however, I was given some real encouragement which was as generous as it was unexpected. The Opposition Chief Whip is not generally made a Privy Councillor because of his job. On the other hand, it is a great help to him in his own party and in Parliament as a whole to have the prestige and trust that goes with this honour. Harold Wilson appreciated the importance of Parliament as an institution. As I gladly recognize, he is also a generous man in many ways. He decided to recommend me for a Privy Councillorship in the New Year's Honours List of 1967. I certainly appreciated this gesture and the honour which, incidentally, was kindly received not only in my own party but in Parliament as a whole. It is at moments such as these that one realizes the value of Parliament's corporate spirit, which extends far beyond the narrow area of party battle.

In 1966 and 1967 we settled down in Parliament to the routine task of parliamentary Opposition in debates and on the Government legislation programme. There were, however, signs of increasing problems over immigration and race relations. Once again I realized that this meant dangers ahead for the Conservative Party. In 1962 the then Conservative Government had imposed some controls on Commonwealth immigration through their Act of that year. The Act has since been widely regarded as too modest, but at the time it aroused strong emotional opposition and internal strife inside the Conservative Party. However, by 1967 a considerable body of opinion believed that these controls were inadequate.

At the party conference that year Duncan Sandys initiated a campaign which warned of the alleged dangers of a mass movement of Asian immigrants from the newly independent territories of Kenya and Uganda. On independence, large numbers of settlers had opted to retain British nationality, rather than adopt a new African nationality. Duncan Sandys was strongly supported by Enoch Powell who, although he had returned to the Shadow Cabinet as defence spokesman, was taking an increasing interest in immigration issues. In February 1968, for example, he spoke of the sense of hopelessness and helplessness felt in the West Midlands over immigration. At this time the level of immigration and potential future movements also alarmed Jim Callaghan, then Labour Home Secretary. In late February, Callaghan brought forward the Commonwealth Immigrants Bill to impose for the first time a specific annual immigration quota on British passport holders from East Africa. The Shadow Cabinet agreed to back the Bill, although Iain Macleod led fourteen Conservatives into the lobbies against it. The Bill was rushed through both Houses and became law within six days of its publication on 1 March.

This emergency Bill was widely criticized. Only five weeks later, the Wilson Government published, partly as a counterweight, a Race Relations Bill to prevent various forms of discrimination. This time Conservative opinion was split three ways. The whole party wanted to maintain good race relations but there were differing views as to how that could be achieved. Some favoured the methods enshrined in the Bill; some were uneasy; others, such as Enoch Powell, were bitterly opposed to the principles of the Bill.

In order to reflect the balance of opinion in the Party, the Shadow Cabinet decided to propose at the second reading a reasoned amendment warning of the specific dangers that might arise from the Race Relations Bill. Enoch Powell helped to draft that amendment. It was therefore expected that he would support the Shadow Cabinet line. The second reading of the Bill was scheduled for 23 April. It was decided to impose only a two-line whip for our amendment.

I remember leaving the meeting after the Shadow Cabinet on Wednesday 17 April had drafted the amendment, hoping against hope that as a compromise it would keep some semblance of party unity. I was pleased that Enoch Powell had committed himself to it, as I knew how strongly he felt. I was therefore all the more distressed when I heard his speech in Birmingham on Saturday 20 April. I felt that as Chief Whip he should have told me about it in advance, particularly as I had always had good and courteous relations with him. When I discovered that he had not told Ted Heath or the Shadow Home Secretary, Quintin Hogg, I was totally outraged. Frankly, I knew then that I could never bring myself fully to trust him again.

Predictably, against the emotional background of race relations, the lurid language in his speech caused a violent storm. Feelings ran high on both sides, particularly in the Conservative Party. Ted Heath himself, and Quintin Hogg who had the delicate task of keeping the Party together, were inevitably furious. Other members of the Shadow Cabinet, especially Iain Macleod, Robert Carr and Edward Boyle, made it clear that they could not remain in the Shadow Cabinet unless Enoch Powell resigned.

I spent most of that Sunday with Ted Heath and greatly admired his courage at this moment of crisis. He knew the likely strength of support which Enoch Powell would receive from the Conservative Party in Parliament, in the country and indeed from many outside our party ranks altogether. On the other hand, he personally knew that he could not support the tone of the speech any more than could many of his leading colleagues. And so he rang up Enoch Powell on the Sunday night and asked for his resignation. He then put out a dignified statement which criticized the speech as 'racialist in tone and liable to exacerbate racial tension'. This was supported by the Shadow Cabinet on the Monday, which backed Heath's firm and courageous stand.

Meantime, with the Race Relations Bill to be debated on the Tuesday, the storm broke. The Conservative Party was desperately split. Many people outside our party ranks, including the marching London dockers and Smithfield porters, supported Enoch Powell. Inevitably Ted Heath's leadership was threatened by the emotional outburst. Matters worsened on the Tuesday. On the second reading debate on the Bill, another Shadow Cabinet member, Edward Boyle, voted with the Government in defiance of the Party whip. Ted Heath's critics complained that Edward Boyle received no public reprimand and said that he too should have been dismissed like Enoch Powell. They pressed this line at a meeting of the 1922 Committee on 25 April. They were, in *The Times*' phrase, 'routed'.

Thereafter we simply had to ride out the storm. Our difficulties with the Race Relations Bill did not end there. On the third reading in July we again decided not to whip against the principle of the Bill. Over forty back-benchers opposed our line and divided the House against the Bill, as a result of which I was criticized for that decision. In fact I was simply carrying out a Shadow Cabinet decision. It was indeed the only possible line for the Party at that time. Moreover, genuine though our angry back-benchers were in their convictions, it cannot in retrospect be denied that the kind of discrimination which the 1968 Act aimed to deal with was – and is – intolerable. The Conservative Party has argued for a quarter of a century that firm control of immigration is essential to good race relations; similarly it has fought for equal treatment for all our citizens before the law. I believe that balance was, and will continue to be, the right one. I have stood by it ever since and, of course, frequently the same critics have subsequently disagreed with me, particularly when I was Home Secretary.

Feelings in the Conservative Party continued to run high on immigration and race issues throughout the rest of the Parliament. But we were compensated by troubles within the Labour Government. We had by-election and local government election successes and the standing of the Party improved throughout 1969.

In Parliament there were two developments which had a considerable, even if negative, influence on events in the end. These were Dick Crossman's plan for the reform of the House of Lords and Barbara Castle's proposal named 'In Place of Strife' for the reform of the trade union movement. Their influence was negative because both were in fact eventually abandoned. But they did have a damaging effect on the standing and prestige of Harold Wilson and his Government, which clearly redounded with advantage to the Conservative Party.

A White Paper on the future of the House of Lords was published in March 1968. The plan would have phased out the right of hereditary peers to sit in the chamber. It would have created a new two-tier House of Lords, comprising 'voting' and 'non-voting' members. 'Voting' members would have been expected to play a full-time role. There were to be about 230 of them, distributed between the parties to give the Government of the day a small majority over other parties, but not an overall majority if a small number of cross-benchers were taken into account. Other members of the House, including existing hereditary peers, could move motions, sit on committees and ask questions, but would have no vote on legislation. The reformed House would have the power of at most six months' delay on legislation.

Given the detailed discussions that had taken place before the Crossman plan was produced, it appeared possible that there might be agreement on it. When the White Paper was debated in the Lords in mid-November, Lord Carrington, then Leader of the Opposition, spoke in favour of it for the Conservative Party. Although Lord Salisbury and others opposed what they felt would be too great a reduction in the power of the Lords to check Government legislation, the motion giving general approval to the proposals was passed by 251 votes to fifty-six.

It was to be on another feature of the proposals that problems arose. This related to the simple issue of who would designate the new class of 'voting' peers. The White Paper had envisaged a committee with an independent chairman of 'national standing', backed by party representatives as well as other independents. Many ordinary Members of both Houses felt that such a committee would amount to little more than a figleaf to cover a further extension of the powers of patronage of the party hierarchies and of the Whips. When the issue was debated in the Commons on 19 and 20 November 1968, the Labour back-bencher, Willie Hamilton, tabled an amendment to reject the White Paper. He struck a chord with back-benchers on both sides in describing the plan as a conspiracy between the two front-benches. These were not the only grounds for worry. Many Conservatives were opposed in principle to the very idea of reform. The two forces combined to challenge the Crossman deal. The Hamilton motion was lost by 270 votes to 159, but 103 Conservatives gave him their support.

In the Conservative Party we were under no illusion that a significant number of our back-benchers could not support the reform plan which came forward for second reading in the form of a parliamentary Bill on 3 February 1969. I warned Ted Heath of the extent of the opposition within our party. He decided that the Opposition front-bench, which had after all been represented in the Inter-Party Conference, should support the Bill. However it was decided that back-benchers on our side should be allowed a free vote. On the Labour side Harold Wilson was faced with the resistance of a group of two dozen or so left-wingers led by that most unlikely defender of the House of Lords, Michael Foot. They bitterly opposed the extension of the power of patronage and the creation of a class of 'voting' peers, whom Foot described as a potential 'seraglio of eunuchs' dependent for their seats in the Lords on their party Leaders' whim. The Bill was given a second reading by a majority of 150, but this time 105 Conservatives voted against it, together with twenty-seven far-left Labour MPs.

Many of the Bill's Conservative opponents were as implacably opposed to the idea of any change in the House of Lords as the Labour Left were to having any House of Lords at all. They were agreed only on the need to defeat the Bill. A strange alliance of Labour Left and Tory Right was formed – to formidable effect. The likes of Michael Foot, Enoch Powell, Eric Heffer, John Boyd-Carpenter, Robert Sheldon and John Peyton joined together to put up bitter resistance throughout the committee stage. Hosts of amendments, filibusters and continuous points of order were raised to delay the Bill's progress. The more the measure was debated, the greater the opposition to it seemed to become. In two months only four of the twenty clauses had been dealt with. As the Bill was being taken on the floor of the House, it was eating up parliamentary time and damaging relations within the Labour Party. The Government finally accepted the inevitable.

Subsequently Peter Carrington chided me in a friendly way, saying that I had considerable responsibility for the Bill's failure. 'Surely,' he said, 'a Chief Whip who was any good would have tried harder to get his troops into the lobby in favour of a Bill supported by his own front-bench! At least he could have stopped the filibustering tactics!' Certainly I could have tried harder, although I believe I would not have succeeded against the type of opposition emanating from our own back-benches. But I never accepted the charge that further effort would have been wise for an Opposition Chief Whip in my position. After all, it was a Government Bill. The Labour Party was splitting its own members and so weakening its general position in the years immediately leading up to a general election. Equally, if I had tried harder, I would have aroused similar reactions on the Conservative back-benches and so neutralized any advantage we had gained. Furthermore, some of the opponents in our party were still all too ready to attack Ted Heath's leadership on the race issue, and would have used divisive action to this end. Not for the first or last time in my life I concluded then that masterly inactivity can have considerable advantages. Certainly it proved so in this case. And, with the benefit of hindsight and my subsequent experience, I am convinced that the House of Lords is far more valuable as it stands.

Harold Wilson abandoned the Bill nominally to allow time for legislation on Barbara Castle's proposal in a White Paper for the reform of the trade unions. These proposals were equally ill-fated and even more divisive in the Labour ranks. In a short time they were dropped. From this blow the basic prestige of the Wilson Government never really recovered.

Despite these setbacks, however, the Labour Government suddenly found itself in May 1970 with a renewed lead in the opinion polls. This was the first time it had been ahead since February 1967. An election could have been delayed until April 1971, but with the improvement of the Government's position, Harold Wilson believed that he had what has come to be known as a 'window of opportunity'. Accordingly, he called an election for 18 June 1970. At that time opinion polls were very much in the ascendancy and had acquired an air of infallibility. Looking back, that seems extraordinary, because they were neither as frequent, as widespread, nor as sophisticated as they are today. Nevertheless, Harold Wilson and the Labour Party were confident in their predictions and, fortunately from our Conservative point of view, somewhat complacent. We, for our part, were apprehensive, particularly as our internal tensions lay not far below the surface. We had, however, achieved a greater degree of unity on policies as a result of a successful Shadow Cabinet weekend conference at Selsdon Park at the end of January.

The general election of 1970 was notable both for the greater extent of its domination by opinion polls and for television and advertising techniques. Tony Barber, the Chairman of the Party, enlisted my assistance as Chief Whip at Central Office in order to deal with the television problems. I thus spent more time in London away from my constituency. I also worked closely for the first time with Geoffrey Tucker, who was then our Director of Public Relations. His skill in this field has since been fully recognized and appreciated, but I learnt during this general election just how important a part he played in our Conservative victory. He understood that the Labour Party was vulnerable because Harold Wilson had decided to fight a complacent campaign, relying not on his Government's future plans but on his own record.

Our Conservative campaign therefore concentrated in large measure on the issue of rising prices under Labour. I have a vivid memory of Geoffrey Tucker constantly armed with a shopping basket showing how much each item in it had risen over the years of the Labour Government. He was convinced that housewives would be swayed in this way, and they were.

Ted Heath's television campaign was well planned and he personally came across extremely successfully, thus scoring heavily over Harold Wilson, then regarded as almost invincible. In the campaign Geoffrey Tucker, ably supported by two top advertising professionals – Jim Garrett, head of a successful film production company, and Barry Day, creative director of a leading advertising agency – broke new ground in the use of television in this country to project a political party, its Leader and its policies.

In addition, the traditional party political broadcasts were turned into a series of television 'programmes' which commented on the campaign issues as they emerged. Christopher Chataway and Geoffrey Johnson-Smith – two of our MPs who had previous reputations as broadcasters – linked our programme, *A Better Tomorrow*, and gained very respectable ratings in so doing. The programmes even contained pointed anti-Labour 'commercials'. During the 1979 Election much was written about the Conservative use of media and advertising, but the seeds were undoubtedly sown in this election.

Nevertheless, relying as we did on the polls, there was little to lead us to comfortable conclusions during the campaign. Indeed, I confess to many private moments of pessimism and gloom when I was only too pleased to leave the hothouse atmosphere of the Central Office in Smith Square for the peace and confident spirit of my own constituency.

After the election was over I recall many of my colleagues saying that they knew we were going to win throughout the campaign. It is sometimes easy to be wise after the event, particularly when the pollsters have on the whole taken a bloody nose. I must say I wish I had had such confidence. On the contrary, I remember the Monday night of the last week, when I heard with total dismay that the Labour lead in the poll had increased to 13 per cent. I imagine that even Ted Heath, whose courage and determination in all circumstances were an example to us, must have suffered some despair at that moment. I also recall the other side of the coin, early on the morning of polling day itself, when I was rung up and told of a final poll by Tommy Thomson's organization, ORC, actually putting the Tories in the lead. I made some frantic telephone calls to gain publicity as last-minute encouragement. However, I must accept that I did not really believe it.

How was it then that the Conservatives actually obtained a majority of thirty-two? With the benefit of hindsight and the experience of subsequent elections, I would suggest a few tentative reasons. First, a Prime Minister should never believe that a sudden change in public opinion offers a secure enough basis for calling a snap election. There needs to be a steady trend for some months, preferably substantiated by similar indications from by-elections and local elections in favour of the Government. Second, as Margaret Thatcher has so triumphantly proved, a Government seeking re-election must not fight on a complacent ticket, looking backwards and relying on its record. Instead it must seek a mandate for a forward-looking programme building on its achievements. In 1970, the Labour Party campaign was based on complacency, and Harold Wilson projected an over-confident image. Ted Heath exploited this position with great success and our Conservative campaign had a vision for the future. Contrary to the views of many who fought this election, I believe therefore that the campaign did substantially affect the result along these lines.

In my own constituency my wife worked extremely hard. I did some whirlwind tours through the villages and held a few meetings in the towns when I was able to get away from London. My organization worked very well under Norman Dent. And in the end my majority was substantially increased.

Friday 19 June was the most exciting day in my life. Suddenly, contrary to all my expectations, the long years of Opposition were over and the hard slog as Opposition Chief Whip had paid a dividend. In those days my constituency count did not finish until the Friday afternoon. Ted Heath required me urgently in Downing Street to discuss the formation of his Government. As I flew down from Carlisle I was thinking about the prospective Government and had little time to contemplate my own personal future. I did not therefore experience at that time the real thrill of anticipation at becoming a Cabinet Minister. As I look back now, after some twelve years' service in Cabinet, I realize the remarkable nature of the institution and the great experience it provides. It is not just the feeling of history which pervades the Cabinet room, where so many momentous decisions have been taken, nor is it simply the realization that you are at the centre of events and sometimes at moments of historic importance. There is also the valuable feeling of comradeship, strangely combined with the inevitable clash of powerful personalities. Then there is the challenge of deciding on the right tactics to be employed, both when to speak and when to be silent.

A wise Cabinet Minister thinks carefully about all these matters and discusses his plans with those of his colleagues closest to him. But of course there are times when emotions take over and well-laid plans are abandoned. All this adds up to the simple fact that the Cabinet is essentially a human institution, which should be studied and enjoyed, but never treated lightly by any Cabinet Minister.

I was delighted to become also Lord President of the Council and Leader of the House of Commons. Strangely, I became Lord President of the Council again in 1983 as Leader of the House of Lords. I therefore held this ancient office, which was basically of a ceremonial order, for just over six years in all. The holder is ministerially responsible to Her Majesty The Queen for the running of the Privy Council and its meetings. But his duties are not onerous, as he is excellently served by the Clerk and a most efficient office with a long tradition of ceremonial service behind them. The Lord President thus has time for his other governmental and parliamentary duties which, as far as the House of Lords and the House of Commons are concerned, always seem to be on the increase.

In 1970 I was extremely lucky, for my Deputy Chief Whip in Opposition, Francis Pym, became Government Chief Whip. He and I had worked closely together over the years and I had the highest regard for his knowledge of the House of Commons and for his skill in management there.

We were soon faced with some of the most difficult parliamentary problems. The first major one concerned Britain's entry into the European Community. Ted Heath, who had conducted the negotiations during the Macmillan Government in the early 1960s, was determined to succeed this time in leading Britain into Europe. Success in negotiations was, however, only the beginning of a major parliamentary task. Both parties were split. The vast majority of our Conservative Members of Parliament supported Ted Heath, but we had some dedicated opponents who were against entry on sovereignty grounds. On the whole, the Labour Party was either opposed to entering or lukewarm, but there was a small minority of Labour Members – led with considerable skill and complete commitment by Roy Jenkins – who were dedicated Europeans. The parliamentary arithmetic was therefore extremely difficult, for there was no clear parliamentary majority and the results depended on the determination with which the dedicated Members in either of the major parties were prepared to defy their Leaders.

The negotiations themselves were satisfactorily concluded, largely through the skill of Ted Heath himself and Geoffrey Rippon. As a result, on 17 June 1971 Ted Heath was able to make the historic statement in the House of Commons that negotiations were nearing success and that a White Paper on Britain's entry to the Community would soon be published. That paper emerged in July. It formed the background to the debate on the principle of entry which began on 21 October.

While the negotiations in Europe were proceeding, equally intensive negotiations were taking place at Westminster where the pro- and anti-European camps were preparing their battlelines. Within a month of the new Parliament meeting, forty-four Conservative back-benchers had signed an Early Day Motion, effectively saying no to Britain's entry. At the same time the Conservative Group for Europe, the umbrella group for pro-Europeans, was actively seeking to recruit those sitting on the fence. Meanwhile, by design or perhaps by indecision, the Labour Party remained uncommitted. So long as Labour hesitated, the temptation for Conservative doubters to break ranks remained strong. In mid-1971 when the negotiations reached a climax we at home still could not be certain that there was a majority in the House of Commons for entry. Francis Pym strongly advised that it would be unwise to seek a vote in favour of entry before the House went down for the recess in the summer. I had no doubt that such advice was correct, particularly as my old fear of July as a difficult parliamentary month was once more to the fore.

Strong though it was in a section of the Party in the House of Commons, the anti-Market view was never of overwhelming influence in the Conservative Party as a whole. At the party conferences in the autumn the Labour Party developed its policy of renegotiation, and the mass of the Tory Party gave Ted Heath strong support for entry. He felt that the Parliamentary Party too should give him its support in what was, to him, the single most important task facing the Government. But the fact was that nothing would have persuaded many of those on our side who were opposed in principle to what they saw as a surrender of sovereignty. Equally, no opportunist argument was going to persuade those in the Labour Party who believed that international co-operation was the right way forward to oppose the principle of entry, simply because it had been negotiated by the Conservatives.

Summing up these conflicting trends, Francis Pym advised that the right course would be to allow our Members a free vote. We might lose more Members than we would otherwise, but he believed that it would make it easier for Labour MPs to abstain or to vote in our lobby for the process of entry. This was agreed by the Cabinet, and it certainly turned out to be a wise and politically prudent decision.

Personally, my strong support for joining Europe was based more on broad foreign policy than on economic grounds. Having lived through the 1939–45 war, I was desperately keen to ensure that no further world wars would start through quarrels in Western Europe. European unity, embracing France and Germany particularly, provides a major insurance against such an eventuality. Britain's membership of the European Community clearly makes a significant contribution to this ideal. I still hold this view today, and I only hope that the great gains of a united Europe will not be submerged in petty disagreement about economic details.

The debate on the principle of entry took six days in the House. At the end, on 28 October, we had a majority of 112. The Treaty of Accession was signed in January 1972, but we all knew that that was not the end of the matter. The Treaty of Accession had to be ratified in a parliamentary Act. This meant that we had to present a Bill to Parliament which would inevitably involve long and complicated discussion. It was obvious that we could not expect the Labour voters who had supported us on the simple principle of entry to continue to give support in similar numbers throughout the passage of a difficult Government Bill.

The Bill could have been several hundred clauses long. Equally, some argued strongly that it should be simply a one-clause enabling Bill, in order to limit scope for amendment and delay. A one-clause Bill would, however, have been deeply resented in Parliament and might have jeopardized the whole crucial principle of entry. So a compromise was reached – a short twelve-clause Bill was presented to the House for second reading on 15–17 February 1972.

Intensive efforts were made to cement Government support on what, given whipped Labour Opposition, was bound to be a touch-and-go vote. Ted Heath put the whole future of the Government on the line by saying that he would resign if the Bill was rejected. It passed by just eight votes – 309 to 301, with fifteen Conservatives in the Labour lobby. It was an historic night.

The Bill was hard fought-over for five months throughout its remaining stages. There were no less than eighty-eight divisions concerned with this relatively short Bill and in all of these there were votes against the Government by Conservative back-benchers. In some of those votes the Government majority fell to only four or five. The successful passage of the Bill leading to Britain's entry into the European Community was a remarkable achievement by the Heath Government. Ted Heath himself deserved great credit not only for his inspiration but also for his courage and determination throughout a long battle. Geoffrey Rippon was extremely skilful in the negotiations and in the detailed handling of the Bill. But those who appreciate the problems of parliamentary and party management will also want to give credit to Francis Pym for his achievement as Chief Whip.

One other major problem arose from our Conservative election manifesto commitment on trade union reform. The Wilson Government had failed to carry through Barbara Castle's proposals, 'In Place of Strife', in the previous Parliament, and so there was strong support in our party for immediate action. Looking back, we now know that trade union resistance to such change was not only very strong but also still commanded substantial support in the country. It needed further hard experience, culminating in the Winter of Discontent in 1978 under Jim Callaghan's Government, before the British people were ready to give continuous backing to a Government for trade union reform. Later experience also suggests that the 1970 plans attempted to do too much at once.

However that may be, the Bill that came forward for second reading on 10 December 1970 aroused great passion and bitterness in Parliament and indeed in the trade union movement throughout the country. Soon, in January 1971, I had to announce as Leader of the House a guillotine motion. It is strange to reflect today that, inspired by Michael Foot's example as Leader of the House in the Labour Government from 1974 to 1979, 'guillotines' – or timetable motions, as they are officially called – are now everyday occurrences. Indeed, there are those who even advocate timetables for all Bills. That was certainly not so in 1971. Despite a most generous allocation of time, my announcement was greeted with a storm of protest which certainly caused me, as indeed it would any Leader of the House, considerable nervous apprehension. How lucky Leaders of the House are today in this regard.

At the end of the debate on my motion some forty Labour Members stood in front of the mace, defied the Speaker, and the sitting had to be suspended. Finally, after many hours of debate, the Report Stage finished at midnight on 23 March. The Labour Opposition decided to challenge by division all the amendments that had not been debated, in order to prove that the Bill had been inadequately discussed. We therefore had to have fifty-seven separate divisions on the undebated amendments, the largest number in any single sitting of the House of Commons, and I imagine that record still stands today. The whole process lasted over eleven hours of continuous voting. It would in fact have gone on longer, had a large number of Government amendments not been withdrawn and subsequently passed in the House of Lords. Even when the Bill returned from there at the end of July, there was fierce controversy still over the use of the guillotine. It is certainly ironic that Michael Foot, of all people, should have succeeded in changing the whole climate of opinion on restricting parliamentary debates. Even more so when the Industrial Relations Bill of 1971, which he so strenuously opposed, provided almost the last major storm over the old guillotine procedure.

The Irish Question

During the time while I, as Leader of the House of Commons, was closely involved in the European Communities Bill, the situation in Northern Ireland was seriously deteriorating. I was not directly involved in the major responsibility, as this was borne by Ted Heath himself, Reggie Maudling as Home Secretary and Peter Carrington as Secretary of State for Defence. But I attended many Government discussions and came to learn something of the mounting difficulties. Even then, however, I certainly never imagined that shortly the troubles in Northern Ireland would dramatically change the course of my political career.

During 1971 the situation there was steadily going from bad to worse. In March of that year James Chichester-Clark resigned as Prime Minister at Stormont, partly because of difficulties inside the Unionist Party but also, as he stated in his resignation statement, 'in order to bring home to all those concerned the realities of the present constitutional, political and security situation'. I was a great friend of his brother Robin, one of Ulster's Westminster MPs. He had been a Whip with me in previous Parliaments and had kept me closely informed on Northern Ireland. He was in no doubt of the gravity of the situation, which Brian Faulkner then took over. I knew that James Chichester-Clark was a brave, honest and wholly straightforward person and his obvious dismay at the situation worried me greatly. Reggie Maudling, whose political brain I greatly admired, was also deeply pessimistic. Nevertheless, as I learnt in my close association with him later, Brian Faulkner was a courageous and determined man. He made strenuous efforts to improve the security situation and political co-operation between the Northern Ireland parties. But he was constantly frustrated by increasing violence. In August 1971, following a heavy bombing campaign in Belfast, he asked the British Government to agree to internment. Ted Heath and Reggie Maudling agreed, but I know that they were anxious about the decision.

I later learnt a great deal about the implications of internment without trial. And so, with the benefit of hindsight, I will offer some observations on its implications. Internment without trial is, to risk stating the obvious, a serious decision which can be justified only if it succeeds in reducing violence. It must, however, be accepted that before it can succeed it is bound to increase tension and so initially to provoke the very violence it is designed to lessen. For this reason it is a high-risk policy. If it is to have any hope of succeeding, it must be accompanied by first-class intelligence which ensures that the really dangerous terrorists – and only the really dangerous terrorists – are quickly taken out of circulation. Unfortunately this was not the case in August 1971. Too many were interned and, as I discovered when I subsequently examined the papers after Direct Rule, a large proportion comprised not really active terrorists. The introduction of internment was predictably followed by heavy rioting during which twenty-one people were killed in three days. Thereafter internment did nothing to stem the deterioration in the situation. On the contrary, it remained a source of discontent and a spur to more violence.

In September of that year the British Parliament was recalled for an emergency debate on Northern Ireland. There were discussions between Ted Heath, Jack Lynch – the Prime Minister of the Republic of Ireland – and Brian Faulkner. There were constant contacts between the British and Northern Ireland Governments, with particular talks between Reggie Maudling and Brian Faulkner. All to no avail. At the end of the year Reggie Maudling, as he wrote in his *Memoirs*, was profoundly pessimistic and, as he told me, had increasing doubts about the possibility of maintaining the Stormont system of Government. Of course, with his clear and logical brain, Reggie Maudling found the Irish mentality almost impossible to understand. He could not be bothered with their constant determination to be governed by their preoccupations of the past rather than face up to the problems of the present and the future. He was a very unemotional man himself and simply could not stand emotional tantrums in others.

Then, on 30 January 1972, there came a decisive blow – Bloody Sunday, as it is now called, in Londonderry. At the end of a civil rights demonstration which had been banned, the firing started and thirteen people were killed by British troops. All hell broke loose in the next few days. There was extensive rioting. The Republic recalled her Ambassador to the United Kingdom and declared a national day of mourning. The UK Embassy in Dublin was burnt down. Bernadette Devlin, an Ulster Republican MP at Westminster, physically attacked Reggie Maudling in the House of Commons. There was an emergency debate at Westminster when Labour divided the House. All sorts of extremist statements were made. Nor did Reggie Maudling's announcement of the Widgery inquiry into the shootings do anything to calm the situation.

The violence in Northern Ireland continued to increase, with the Stormont Government looking increasingly beleaguered against the background of an emotionally divided Westminster Parliament. In this atmosphere there was inevitably mounting speculation in the Press of some new initiative by the British Government. Later, the IRA explosion in the Parachute Brigade Mess in Aldershot and the attempted assassination of John Taylor, the Stormont Government Minister, simply added fuel to the flames. That famous and often dangerous phrase, 'something must be done', became the inevitable comment of the moment.

Throughout February and early March there were more talks and discussions and further Press rumours. Brian Faulkner remained convinced that the British Government would not take Direct Rule unless there was a complete breakdown. But I remember feeling that the inevitable contingency planning would have to lead soon to some clear action.

Eventually, on Wednesday 22 March, Ted Heath asked Brian Faulkner and Jack Andrews to London for talks. For the first time I joined Ted Heath, Alec Home, Reggie Maudling and Peter Carrington on the British side. As far as I knew officially at that stage, I had been invited because of the parliamentary implications of any British initiative. Nevertheless I knew that my name had been linked with rumours about a possible Secretary of State. Nothing, however, had been said to me.

At these talks Ted Heath put forward the proposals which had been agreed by the Cabinet. They were a transfer to Westminster of all security powers and responsibility for criminal matters, followed by a constitutional referendum, a move towards ending internment, the appointment of a Secretary of State for Northern Ireland at Westminster, and open-ended talks with the Social Democratic and Labour Party on the form of Government with a view to reaching a community Government. There is no doubt that Brian Faulkner and his team were completely taken aback by these plans and really could not believe that Ted Heath was in earnest. As the talks continued, it became increasingly clear not only that the British Government was quite firm in its intentions, but that Brian Faulkner was not prepared to consider any such plans. He made it perfectly clear, as I remember it, that he could not recommend any such proposals to the Stormont Cabinet because he believed that they would be left in a powerless position. As he has since made plain, he thought the plans insulting and completely unacceptable. Looking back, I greatly regret that this was the result of all these talks.

After all, the basic premise of the British plan had considerable logic, for divided responsibility is always likely to end in disaster. The British Government provided the troops who were employed in an increasingly prominent role as the terrorist situation worsened. The Northern Ireland Government had devolved responsibility for law and order, but they had no constitutional authority to direct the policy to be followed by the British Army, which was playing a major and, at times, dominant part in dealing with violence. Inevitably, as the security situation deteriorated, the actions of the security forces became ever more entangled in the basic controversy of the Northern Ireland situation. This in turn led to severe, even if at times totally unjustified, criticism of troop actions both in the British Parliament and from world opinion. As a result, the British Government found itself increasingly condemned for troop actions when the basic responsibility had been delegated to the Northern Ireland Government. Really neither the British Government nor the Westminster Parliament could be expected to tolerate such a state of affairs for long. On the other hand, from the Northern Ireland Government's point of view, the position of the police was crucial. The Royal Ulster Constabulary, as I came to learn, is a brave and much to be admired police force, often operating in difficult circumstances. But the terrorist situation of 1971-2 was well beyond the capacity of any police force. The proper position of the troops being used in support of the police was therefore steadily eroded. In these circumstances the British Government's plan had to include both troops and police as they worked together in the security situation.

It was clearly very difficult for Brian Faulkner and his colleagues to surrender operational control of the police. In addition, Unionist opinion in Northern Ireland would certainly have been outraged. Nevertheless, I still feel that if there had been more time to consider the proposals calmly, the Northern Ireland Government might have been persuaded. But as always at moments of crisis, time is a commodity in short supply. Once the nature of the talks became public there could be no delay in making a decision. Probably my thoughts years afterwards represent a counsel of perfection, rarely obtainable in practice. Yet some of the more desperate problems at the start of Direct Rule might have been avoided. Certainly later experience convinced me that, for example, Brian Faulkner and a new Secretary of State, whether me or another, could have worked amicably under the British plan. After all, despite the appalling emotional stress caused by the introduction of Direct Rule, Brian Faulkner and I did work together amicably in the period leading up to the introduction of the power-sharing executive only some eighteen months later. And today, relying on my own experience, I believe that Brian Faulkner's untimely death was one of the greatest tragedies of the present Northern Ireland situation. His leadership has been sadly missed.

However all that may be, the talks continued all day on Wednesday 22 March. Clearly it would have been possible to reach some agreement on the minor elements of the plan, but there was never any sign of a compromise on the basic security issue and so, late on Wednesday night, we parted in disagreement. Brian Faulkner and his team returned to Northern Ireland to put the position to his Cabinet the next day. Ted Heath said that the British Cabinet would also meet. However, he made it clear that at that meeting they would certainly reaffirm their position.

That night I remember feeling depressed and somewhat apprehensive, for we were embarking on a collision course full of hazards. Still, I was nothing like as apprehensive as I would have been had I known then about my future role as Secretary of State. On Thursday 23 March both parties reaffirmed their positions. Brian Faulkner resigned but agreed to stay in office until the legislation enabling Direct Rule was passed. He came over to London late in the afternoon to agree on the formalities. It was not until after midnight that these meetings finished.

During the day the gossip about my position had hardened and I remember Robert Armstrong, Ted Heath's Principal Private Secretary, discussing with me the possibility of my becoming Secretary of State. And so when Ted Heath called me in some time after midnight I was forewarned. I had not given it a great deal of thought, but I knew that if I was offered the job I could not refuse. First, I remembered the advice given me by my old friend, Charlie MacAndrew, when I first entered the House of Commons: 'Never appear too eager for any appointment, but never refuse one that is offered to you.' I can faithfully say that I have followed that excellent advice throughout my career. Second, I could never have believed in myself again if I had failed to accept a really daunting challenge. I would have felt that I had been a coward; frankly I would have been. And so I accepted Ted Heath's offer to become Secretary of State for Northern Ireland. There was little to be said, for we both knew each other so well and appreciated the situation. I felt better when I left him, for on such occasions Ted was at his best in a mood of quiet imperturbability and courage. It may seem surprising that I did not ask for time to discuss the appointment with my wife, but I knew what Celia would say and anyway it would not have rung true to Ted Heath, who knew her well enough to appreciate what her answer would be. When I got home and woke her up I found her characteristically more concerned with an urgent family problem which confronted us at that moment. She told me about that and then said that I obviously needed some sleep. On that note she threw herself wholeheartedly into this new and totally unpredictable chapter in our lives. Strangely enough, I obeyed her instructions and slept soundly. I am one of those lucky people who can sleep in almost any circumstances.

I woke up with my previous apprehension replaced by a mood of determination and excitement in the face of a major challenge. And so I was ready to face the public announcement of both Direct Rule and my appointment as Secretary of State. Ted Heath made the statement in the House of Commons at 11 a.m. on Friday 24 March. It is rare for such major announcements to be made on a Friday.

It is recorded, which is hardly surprising in the circumstances, that the House had not been so crowded on a Friday for many years. It is also recorded that while I did not speak I was clearly touched by the reaction to my appointment. Indeed, one comment suggested that I was seen to shed tears. Certainly I felt somewhat overcome, for I have always been affected by the emotional atmosphere of the House of Commons. I have experienced its attitude to me in all its moods, and I have found that appreciation of its feelings very helpful. At times I have been most encouraged by strong support. And when that support comes from all parties, the House of Commons can be a great strength at moments of trial. Ordinary hostility from an Opposition party has to be faced as an accepted part of the party battle. Sometimes there is a genuine hostility behind it, and it is a foolish Minister who does not recognize that and take account of it. Hostility from your own party behind you is both unpleasant and worrying. If one has to ride through it, as I have done on occasions, there is only one rule: you must go out of your way to show your opponents that you bear them no grudge.

On this Friday morning the warmth of the general feeling was overwhelming and that gave me great encouragement throughout the many trials in the ensuing months. It also helped me to bear the understandable and deep hostility of the Ulster Unionists and some members in my own party.

That evening I spoke to the Harrow Central Conservatives. In my speech I said, 'I am undertaking the most terrifying, difficult and awesome task. The solution will not be found by military means alone. It will only be found in the hearts and minds of men and women.' Quite unlike most of my pronouncements, I would not change one word today.

After sixteen further tragic years of killing and suffering in Northern Ireland the position remains the same.

Not the least of our problems that Friday was the establishment of a completely new Government department, controlled by a small number of staff from Whitehall. We had to hope that the Northern Ireland Civil Service as a whole would co-operate with us. Even if they did, we had to understand and overcome all the obvious difficulties and emotional problems which would arise. Luckily Philip Woodfield and another senior Home Office official, Neil Cairncross, joined me as senior members of the Office. Philip Woodfield had had close and friendly contact with the top of the Northern Ireland Civil Service, since he had been dealing with Northern Ireland affairs at the Home Office. He was therefore able to make the transition less painful than it might have been. In addition, I had the great good fortune to be given as Permanent Secretary Bill Nield, a most experienced and eminent Civil Servant.

He and I decided that we must go at once to Northern Ireland the very next day, Saturday 25 March. Our purpose was to meet the Governor, Lord Grey of Naunton, the GOC, Sir Harry Tuzo, the Chief Constable, Sir Graham Shillington, and the Permanent Secretaries in the Stormont Government departments. Our task was to make sure of their loyalty to us and establish with them all a basis of co-operation. It seems bizarre to say this calmly after the event, but in the general turmoil and emotional upheaval even the long-established loyalty to the Crown of the Civil Service and the police could not be taken for granted. Of course we had the General and all his soldiers, but without the civilian support we would have had many grave difficulties.

I had been to Northern Ireland only twice in my life, the first time to attend a friend's twenty-first birthday party just before the war and the second on a golf tour in the 1950s. Needless to say these visits, while they had given me much enjoyment, had taught me nothing about the political problems. And so as we landed at Aldegrove Airport I experienced a feeling of loneliness, comforted only by Bill Nield at his forceful best and the first of the many Scotland Yard detectives who have been such friendly and cheerful companions over the years.

We were formally met by Howard Smith, the British Government representative in Northern Ireland. When we got into the car he handed me the morning edition of the *Belfast Newsletter*, the strongly Protestant mouthpiece. The heading announced that the new Secretary of State for Northern Ireland, Mr Whitelaw, was a prominent English Roman Catholic. I was amazed, because the only previous religious concern about my appointment had been that many years before, my great-uncle had allowed the grounds of our family home near Glasgow to be used for an Orange function. In fact I was brought up a Scottish Presbyterian and joined the Church of England after we moved to Cumbria in 1956. I gave the facts to Howard Smith and said, 'We must instantly deny this story.' He replied sadly, 'You will find in this community that that is easier said than done.' I had many later opportunities to learn the truth of that statement.

Soon, however, I was to be given some encouragement by the meeting with the senior Stormont Government officials. They were obviously deeply worried and apprehensive about the future of their community. But at this moment of extreme trial they unanimously lived up to the best traditions of the Civil Service. Despite their personal misgivings, they were clear that it was their duty to work for the British Crown and the British Government, and that they most certainly did. I remember saying towards the end of the meeting words to the effect that they obviously had not wanted me to come, probably any more than I had wanted to be there, but once all of this had happened it was much better that we should settle down, do our duty together and enjoy it as friends. As I look back on that traumatic day, I know that I feel immensely grateful for the unfailing support and friendship which they gave me at all times.

From that meeting I went straight to Hillsborough Castle to meet Lord Grey of Naunton, whom I had been told was a much-respected and highly popular figure. I was therefore greatly shaken when he turned to me soon after I arrived and said, 'When do you want me to leave?' When I appeared most surprised at his request he handed me a copy of that day's *Times* which said that the new legislation abolished his position and transferred his powers to me. I replied that I would investigate the story and in the meantime I wanted to make one thing quite clear: I trusted that he would stay on because I needed him desperately. We agreed on this and he suggested that I should come and stay with him at Government House. I immediately accepted this kind offer and thus started a friendship that meant a lot to me. He and Lady Grey were most hospitable to me and to my wife on her visits. In addition he continued selflessly with his duties and so provided some vital stability. At the same time he gave me a great deal of sound advice. At that moment I felt for the first time that I had acquired another important ally in my desperately lonely position.

During the rest of the day I had discussions with the GOC, Harry Tuzo, whom I had already met at Westminster meetings. His unfailing cheerfulness and considerable powers of leadership were a great encouragement, both at the start and indeed throughout the time that we worked together. I went also to the RUC Headquarters and met the Chief Constable, Graham Shillington, and his Deputy, Jamie Flannagan, and other senior officers. Again their steadfastness and loyalty were most heartening. Graham Shillington had all the stalwart qualities of the traditional Ulsterman, with a great feeling of loyalty to the British Crown and to his police service, the RUC. He knew his men and could speak for them, which was another priceless advantage at this moment of stress.

Finally I attended a Press conference at Aldegrove Airport. I had been used to the calm, well-conducted, even if sometimes hard-hitting questioning of Westminster Press conferences. This one, therefore, was something quite different. First, it was attended by a large group of correspondents from all over the world. Second, it has to be remembered that on the day after the announcement of Direct Rule such a conference was held in a highly charged emotional atmosphere, even by Northern Ireland standards. Third, I suppose many of those present hoped, and believed, that a new Secretary of State would be a sacrificial lamb to the slaughter. Fourth, to some extent I obviously was just such a victim, for I had no detailed knowledge of Northern Ireland and at that moment only a limited appreciation of the enormous pitfalls waiting to swallow up the unwary. Questions were fired at me like bullets from a machine-gun, couched in the most aggressive, and usually personal, terms. Several questioners spoke at once, there was a general atmosphere of background noise and turbulence and few opportunities to complete an answer without constant interruptions. This all contributed to a bear-garden atmosphere.

Some commentators afterwards said that the Secretary

of State evidently did not understand Northern Ireland Press conferences. How right they were! However, I gradually learnt about such occasions through the expert guidance of my invaluable public relations officer, Keith McDowall. This initiation, though, was an experience never to be forgotten.

As it ended my only comment to myself and to others was 'What a hell of a day'. And I flew home to Cumbria for the rest of the weekend, totally exhausted, thoroughly bemused and yet just a little heartened by the encouraging response from the crucial figures on whom I had to rely, if I was to make any success of what at first sight seemed an almost impossible task.

The next week was one of frenzied activity both at Westminster and in Northern Ireland. From Monday to Thursday I was engaged in piloting the necessary legislation for Direct Rule through Parliament. The second reading was passed in the House of Commons on Tuesday by 483 votes to eighteen with the Ulster Unionists, Enoch Powell and some other Tories voting against it. On Wednesday we discussed the Bill in Committee throughout the night. The House of Lords gave an unopposed passage to the measure on Thursday. And so by Friday I became Secretary of State for Northern Ireland and received my Seals of Office from Her Majesty The Queen at the Privy Council in Windsor Castle.

During that week also I had many discussions with my own Conservative back-benchers and others at Westminster, while my officials continued to establish the new Government department. The general mood on all sides at Westminster was most supportive. The Conservatives were inevitably the most anxious because they had had the closest links with the Ulster Unionists over the years. There was also a small, but vociferous and bitter, group who allied themselves completely with the Ulster Unionists in strong opposition. The Labour and Liberal Parties in varying degrees were greatly relieved that action had been taken. Some of their members had close links with Gerry Fitt and the SDLP and took a strongly anti-Unionist position.

I concluded that I would frequently encounter emotional opposition from both extremes, but that I could rely in general on a broad consensus of support throughout Parliament. This meant that, carefully handled, Westminster was a potential source of strength to me at moments of extreme stress. So it proved. In Northern Ireland during that week there was considerable protest from the Protestants – as was only to be expected – and, perhaps just as inevitably, continued heavy violence as the IRA exploited a moment of stress. There was a general strike and a large Protestant rally at Stormont where, somewhat ominously for me, Brian Faulkner appeared to ally himself with Bill Craig, the leader of Vanguard, who was much more extreme in his attitude at that particular time. Vanguard, a group within the Unionist movement formed in 1972, took a tougher stance than the Faulkner Unionists on co-operation with the Catholic parties. I soon discovered that this was a gesture in the heat of the moment, which came as a great relief to me as Brian Faulkner had loyally promised his basic support, and of course such limited co-operation from a strong opponent meant a lot to me in those circumstances.

The IRA violence continued in its express purpose of inflaming Protestant opinion by killing two men with a bomb outside Limavaddy police station. Tragically also, Major Callander, an Army Bomb Disposal Officer, was killed when seeking to defuse a car bomb in Belfast.

As a result of all this activity I felt apprehensive again as I left Windsor for the weekend in Northern Ireland accompanied by my wife. For the first time we stayed with the Governor and Lady Grey at Hillsborough. I found him a great comfort and source of help, as he quietly educated me about the position with all its complications. On the Sunday I watched some traditional Republican Easter parades in Belfast and Londonderry from a helicopter and was relieved when they passed off peacefully.

The Governor also invited Brian Faulkner and his wife to meet us at Hillsborough, which was much the best way of breaking the ice. I suspect that we all found it an awkward occasion. Both Brian and Lucy Faulkner, whom I came to admire greatly, naturally felt bitter and betrayed. I was nervous because I wanted to establish a working relationship, even if at first it was bound to be cool. Furthermore, there was little basis for agreement since Brian Faulkner and his colleagues strongly disputed nearly every aspect of the British plan which I had been sent to implement. My basic remit was to break the mould of Northern Ireland politics, of which the Stormont Government was a cornerstone. I think we were probably both glad when our rather stilted but polite conversations were over. Equally, we probably learnt enough about each other to begin to establish a relationship which eventually grew into mutual respect and friendship.

On 30 March I took over at Stormont Castle, faced with the task of running a community in a state of the utmost turbulence. At that time someone told me every day that I would wake up to full-scale revolution in the morning. And so I learnt to live by the day. When I went to sleep at night I hoped for the best. When I woke up in the morning to find just the same violence and turmoil as usual, I gained a little relief.

I also remembered my wartime experience and recognized the vital importance of morale at moments of trial. I know that in that respect a leader has to set the tone. I have always appreciated that there is no purpose in gloom and depression in the face of adversity. Team spirit, based on as much enjoyment as possible and a sense of humour, is an essential ingredient in any endeavour.

I have already mentioned some of the officials who joined me. I was also immensely fortunate in my ministerial team: David Windlesham from the Lords, Paul Channon and David Howell from the Commons. Later I was joined by Bill van Straubenzee, John Belstead and Peter Mills. We were a happy group in the midst of tribulation. We worked closely together and I had to rely on them completely because we were separated from each other for so much of the time. We always had to have one Minister at Stormont and one close to Whitehall. And so we were frequently in aeroplanes between Belfast and London.

Early on I realized that if I was to stand the strain and maintain my own morale, which was essential, I had to establish as sensible a routine as possible. This demanded both careful planning and access to aircraft. Here I soon had to rely on the one promise I obtained from Ted Heath when I took the job, namely that I would have the right to an aircraft whenever I wanted it.

The arrangement enabled me to organize my working week between London and Belfast with contingency plans for emergencies. I decided that I must attend the weekly Cabinet meetings on Thursday morning, in order to keep in close touch with my colleagues and to keep up to date with Government business and with Parliament. I was also determined to continue my constituency work, which must always make a prime demand on any Member of Parliament, and to keep in touch with my home and family. The maintenance of one's health and morale also required some relaxation. And so I went home to Cumbria for as many weekends as possible. Throughout, of course, I was in constant touch with Northern Ireland and always had one of my Ministers there when I was away.

Excellent communications made all this possible and have left me permanently intolerant of normal travel arrangements. As I write this I am reminded of it because my train's engine has just broken down in Preston and so we will arrive half an hour late in London at best. But then I have to remember that I am not as important now!

My arrangements thus completed, I had to get to know my staff in London and Northern Ireland, and with them to consider the basis of the problem we faced. My first reaction was one of shock at the depth of the divisions within the Northern Ireland community. It should be stated at once that the problem is caused more by historical background than actual religion. The Protestant element hailed mainly from Scotland whereas the Catholic tradition was based on the indigenous Irish. Ever since the days of William of Orange and the Battle of the Boyne these two communities have lived uneasily together with separate schools and separate history books. For the last hundred years at least they have been caught up in the arguments between Britain and Ireland as to the future government of the whole island. The situation has been such that violence is always just under the surface.

Under the Anglo-Irish Treaty of 1921 the Governments of Britain and Ireland came to an agreement: Southern Ireland would break away from Britain and become an independent country as the Irish Free State, with its strong Catholic majority. The Protestants, who were in a majority in the North, chose to remain a part of the United Kingdom. The boundary between the two was drawn with the effect of creating a Protestant state in Northern Ireland with some 66 per cent Protestants against 34 per cent Catholics. The Protestants were therefore entrenched in command and, alas, the Catholic minority continually felt themselves to be disadvantaged and deprived citizens.

Despite genuine efforts by successive Stormont Governments, the two communities lived increasingly in their own enclaves. This was particularly true of Belfast, where lived roughly half a million out of a total population in Northern Ireland of a million and a half. It was the same in Londonderry with the Catholic estates in the Bogside and the Creggan, which, by the time I came to Northern Ireland as Secretary of State, had become 'no-go' areas outside the control of the troops or police. After the Second World War the Stormont Prime Minister was Lord Brookeborough, a strong, brave and resolute leader much respected in British Government circles as in Protestant Ulster. But, understandably for someone of his age and experience, he did not see the need for fundamental change and probably did not retire soon enough in this new era. As a result, when Terence O'Neill took over as Prime Minister in 1963 and endeavoured, bravely and correctly in my opinion, to institute reforms and improve relations with the Republic, it was too late. Civil rights marches and demonstrations, some fanned by the IRA, and militant opposition from Protestant extremists led by, among others, Ian Paisley, led to increasing violence. Terence O'Neill was undermined and James Chichester-Clark took over as Prime Minister in April 1969 in increasingly difficult circumstances.

By 1969 the violence was such that the Labour Government had to introduce British troops at the time when Jim

Callaghan was Home Secretary. At first, the Catholic community welcomed the British troops but as violent incidents continued in which they became involved, this welcome changed and relations worsened.

Against this background I arrived with a commitment by the British Parliament to exercise control and introduce a new era. Inevitably I had to deal with a bitterly resentful Protestant majority and a suspicious Catholic minority. In the mood of that moment, I had first to calm the Protestants and seek to give hope to the Catholics of a new standing in the community.

Clearly, however, any such political progress was out of the question as long as bitter violence continued. Paradoxically, lasting success against violence depended on improved attitudes in the whole community. Alas, any moves which were likely to encourage the Catholics were almost certain to infuriate the Protestants still further.

As I attempt to evaluate, with the benefit of hindsight, the various decisions I took against this background, I do not intend to indulge in self-justification. Rather I will seek to set out the reasons for the decisions as they seemed to me at the time. I will also examine their impact on subsequent events, both then and in the longer term.

As all these thoughts went through my mind, I realized just why the Irish problem was said to be insoluble. Yet I knew that such a negative attitude must be banished altogether from my mind. Rather I had constantly to remind myself that I would certainly fail ignominiously if I did nothing. I concluded that my first objective must be to enlist the active support of those in both communities who were at least prepared to support a fresh approach. Lord Grey helped by introducing me to influential and public-spirited figures throughout the community whom he

Monkland, Nairn, my home from early childhood until the war

With the father I never knew, William Alexander Whitelaw

Myself, aged three, with my mother

Wedding day at St Giles's Cathedral, Edinburgh, on 6 February 1943

Standing *(far left)* with the officers of 'S' Squadron, 3rd (Armoured) Battalion Scots Guards, in 1942

Field Marshal Montgomery presents me with the Military Cross at Plön in Schleswig-Holstein in May 1945

Driving in as Captain of the Royal and Ancient Golf Club in September 1969 watched by the late Laurie Auchterlonie

On the course at Penrith
Golf Club in September
1976

The start of my political
career – I am adopted as
prospective candidate
for East Dunbartonshire
in 1949

Canvassing with my family in Brampton during the 1955
General Election

The Shadow Cabinet in conference, February 1970

After the debate on Northern Ireland at the Conservative Party Conference of 1972

At a meeting of Ulster party leaders at Stormont Castle in 1973. *(Left to right)* Phelim O'Neill, Brian Faulkner, David Howell, myself, Sir William Nield, Dr Vivian Simpson and Ian Paisley

"And in Northern Ireland, I thought I had trouble"

believed had such feelings. I found their help and advice most valuable. But in the end I had to balance the risks which they clearly outlined on the basis of their own positions.

First I decided that I had to release some of those interned. This would provide clear encouragement for the Catholics and should not infuriate the Protestants too much. It was also manifestly fair and sensible, in so far as the total number interned was far too high and some of the cases were clearly not justified on grounds of violence. There was, therefore, at least a hope that releases could be achieved without any damage to the security situation. At the same time I had to realize that mistakes would be costly if it could be proved that some of those released had returned to violence.

And so my officials and I studied the individual papers with great care. At first we appeared to be succeeding with our early releases. The Catholics were delighted and the Protestants, while angry and suspicious, lacked the necessary evidence of reinvolvement in terrorism. But we had not taken sufficient account of the myths and unfounded stories which are so much a part of life in Northern Ireland. I soon experienced one of these on a visit to Lurgan where I was given a very rough reception. It turned out that a recent bombing in the town was alleged to have been the work of a released internee. Subsequently the story was found to be wholly false. But the damage was done, as the initial publicity was exactly what many critics wanted it to be. What was worse, I was always accused thereafter of causing damage and death by the release of internees in general, for which there was in fact little, if any, evidence. Despite these typical distortions of the facts I continued carefully with the releases.

Then on 27 April I lifted the ban on marches and demonstrations. Undoubtedly these tended to provoke violence but I learnt that they were a part of the community's life and were valued by Protestants and Catholics alike.

These two actions certainly helped me in my relations with the SDLP, the main Catholic party. It must be remembered that they were engaged in a struggle for support within the Catholic community with the Provisional IRA, whose power rested on violence and odious intimidation. I needed to encourage the SDLP to build up their strength and their co-operation with the Government and the security forces.

Despite these efforts, their response continued to be slow and it was not until 26 May, two months after my arrival, that they felt in a position to end their members' boycott of all public offices. This SDLP gesture followed the callous killing by the Official IRA of a young soldier at home on leave in what they described as 'Free Derry'. This action was received with outrage on all sides. As a result the Official IRA called off their violent campaign and never subsequently resumed it. The Provisional IRA had also condemned the murder and their further reaction was anxiously awaited by the SDLP and many others in the Catholic community.

In the event they made no ceasefire statement. They did, however, set out 'demands' which they claimed could form the basis of a truce. These were: the release of all internees; the withdrawal of British troops to barracks; and an amnesty. Some of the SDLP wanted to explore whether the Provisionals too, against this background, could be induced to accept a ceasefire, pending peaceful negotiations for a lasting settlement. On 13 June the Provisional IRA had publicly invited me to meet them in 'Free Derry', an offer which naturally was firmly rejected. However, the Provisionals' statement made no mention of the ending of internment as a precondition. This omission allowed the SDLP off its self-imposed hook without exposing them to charges of 'weakness' from the IRA. It opened the way to direct talks between me and the SDLP leaders while internment was still in being. We met in London on 15 June, which was a crucial breakthrough.

We had a further meeting four days later. The SDLP were anxious to show some benefit, as they called it, from the talks. In the Crumlin Road jail, a group of IRA prisoners had gone on hunger strike to demand special 'political' privileges. The hunger strike as a tactic was all too familiar in Ireland. However, the issue had inflamed Republican opinions. Already riots had followed a rumour that one of the hunger strikers had died. The SDLP felt that they could not continue the talks unless a concession was made. They also felt that the concession might bring pressure to bear on the Provisionals within the Catholic community. Against that background, I agreed to the limited concession of 'special category' status, allowing more visits and the use of civilian clothes for eight Republicans and forty Loyalist prisoners.

In the circumstances of that moment the decision seemed a fairly innocuous concession, although I was clearly warned by my officials of its dangers *vis-à-vis* the prison system throughout the United Kingdom. It helped my relations with the SDLP in a limited way. Alas, though, it did establish a practice which caused my successors considerable trouble. I conclude today that its immediate impact was limited and it was later found to have been a misguided decision.

However, the SDLP engaged in further talks as a result. And they in their turn had contacts with the Provisional IRA. All these discussions led to a hope which gained strength throughout the community that talks might replace violence. Many in the Protestant community, however, remained firmly against any such idea and continued to be sceptical and fearful of a sell-out.

On 22 June the Provisional IRA announced a ceasefire. In typically callous fashion so-called 'offensive action' continued until the very eve of the ceasefire. A soldier was murdered in Belfast only a few minutes before midnight on 26 June, the time chosen by the Provisionals for the beginning of the truce. Nor was there any slackening in the spate of sectarian killings by both sides. Little serious effort was made to ease tension. Only three of the barricades in the no-go areas were removed. And indeed the arrogant political 'demands' of the IRA were unchanged.

The IRA ceasefire was nevertheless welcomed throughout Britain and Ireland, although it aroused extreme Protestant reactions. It was mistakenly felt in Ulster Protestant circles that the ceasefire had been bought at the promise of a softly-softly approach on terrorism. Nor did my efforts to woo the Catholic population away from terrorism mean that the will of the silent Protestant majority went unrecognized. I knew full well the appalling toll that IRA terrorism had exacted on the RUC and on the Protestant population. My office was as open to Protestants through that spring as it was to Roman Catholics. By mid-April Brian Faulkner and the mainstream Unionists had held talks with us, although I have to admit that Unionist suspicion understandably remained strong until more intensive talks began in June. Ian Paisley, who was initially critical of the negative Unionist response to Direct Rule, came to meet me on the first day of the IRA ceasefire on 27 June.

Inevitably there was an upsurge of Protestant reaction on the streets. We saw the emergence of so-called 'Tartan gangs', young hooligans who took violent action against Catholics. We saw the beginning of a despicable campaign of sectarian murders of Catholics by Protestants, which drew the inevitable odious response from the IRA. We also had to face the growth of paramilitary demonstrations by the Ulster Defence Association on the streets.

A particularly inflammatory point for Protestant militants were the so-called no-go areas that I had inherited in the Bogside and the Creggan in Londonderry. From mid-May the UDA staged weekly demonstrations by erecting temporary barricades of their own. I met the UDA leaders in mid-June. They arrived looking quite absurd in hoods and sun-glasses. I told them that I would not allow the erection of permanent barricades of their own. And they indeed agreed to postpone their action. However, after the announcement of the Provisional ceasefire, they revived their threat. On the evening of 30 June, UDA men hijacked almost eighty vehicles and worked with pneumatic drills to prepare selected roads in Belfast for concrete and metal barricades. Work continued over the weekend. While other temporary barricades were removed, the UDA declared permanent barricades in the Shankhill Road, Oldpark and Woodvale on the evening of Sunday 2 July. It was a direct challenge to the Government and to the rule of law.

This was a prelude to the so-called Ainsworth Avenue incident on the evening of Monday 3 July. Back in April I had made it clear that I would tolerate no further 'no-go' areas from any party; there was no change in this position.

In Ainsworth Avenue the UDA was attempting to erect a barricade that would have enclosed about fifty Catholic families. They were warned by the Army that they could not proceed, but still insisted on bringing forward pneumatic drills and ordered British troops to withdraw. The officer commanding the troops on the spot sensibly played for time by opening negotiations. But a compromise suggestion that a permanent barricade be erected, manned by the Army rather than the UDA, was not acceptable to me. Such a solution would almost certainly have led to violent Catholic reaction, because it would have exposed those Catholic families to inclusion in a Protestant area.

As a result the situation would have been represented in the Catholic community as a British Government surrender to Protestant power. The Provisional IRA would have moved in as protectors of the Catholics and would have thereby regained flagging support. In short, this comparatively limited incident would have acquired lasting psychological importance. Neither the Army Commander, my officials nor I were under any illusion: we could not give way.

That night I was having dinner outside Belfast with Sir Robin Kinahan, a leading industrialist. He had been most helpful to me and had agreed to serve on the Northern Ireland Commission which I had set up with combined Protestant and Catholic membership. I was called from dinner to speak on the telephone to the Army Commander, General Ford, as he himself had gone to the scene as tension mounted. He told me that he could not contain the situation unless he had my permission for the troops to fire on the UDA if they advanced. Otherwise the troops would be overwhelmed by sheer weight of numbers. In reply I asked if I could have a short time to consider such a major decision, by which British troops might fire, and presumably kill, Protestants in a street battle for the first time. I pointed out that if such a threat was not successful in deterring them, I really ought to consult at least the Prime Minister and the Defence Secretary before the troops actually fired.

Robert Ford replied that he much regretted there was no such time. Unless he had my immediate authority, he would have to make concessions as the situation was rapidly getting out of control.

I had no illusions about the major importance of my decision and of the possible consequences. I remember hesitating for a moment, feeling very sick and then saying, 'Very well, Robert. You have my permission for the troops to fire. I pray it will not be necessary.'

'So do I,' said an equally anxious voice at the other end of the phone.

I went back to the dinner table evidently looking very white. 'Are you all right?' my host asked.

'I think so,' I replied, 'but perhaps I may have a strong drink.'

Meanwhile Robert Ford played the hand brilliantly. He informed the UDA leaders that he had my permission for the troops to fire if their members advanced. The UDA leaders were apparently incredulous. 'Surely the Big Man,' as they called me, 'didn't say that.' Robert Ford confirmed that indeed I had done just that.

Eventually the UDA backed down in the face of General Ford's firm line. Efforts to set up barricades were abandoned. The paramilitaries dispersed and the Army agreed to mount a security check-point in Ainsworth Avenue itself. That UDA men were permitted to move unarmed in a road behind an Army check-point was a far cry from an armed force manning a permanent concrete barricade, which had been the UDA objective.

Press comments at that time did not reflect the real risks that we had been forced to take, nor the extent of our success. The reason for the understatement was simply that we decided not to tell the full story, which in fact exposed a major decision of emotional content which would surely have had considerable repercussions if fully appreciated. It was better, then, to allow the UDA to claim a meaningless concession, for their leaders knew the truth and so did the Catholic families involved. Curiously, that awful moment assisted me greatly thereafter in my dealings with the militant Protestants. They realized that I was prepared to stand up to them.

Operation Motorman and the Darlington Conference

While the crisis with the Protestants was in progress, I had another momentous decision on my mind. Once the Provisional IRA had declared a ceasefire, I was being widely urged to take the opportunity to meet them in order to find out their intentions. I discussed the balance of arguments with my officials, and of course in the end I sought the agreement of Ted Heath and my senior colleagues before the meeting took place. However, in view of its intensely controversial nature and the extremely difficult and narrow balance of arguments, I must make clear even now that the decision was my own. The debate, as I saw it, was as follows.

There was a desperate longing on all sides for an end to the senseless violence. Those who favoured a meeting with the Provisional IRA believed that no opportunity should be missed, and they would have been bitterly critical of a British Government which refused to talk once a truce had been declared. They included in Northern Ireland the Catholic community led by the SDLP, and a sizeable group of Protestants, mainly those in the business community not closely associated with politics. In the rest of the United Kingdom I knew that I would lose the support of the Opposition parties at Westminster if I turned down a meeting, particularly since Harold Wilson, as Leader of the Opposition, had already met the Provisional IRA leaders in Dublin in March. Nor did I feel that a British Government would find it easy to explain to world opinion, particularly the Irish community in the United States of America, why it would not talk once the terrorist action had been stopped, even if only temporarily.

On the other hand, those against a meeting relied on the traditional and extremely valid arguments that there should be no negotiation or discussion with those engaged in terrorism. They included in particular the Unionist Party in Northern Ireland and a substantial body of members in the Conservative Party at Westminster, with considerable backing in the rest of the United Kingdom. It has to be said that the opinion against such meetings was nothing like as strong then as it is today. But then those who hold such a view will certainly claim that the passage of time has proved them right.

My initial instinct was against a meeting, particularly because I was sensitive to feelings in my own party. But as the discussions continued with my officials, and strongly held and contradictory views were expressed, I was persuaded that a refusal to talk would leave the political initiative in the hands of the IRA. Equally, if I agreed to talks which then failed through their intransigence, at least I should be able to gain support for stronger security action, particularly from the Catholic community in Northern Ireland and from all those who were urging a meeting on me. Finally I decided that I wanted to go ahead and asked Ted Heath if I could hold a secret meeting of an exploratory nature. He immediately gave me his agreement and support.

My Minister of State, Paul Channon, and I met leaders of the Provisional IRA at his house in London on 7 July. The meeting was a non-event. The IRA leaders simply made impossible demands which I told them the British Government would never concede. They were in fact still in a mood of defiance and determination to carry on until their absurd ultimatums were met.

Two days after the talks the IRA manufactured a pretext for breaking the truce by staging a confrontation with the Army over a housing issue and opening fire on the security forces. Late on Sunday night they issued a statement in Dublin which revealed that our talks had taken place. I learnt the news on my wireless at home in Cumbria in the early hours of the Monday morning. I knew that I was facing a major storm and my first reaction was that I ought to resign, since I would certainly forfeit any remaining vestige of confidence in the Unionist population in Northern Ireland.

Needless to say, even I failed to sleep any more that night. I got up still resolved to ask Ted Heath to accept my resignation. However, before doing so I decided that I must fly straight to Northern Ireland as I had previously planned, there to see the Governor. That proved to be a wise decision, for Ralph Grey gave me immense support and encouragement. He accepted the strength of Unionist wrath but reminded me of the substantial body of opinion which had urged talks in the interests of peace. I asked him to fly over with me to see Ted Heath and said that I would certainly face Parliament before making any decision about resigning.

On the flight I remember him most helpfully drafting notes for my parliamentary statement. We went immediately to No. 10 Downing Street to see Ted Heath, where Ralph Grey again counselled strongly against my resignation. I thus faced Parliament that afternoon still undecided about my position but with my morale greatly improved by

Ted Heath's calmness and indeed by Ralph Grey's encouragement. I made a statement in a subdued House of Commons – there was some criticism from our backbenchers but overall the tone in Parliament was extremely sympathetic and understanding. So it was on the whole in the Press.

All, however, were now agreed with my own view that a tough security response was essential to send an unmistakable message to the IRA and to both communities in Northern Ireland. At the same time I was anxious to press forward with my other objective of holding a conference of all the legitimate political representatives of the Northern Ireland parties.

I have no doubt looking back at that period, that I was extremely fortunate over this incident. If, as a result of deciding in favour of a secret exploratory meeting, I had become involved in further discussions with the IRA leaders, I would eventually have landed myself in great difficulties. Clearly those ought to have been the IRA tactics. As it turned out, by returning to violence almost at once, they presented me with a considerable advantage. They proved that they were intransigent and that it was the British Government who really wanted an end to violence. Many in the Catholic community appreciated this and gave me increasing support for tougher security action. They also turned against the IRA and looked more to the SDLP, who became stronger, more self-confident and thus more co-operative in their relations with me.

Of course this substantial gain, which was actually one of the main aims in my mind in having the talks, had to be set against the fury and resentment in the Protestant community. But once again I would have an opportunity to reassure them if the security forces could achieve some clear success.

And so I gained from what might easily have proved a dangerously mistaken decision. I was also able to say at this time, with the utmost conviction, that I would never again consider any such meeting with the IRA leaders. For the future I had learnt a lesson which taught me all too plainly the dangers and risks of dealing with terrorists.

But in July 1972 there was no time for such reflection. I had to act quickly and decisively on the security front. In particular, the Army had to regain control of the no-go areas in the Bogside and Creggan in Londonderry. They were not only, rightly, a target of Protestant anger but also a symbol of weakness and failure in British rule. They were areas in the United Kingdom of Great Britain and Northern Ireland which the British Government did not control.

No one was under any illusion that the task would be an easy one. The re-establishment of control required a major military operation. Fortunately, once again at this moment, the IRA leaders gave me further propaganda assistance. While the planning for the Londonderry operation was in progress they unleashed a savage bombing operation in the centre of Belfast on 21 July. There were twenty bomb explosions in just seventy minutes within a mile of Belfast city centre. Nine people, including two children, were killed and 130 injured. I was in London at that moment for various meetings, as it was a Friday. I flew back immediately, for there was no doubt of the alarm and distress which were sweeping throughout the Northern Ireland community at all levels. Peter Carrington, Secretary of State for Defence, offered to come with me as major military action was necessary. I was extremely grateful to him and in the end his presence was invaluable to me.

When we arrived at Stormont Castle in the evening we found from reports that there was considerable alarm and despondency among many on all sides. It was one of those moments when calm and strong leadership is vital. No one could have been a better companion in such a situation than Peter Carrington. Equally, it was perhaps important that we had both had substantial experience of war and battle conditions. Fortunately too we had Harry Tuzo as GOC, for his personality and powers of leadership were invaluable in such circumstances.

Our detailed plans for clearing the no-go areas were well advanced but we could not accelerate them further. Nevertheless we had to take immediate strong action in Belfast that night, and the whole population throughout Northern Ireland had to know what we were doing otherwise a situation of near-panic could have developed. Harry Tuzo and the Army achieved a remarkably quick and major deployment of troops on to the streets. I did a radio broadcast. The immediate actions during the night did not achieve many tangible results but they had the necessary immediate effect on badly shaken morale.

The general revulsion against the IRA which resulted from the bombing encouraged me to hope that the climate was right for the major action in Londonderry and the rest of the province. Moreover, we did not have to wait long for this operation, codenamed 'Motorman', which was scheduled for 31 July, just ten days ahead.

Those of us on the spot recognized that Operation Motorman was a vitally important action that simply had to succeed. Nor was such success as easy as many people and much Press comment after the event assumed. The Bogside and the Creggan estates represented a substantial and self-contained area of Londonderry. They were close to the border with the Republic and therefore offered an easy escape route through open country just behind them. For almost a year they had been under the control of the IRA, who were strongly entrenched behind substantial barricades. The wholly Catholic community was controlled by the IRA through the power of strong intimidation. There were also people, not necessarily ideological supporters of the IRA, who were gaining in such circumstances through protection rackets and other Mafia-style activities in a community outside the rule of law.

The Army, moreover, had to regain control of this large built-up area with the minimum of civilian casualties. Therein lay the real problem. If the IRA activists decided to fight and large numbers of the Catholic population supported them by obstructing the entry of the troops, the Army could have experienced substantial difficulties. And of course the greater the resistance confronting the Army, the more likely it was that there would be substantial civilian casualties. We also had to accept that mounting an operation involving a large number of troops and equipment, at the same time as maintaining an element of surprise, would have been difficult in any event. In Northern Ireland, where rumours and gossip are the bread of life, it was virtually impossible.

We decided to maintain the element of surprise as long as we could. I played my part in the preceding days by appearing ostentatiously in London on the Thursday and Friday and then in Cumbria and at a well-attended game fair in Durham over the weekend. Then on the Sunday evening I returned to Northern Ireland in order to make a special statement.

We had decided to make known our general intention to act. I therefore announced on the radio that the Army would be conducting substantial operations and warned people to stay off the streets. This action was subsequently criticized because it was said that it gave a warning to the IRA leaders who were then able to escape over the border nearby. We of course appreciated that that was liable to happen. Our reasoning was that we must stick to our main purpose, which was to establish control of the whole area of the Bogside and the Creggan. If we were to succeed in that we did not wish the troops to be burdened by crowds on the streets, which would inevitably lead to casualties as well as delay. Therefore, whatever the views of our armchair critics, I remain convinced that it was right to make the sort of warning we did.

The operation was due to start at daybreak on the Monday. I stayed the previous night at Stormont Castle and went to the Army Headquarters at Lisburn before the Army moved off. For some time Harry Tuzo and I sat in his office in considerable suspense. Was the Army being obstructed? Were civilians lying on the streets? Was the IRA going to organize resistance? These were the questions going through our minds. The Bogside and Creggan areas had been occupied and controlled by the IRA for so long that they had to be treated as enemy territory. We feared that the population as a whole would be instructed to obstruct the entry of troops by mass demonstrations and even by actually lying down on the streets in front of advancing vehicles. For the first time I realized what it must have been like for Army Commanders during the war; equally for the first time I had some considerable sympathy for them.

At first we could get no reply from Robert Ford who was commanding the troops on the ground. The reason was simple. As one might have appreciated, that brave and powerful soldier had driven in to the area at the head of his troops and was temporarily out of wireless contact. However, he did not keep us long in suspense and we soon had the welcome news we sought. There had been no real resistance and none of the obstructions which we had feared. The Army was almost at once in full control of the area. Later on some shots were fired at the Army and two civilians died in return fire. Thanks to a well-planned and well-executed operation we had succeeded beyond our wildest dreams.

Through Operation Motorman we removed the blot of the no-go areas – so long a major source of irritation. Most important of all, this was achieved with virtually no casualties. Great credit was due to General Tuzo, General Ford and all the Army. Even the fact that the IRA planted three car bombs, which caused considerable destruction in the peaceful village of Claudy twelve miles from Londonderry, could not detract from a major security success.

Once again there was no time for reflection or congratulations. But it was certainly with a feeling of relief that I felt able to turn to the next political move. On 11 August I issued an invitation to the leaders of all the constitutional parties which had been represented in the old Stormont Parliament to attend a political conference on the future of Northern Ireland on 25 September.

My officials searched for a suitable site from a security point of view, which we had decided should be in mainland Britain. They found an ideal one in a newly refurbished, but as yet unused, hotel called the Europa just outside Darlington. They reported to me that there was only one snag. The hotel was surrounded by a golf course which would have to be closed for a few days during the conference. The Blackwell Grange Golf Club had little alternative but to agree, although in fact they were immensely co-operative. I thus became what must surely be the only past Captain of the Royal and Ancient Golf Club who had actually closed a golf course. The club was kind and generous enough to mark the occasion by making me an honorary member – a gesture which I much appreciated.

The Unionists, Alliance and Northern Ireland Labour Parties all accepted immediately. I thought that Ian Paisley would accept, in order to use the conference for propaganda purposes, but I did not then understand the nature and capacity of this extraordinary character. He has an unrivalled skill at undermining the plans of others. This, coupled with his large build and booming voice, make him a dangerous opponent. He can effectively destroy and obstruct, but he has never seemed able to act constructively. As far as the proposed conference was concerned, he used a shooting incident between the Army and a UDA mob attacking a police station as a pretext for demanding an inquiry into the incident, which he knew was a ludicrous request. When I refused, he announced that as a result he would boycott the talks. This did not really matter for, as I subsequently learnt, he would certainly have indulged in disruptive propaganda.

The refusal of the SDLP to attend was much more worrying, for they were the only constitutional party which was recognized as enjoying substantial Catholic support. They based their refusal on the continuation of internment and were unmoved by the announcement that future decisions on internment would be made by a judicial tribunal rather than executive power. I was particularly upset by this aspect, because I had made great efforts to obtain this important and significant change.

Both parties did send in plans and some papers, but it was personal contact, personal discussion and argument which were really needed at this stage. To that extent, the value of the conference was seriously undermined before it started.

In the event, however, the Darlington Conference, despite the limited attendance, proved more successful than I expected. In a way it became a watershed in the process of achieving a broader political dialogue. For too long Northern Ireland had been in the news only for acts of violence. Now a huge media circus focused on the process of political discussion. The Unionists in Ulster as a whole could be in no doubt that their voice was heard and many were impressed by the coherence and good sense with which their case was put. This, I believe, was helpful to those Unionists who wanted to seek a political solution at a time when the Vanguard Movement was trying to rally the population to take direct unconstitutional action. The Alliance and Northern Ireland Labour Parties also gained valuable publicity for moderate policies which had seldom been heard previously in Northern Ireland politics.

Perhaps just as important my Ministers, officials and I established personal contacts and understanding with the Northern Ireland politicians who attended. I believe that this improved relationship after the traumatic events of Direct Rule helped us all and made further discussions much easier.

Meanwhile on the security front there was a modest improvement in the level of violence over the autumn months following Operation Motorman. In particular, the security forces were having greater success against the IRA. In the four months up to Motorman there were almost 5,500 shooting incidents. In the four months following, the number of incidents was almost halved. In July alone there had been ninety-five deaths. By September the number was down to forty, and in November to twenty. When such figures are set out sixteen years later they serve to indicate the desperate level of violence with which we were confronted. It seems almost incredible today to appreciate that at the time they were regarded as an improving climate in which to seek political progress. I remember reflecting that at least no one suggested any longer that there would be civil war in the morning. Perhaps I myself had become accustomed to strain and anxiety, although I was never able to calm my feelings of despair when I heard of casualties among soldiers and innocent civilians. Once again I experienced sympathy for wartime leaders.

As always there was no time for such reflections. I had immediately to build on the Darlington Conference and thereby retain the political initiative. On 31 October I published a paper for discussion which set out in detail the full range of constitutional options put forward in Northern Ireland as a focus for further political discussion. The speed with which the paper was produced was a tribute to all those who worked on it. Ken Bloomfield in particular, now head of the Northern Ireland Civil Service, was a most valuable adviser.

The paper was not prescriptive but it underlined both the Border Pledge – the undertaking that there would be no removal of the border without the consent of the majority of the population in Northern Ireland – and the need for those in the North to have a dialogue with those in the South, because so many of the problems ran across political frontiers. We encouraged the idea that some kind of devolved Government which recognized minority concerns was the best hope. I believed that we could create a system which would enjoy the support and respect of the overwhelming majority on both sides of the divide. Immediate reaction was encouraging. All parties, including the SDLP, made a relatively positive response. But the key task was to convert the general principles and the range of options in the discussion paper into specific White Paper proposals as soon as possible.

The first requirement was to give effect to the Border Pledge, which was repeated by Ted Heath when he visited Northern Ireland for two days in November. This was all the more important because the Darlington Conference had agreed, whatever else was disputed, that Northern Ireland should remain a part of the United Kingdom until the majority of the population agreed otherwise. That had long been a fundamental Unionist principle. It was enshrined in the legislation governing the constitutional framework of Northern Ireland. There was no doubt how Ulster would vote in a referendum on this issue because of the balance between the two communities. However, in the context of Unionist concern over our motives, it was clear that a vote on this question would be both helpful and valued. It would also counter any idea put about by the IRA and its sympathizers that the British Army was somehow an occupying force holding an unwilling majority under a colonialist yoke. We therefore announced that a Border Poll would be held on 8 March 1973.

I visited many polling stations on the day and was struck not only by the determination of the Protestants to vote but also by their obvious satisfaction in doing so. As a means of improving Protestant morale there was no doubt of its effectiveness, despite the certainty of the result. And despite SDLP calls for a boycott, there was some evidence that a significant number of Catholics had answered yes to the question 'Do you want Northern Ireland to remain part of the United Kingdom?' Over 600,000 people voted: almost 58 per cent of the whole electorate opted for Ulster to stay in the United Kingdom.

As I had hoped, the Border Poll also changed the climate of political discussion. It made clear that a solution had to be found within the United Kingdom, although such a solution would not exclude constructive co-operation between North and South. Above all, when taken with the known imminence of a Government White Paper, it put pressure on all parties to devote their energy to influencing our thinking in that White Paper. There was little difficulty now in persuading even reluctant partners to talk. The poll also put an end – at any rate for the moment – to the vague but nevertheless dangerous talk about Ulster opting for independence outside the United Kingdom.

We published our White Paper on 20 March. The basis was to be a legislative Assembly of eighty members to be elected by proportional representation. The office of Governor would be abolished but that of Secretary of State would continue. The new Assembly would have powers over a wide range of policy matters. However, electoral arrangements, the judiciary, prosecution and emergency powers would be permanently reserved to Westminster, while other powers over the police, criminal law and prisons would be temporarily reserved until the British Government was satisfied that they could be transferred. It was proposed to set up a new Council of Ireland as a forum for discussion between North and South, but it was reaffirmed yet again that Northern Ireland would remain part of the United Kingdom so long as that was the majority wish. As I said in a broadcast to the people of Northern Ireland, 'What we have tried to do is to present the people of Northern Ireland with an opportunity: a chance to free themselves of violence, of sectarian strait-jackets, above all of the sterile politics based solely on the border.'

Certain matters of course remained unresolved – above all how the Assembly would conduct its business and how the executive to govern Northern Ireland would be formed. I believed that it was essential to give time for further discussion on those issues. Talks across the sectarian divide were too recent, relationships still too brittle, for it to have been possible to resolve these matters, or the issue of the temporarily reserved powers, before the White Paper was published. If devolved Government were to have any meaning, and if it were to be successfully conducted, then Ulster politicians working with us must find Ulster solutions. But as we declared in the White Paper, 'It is the view of the Government that the executive itself can no longer be based upon any single party if the party draws its support and its elected representatives virtually entirely from one section of a divided community.' It was essential that responsible Nationalists and Unionists should work together to devise a practical form of Government for the beleaguered communities for whom they proclaimed their concern.

The reaction to the White Paper was encouraging. The extremist elements among the Unionists summoned a rally in Belfast on 24 March. In the event, only 2,000 people appeared. The Provisional IRA pledged the continuance of their murderous campaign, which has never since ceased; agreement is anathema to the terrorist mind. But for the rest, the White Paper did seem to offer a way forward. Above all, Brian Faulkner's Unionists and the SDLP expressed their willingness to negotiate a way forward on the basis of the White Paper. Elections for the new Assembly were set for 28 June.

As we embarked on this new and vital phase in our political efforts, I was under no illusions about the major difficulties ahead. Some of the questions in my mind could easily be answered. There was no chance of Ian Paisley and the Democratic Unionist Party backing the White Paper proposals. On the contrary, the very existence of the White

Paper gave Ian Paisley one of those opportunities for destructive action which he most relishes. A 'sell-out', a secret plan devised by the wicked British Government in collusion with Dublin, and even with the Pope and the Vatican, would of course be in the forefront of all that he said. I could almost write the phrases in his denunciatory statements. I found these sad reflections, because I knew how much effect Ian Paisley would have on Protestant opinion. I wondered even then if I could persuade him to use his powerful personality constructively for, away from political discussion, I found him friendly and engaging. As usual such hopes were soon overtaken by his next dramatic and outrageous outbursts.

I knew that the SDLP, while in principle anxious to co-operate, would have internal difficulties over policing and the continuation of internment. They would also require some comment on the part of the British Government about co-operation with the Republic which would arouse Protestant Unionist suspicion. I knew too that I could rely on support from the Alliance Party, but wondered whether they would get enough support at the polls to give them influence. Lastly I was only too well aware that Brian Faulkner, on whom I believed the whole success of any joint endeavour between Protestant and Catholic politicians depended, would have substantial difficulties inside the Unionist Party. The extent and nature of these difficulties remained the most fundamental problem.

Many Unionists had sincere objections to our ideas. They still resented the suspension of Stormont and now regretted the proposal to abolish the office of Governor. They also wanted to see control over policing returned to the executive. Nevertheless, many of them felt that our proposals offered an acceptable basis for further discussion and represented a move back in the direction of returning responsibility to Northern Ireland. As a result, on 27 March the Unionist Council met in Belfast and authorized Brian Faulkner to have talks with me, even on the issue of power-sharing. A motion to reject the White Paper was defeated by 381 votes to 231.

Alas, this meeting led to a further lasting split inside the Unionist Party. On 30 March William Craig announced the formation of a new political party, the 'Vanguard Unionist Progressives', who would fight elections against the Faulkner Unionists. Their aim would be to 'make the Assembly a nonsense'. Craig and his group seemed to feel that the White Paper proposals might be set aside. There was, on the other hand, no question of our negotiating the fundamental basis of our constitutional proposals. I made that absolutely clear early in April. I did not want the waverers among the Unionists to feel that there was something to be gained by the old negative tactics. At the same time we wished to give the more flexible Unionists reassurance on those points that were fundamental to them – namely that the majority should determine the future place of Northern Ireland in the United Kingdom; that there should be the prospect of returning police powers to Ulster when the situation was right; and that should the SDLP take part in the executive, they must end the rent and rate strike and accept the principle that a united Ireland could only come about peacefully through the will of the majority. Concurrently we made various efforts to help the SDLP in their task. For example, in April we removed the requirement that local councillors, school teachers and public sector employees should swear allegiance to the Crown.

Of course I realized that it would be difficult to achieve common ground, but I became at that moment slightly more optimistic. Many of the expected difficulties had arisen but the response from Brian Faulkner, Gerry Fitt and Oliver Napier at the head of their parties gave me hope that common-sense co-operation against violence and for the Northern Ireland community was possible. Hindsight, however, leads me to the conclusion that such thoughts were too optimistic as far as Unionist opinion was concerned. As a result I probably did not give enough thought to helping Brian Faulkner. Should I, for instance, have allowed three months to elapse between the publication of the White Paper and the Assembly elections? Certainly that did give time for divisive tendencies to appear in the Unionist Party, but at that moment we thought we were moving as fast as we could. After all, we were engaged in preparing the Constitution Act, which was not published until 15 May. We had also scheduled the local elections in Northern Ireland for 30 May. Nor should our Government administrative problems be underestimated. Indeed, it was a remarkable achievement on the part of my Ministers and officials – both in Belfast and London – that the Green and White Papers, the various parliamentary procedures at Westminster and the election arrangements Northern Ireland were all ready on time. Looking back on it I am frankly amazed at what was done under the great administrative skill of my Permanent Secretary, Frank Cooper.

I believe that we would also have been under severe criticism from the Northern Ireland political parties if we had appeared to rush the elections. Despite all that, I feel now that I should have had more discussions with Brian Faulkner about the impact of these decisions on his internal party difficulties. Certainly these developed and in the final event may have reduced his support in the new Assembly as it emerged from the elections on 28 June.

I have also read criticism of the way in which Brian Faulkner handled his party in discussions leading up to the election and so alienated some opinion. Frankly I do not believe that such criticism is really justified, or that the timing of the Assembly election was crucial. The divisions in the Unionist Party were far more fundamental and went to the root of the controversy of the continuing Northern Ireland political situation to this day. Under the circumstances I am convinced that Brian Faulkner handled his party bravely and skilfully. At any rate he gained a result which, however tenuously, made the formation of the power-sharing executive possible. Certainly the results of the local elections on 30 May were reasonably satisfactory from his point of view. The Unionists won 210 out of 519 seats contested; other Loyalists eighty-one; the SDLP eighty-two; the Alliance sixty-three; other parties eighty-three.

The campaign for the Assembly election then began in earnest. It was punctuated by the continuing ruthless violence of the Provisional IRA, including a murderous explosion at Coleraine which killed six people and injured thirty-three. But politicians and people throughout Ulster entered with enthusiasm and vigour into the naturally heated campaign. I was in truth particularly heartened by the manifesto of the SDLP, which affirmed their willingness to take part in the executive and to take the necessary oath, which implied acceptance of the majority determination of Ulster's future.

Polling day on 28 June – incidentally my fifty-fifth birthday – was bright and sunny. Almost three-quarters of the electorate turned out to vote. Of the seventy-eight seats at stake the SDLP won nineteen, the Alliance eight and the Northern Ireland Labour Party one. The Loyalist Coalition led by Paisley and Craig took eighteen seats. The Faulkner Unionists took twenty-two. The remaining ten were held by Unionists who had refused to sign the Faulkner 'pledge'. This was a difficult result. There was hope of creating a clear majority for forming a stable power-sharing executive, but unless Brian Faulkner could bring on board some of the middle-ground Unionists he would hold only a minority of the Unionist seats.

I called in the leaders of all parties one by one on 2 July to test their willingness to try and form an executive. No concrete action could be taken until after the Constitution Act received the Royal Assent on 18 July. In any event, I was not prepared to negotiate individually with the parties on particular issues ahead of all-party talks leading to the formation of an executive. My primary objective was to create the forum for such all-party talks without agreeing to preconditions unacceptable to other parties. I was convinced that if I did that, later discussions would be stillborn.

The first meeting of the Assembly on 21 July was badly disrupted by Loyalist wrecking tactics. The Assembly then became bogged down in discussion of Standing Orders. By this stage Brian Faulkner had completely failed to win over the 'unpledged' Unionists. They formed a new grouping led by Harry West and John Taylor. The future of our initiative now lay in successfully producing an agreement between Brian Faulkner's group, the SDLP and the Alliance. The executive must then prove itself in action and so broaden support in the Protestant community. Ted Heath met party leaders on a visit to Northern Ireland on 28 August. He urged them to concentrate on forming an executive. I conducted some exploratory talks with representatives of the three main parties concerned in September and the key talks opened at Stormont on 5 October.

Looking back I recognize these talks, which continued for nearly two months, as one of the most fascinating periods of my political life. Whatever may have happened since, the fact that they ended in agreement represents a considerable achievement on the part of the Northern Ireland political leaders who participated. They were prepared to sink their substantial differences in the interests of giving a constructive lead to all the people of Northern Ireland. They were also prepared to work together democratically in unity against the men of violence. Subsequently, of course, their efforts were defeated not democratically but by industrial action in the Ulster Workers' Council strike. Thereafter their work has been belittled and even derided. This is tragic, because the need for similar leadership becomes ever more necessary, and indeed ever more demanding, as the toll of violence continues today. In these pages I therefore want to record my gratitude to them all by name. The Unionist team led by Brian Faulkner included Herbie Kirk, Roy Bradford, Basil McIvor, Leslie Morell and John Baxter. The SDLP team led by Gerry Fitt was composed of John Hume, Austin Currie, Paddy Devlin, Eddie McGrady and Ivan Cooper. Oliver Napier led the Alliance team with Robert Cooper and Basil Glass as his assistants. David Howell and Bill van Straubenzee attended as my Ministers, and my officials who gave invaluable assistance were led by Frank Cooper.

On that day we met for the first time in a tense and nervous atmosphere. The members of the various delegations either did not know each other at all or had been resolute opponents in the old Stormont Parliament. They had to overcome many prejudices of the past and put some unhappy memories out of their minds. I feared that we might break up almost as soon as we started, and so told the staff to be prepared for an early lunch adjournment. I hoped that a break for food and drink might help to improve personal relationships. And so indeed in the end it did. Thereafter I gave great attention to the catering arrangements for our meetings as I believed that they helped to establish a friendly team spirit. I maintain that time and thought spent on promoting human and personal relations in any discussion or negotiation is seldom wasted.

At any rate our discussions on the Friday left us in a reasonably optimistic mood. We had succeeded in breaking the ice and in defining the major areas of disagreement, which were policing, detention and the Council of Ireland. They were obviously difficult points but the mood of the meeting clearly indicated a desire to resolve them. Most significant of all, we agreed to maintain strict confidentiality for the duration of the talks. Such a requirement was clearly important to progress, but its fulfilment was, if anything, more a pious hope in Northern Ireland than it would even be at Westminster. I am delighted to say that my fears in this regard were unfounded and there were no substantial leaks during the talks. This became a crucial factor in their success.

So did another development from the first meeting: the setting up of a sub-committee under David Howell to propose a social and economic programme for a political executive. David Howell had been a tower of strength on the economic front since Direct Rule and had, in fact, achieved considerable success in improving the very depressed Northern Ireland economy. This sub-committee was working in a less contentious area and so made considerable progress towards establishing a sense of unity at least in this one area. Yet I understand that it had its own turbulent moments, surfacing in antagonism between Roy Bradford and Paddy Devlin, before it was able to endorse its final report.

The main meeting meanwhile had many difficult discussions on detention, policing and the Council of Ireland. Gradually, by means of adjournments and skilful redrafting of papers by Frank Cooper and my officials, we reached comparatively agreed positions – except on policing, which remained a major sticking-point until the final days.

I cherish one exchange during these meetings which I feel sure my old friend, Paddy Devlin, will not mind me repeating. As I remember, it went as follows. Paddy Devlin, angered at not getting his own way, exclaimed, 'Mr Chairman, you are a bloody [I think he probably said worse!] Chairman.'

'That may be,' I replied, 'but your language is unnecessarily rude and your other intervention quite valueless because I am the best Chairman you have got and indeed the only one you are likely to have!'

An hour later Paddy Devlin was delighted when he got his way on some other point. 'Mr Chairman,' he exclaimed in delight, 'all our progress is due to your remarkable skill as Chairman. We are deeply indebted to you.'

'That also may be,' I replied, 'but it is now a suitable moment for lunch and possibly for a drink.' That turned out to be a good day but many others were extremely trying.

As November drew to its close I realized that time was no longer on our side. If we did not come to a conclusion soon, disagreements would emerge in public because the confidentiality agreement was bound to break.

In addition to the problems on law and order, the composition of the new executive emerged as a major area of potential disagreement. The Constitution Act provided that the executive should consist of twelve members and the number allocated to each party was bound to be keenly contested. The Unionists wanted seven members. They based their claim on the provision in the Constitution Act that the executive must be widely accepted. Brian Faulkner claimed emphatically, and correctly, that the executive would not be widely accepted unless it had a Unionist majority. Gerry Fitt for the SDLP said that his party must have five seats, and Oliver Napier for the Alliance said that he could not accept less than two.

Our meeting on Monday 19 November, which had been widely predicted as a make-or-break session, therefore ended in stalemate. The talks were on the verge of collapse. Furthermore, the Unionist Council was meeting the next day, when Brian Faulkner's opponents were determined finally to undermine his negotiating position. I recognized that at this meeting he would have to restate his position that the Unionists must have a majority on the executive. But I stressed that he would not be able to claim that that had been agreed in the talks. Although he was put under considerable pressure by his critics he was as good as his word.

It was clear that unless we could reach a final agreement the following day, Wednesday 21 November, our talks had finally broken down. This was also inevitable since I had undertaken to report the position to Parliament at Westminster on Thursday 22 November. In any event, if one more day of talks did not resolve the disagreements, then further discussion would be useless.

That Wednesday I woke up in a very depressed mood. I rang Ted Heath early and told him that I would be coming back that afternoon and that I was convinced I would be reporting failure. He accepted my news with a note of resignation and depression in his voice, for he was facing many other problems at that moment. As always on such occasions he said little, but curiously he made me feel all the more determined not to fail him and my Cabinet colleagues.

In the morning our talks settled amicably most of the outstanding points in the draft agreement. During the day I had private talks with Gerry Fitt and John Hume on the law and order issue, and finally persuaded them that the police must continue to be called the Royal Ulster Constabulary. I understood that this was a difficult point for their party to accept. I also knew that it was a complete sticking-point with the Unionist Party and with a large section of the Conservative Party at Westminster. It was therefore an essential feature of the agreement.

But the composition of the executive still remained to be settled. Since the failure to agree on Monday, my Ministers, officials and I had inevitably discussed this issue in great detail. We came to the Wednesday talks, as Brian Faulkner described it in his memoirs, 'with a few tricks up our sleeves'. I was therefore able to point out at the start of the afternoon meeting that we could amend the Constitution Act to change the executive members from twelve to whatever number we felt necessary. There could also be flexibility on the number of members holding office outside the executive. This would mean that on the executive itself, where all decisions would finally be made, as in a Cabinet, there would be a Unionist majority. At the same time within the administration as a whole there could be a more even spread of positions. This flexibility broke the original stalemate and there now followed several hours of bargaining, with adjournments of the conference sessions for party discussions and private talks between the individual parties and me. As on all such occasions there were all kinds of alarms and digressions.

Throughout I stuck to one feature of my plan. The talks had to end that day – whether in agreement or failure – as I had to leave for London that evening. In order to underline this point I allowed my helicopter to land on the lawn outside Stormont Castle at the scheduled time. Its arrival concentrated minds wonderfully. I was immediately asked if I intended to leave. I replied, 'Certainly, unless I can sense some signs of agreement.' I then gave instructions to the helicopter to go away and come back in one hour's time. When it returned, agreement still had not been reached but it was in sight. Fortunately the helicopter could land just outside the conference room. Under such circumstances there would seem to be few better means of resolving issues, particularly of course if there is a basic will to agreement. On this occasion that basic will did exist. Frankly, no agreement of this kind will be reached in the future without such an underlying determination. Finally around 7 p.m., and certainly long after I had had to make special late-night landing arrangements in London, agreement was reached. The Act would be amended to provide for a maximum of eleven voting members, of whom six would be Unionists, four SDLP and one Alliance. There would be four more executive members of the administration, two of whom would be SDLP, one Unionist, one Alliance, and the Chief Whip for the executive would be one of those four.

There was considerable euphoria as we went out on to the steps of Stormont Castle to announce our agreement to the waiting media. It should have been one of the great moments of my political life, as I basked in the universal congratulations. But suddenly a nagging thought came into my mind. I remembered a wise saying which I had learnt from my old friend Edward Boyle: 'Nothing in politics is ever as good or as bad as it first appears.' It was a phrase I had used so frequently that it became a joke among those who worked with me, particularly in the Opposition Whips' Office between 1964 and 1970. Now it came back to haunt me at a crucial moment of possible success. And how right it proved to be. Luckily for me, this old saying kept my feet on the ground in the ensuing period.

I received a great welcome when I announced the details of the agreement in the House of Commons the next day, Thursday 22 November. The Press comments were so favourable that when I look at them now I wonder if they can be describing the same person that I have sometimes read about in their columns since. But then that is the fate of all politicians and one must learn to accept the good with the bad in Press treatment.

The agreement on the formation of the executive was in a sense a culmination of many months of effort. Naturally those of us involved felt great satisfaction. Equally we realized that it was only the beginning of a difficult challenge. The executive was implacably opposed by men of violence. It would also inevitably have to confront the head-on challenge of a major section of 'Loyalist' Unionist opinion. It would need strong backing from the British Government if it was successfully to face those challenges.

This event was to be followed by tripartite discussions including the UK and Eire Governments and members of the Northern Ireland executive at Sunningdale on 6 December. These covered the all-Ireland dimension to the agreement, which was later used as the reason for destroying the executive part of the deal. Before that time, however, events had again forced a sudden shift in my political career. The Government was moving into what was to be a damaging confrontation with the National Union of Mineworkers. Ted Heath felt that the agreement on the power-sharing executive provided him with an opportunity to bring me back to Westminster. He wished to involve me in the critically important areas of counter-inflation and trade union policy. So it was that on 2 December it was announced that I would become Secretary of State for Employment. Francis Pym was named as my successor in Northern Ireland.

At the time I felt that those of us who, as Ministers and officials, were the pioneers of Direct Rule had at least carried out our initial remit. We had broken the mould of Northern Ireland politics based on sectarian division, and we had helped to provide an opportunity for Northern Ireland politicians across the divide to work constructively against the men of violence. Personally I never accepted the more optimistic and flattering comments of the moment which said that we had changed the course of Irish history. I felt even then that I would probably go the way of my many predecessors who had ultimately been seen to fail.

But I did hope that our power-sharing executive, certainly a very tender plant seeking to establish itself in a harsh climate, would at least survive for some time. I was certainly convinced, as I remain today, that if only it could have lasted a few years the mould would have been truly broken. I felt that, given a year or so of Protestant and Catholic political parties working together, the unfortunate people of Northern Ireland who had suffered so much would be given a new opportunity and fresh hope. For these reasons it was the greatest disappointment of my political career when the executive was brought down, not by democratic means but by violent industrial action in the 1974 Ulster Workers' Council strike. My first reaction was one of intense bitterness, but soon I realized that such feelings only hurt oneself and distort one's judgment. I hope therefore that I never showed my resentment publicly, nor indeed privately to those who, by that time, held responsibility in the new Labour Government, namely Prime Minister Harold Wilson and Secretary of State Merlyn Rees, a particular friend of mine then and now. Since then I have been able to analyse the position reasonably dispassionately and certainly to listen to the views of those who were involved. At this distance of time I therefore feel able to give my own opinion.

First, I am convinced that the timing of the British general election in February 1974 represented a grave risk to the new Northern Ireland executive so early in its life. Of course there were many other considerations behind the timing of that election. But it is no secret that my successor, Francis Pym, and I were both unhappy about it from the Northern Ireland point of view. The main reason was simple enough. Those, like Brian Faulkner and Gerry Fitt who were partners in the new executive, were leading parties – the Unionists and the SDLP – which were bound to fight each other in the Westminster election. Worse still, the Democratic Unionist Party under Ian Paisley and those Unionists who were seeking to undermine Brian Faulkner had a glorious opportunity to campaign against the executive. Furthermore, the large Northern Ireland constituencies which were fought, correctly in my view, in the Westminster election on the 'first past the post' basis inevitably favoured the more extreme Protestants such as Ian Paisley, who were masters of destruction and scaremongering politics. The election itself justified all these fears and seriously undermined the authority of the executive.

The result of the election caused even further damage. Harold Wilson's Labour Party was somewhat unexpectedly elected without an overall majority, and his Government was inevitably concerned with establishing its authority. Difficulties caused by a major strike in Northern Ireland represented a distraction which they understandably felt was likely to divert them from their main purpose. In addition, although Harold Wilson and Merlyn Rees while in Opposition had generously supported my efforts, they clearly did not feel as committed to the new executive as those of us in the previous Conservative Government who had been instrumental in founding it. To put it more colloquially, we had feelings of parents for the new child which our Labour successors naturally did not possess. I know they believed that the executive was doomed sooner or later anyway. As a result I believe that they gave in too early to the violence of the Protestant workers. I still maintain, for the reasons I have given, that the power-sharing executive's continued existence would in the long run have repaid a far more determined reaction from the Labour Government. The final irony is that it was a Labour Government, traditionally most critical of the Ulster Protestants, who gave way on this occasion to Protestant violence.

Some time in the future, sooner rather than later I hope, another effort will be made to establish a broadly based administration in Northern Ireland. I believe this because I fundamentally disagree with those who favour complete integration of Northern Ireland in the United Kingdom. My reasons for opposing this solution are that Northern Ireland is not the same as, and has different priorities from, the rest of the United Kingdom and that the Northern Ireland people, Protestant and Catholic alike, have a different identity of which they are justly proud. They do live on the other side of the Irish Sea and they do not want to be wholly dominated by Westminster. They yearn for their old administration. It can be formed in modern conditions only if more people like Brian Faulkner, Gerry Fitt, John Hume and Oliver Napier are prepared to work to unite once again in joint leadership against the men of violence. But let leaders in the United Kingdom, whether in Britain or Northern Ireland, be warned. Success in any such endeavour would be as hard in the future as we found it in 1972–3. And on the road there will be troubles again such as the Ulster Workers' Council strike. These too will have to be met with complete resolution if any lasting success is to be achieved.

A State of Emergency

I returned to London as Secretary of State for Employment at a time when the critical confrontation with the miners was moving into a serious phase. In the years since then I have often been told that I should never have been brought back from Northern Ireland at that moment. I shall now try to answer that question with the benefit of hindsight. In doing so I shall attempt to examine my own state of mind at that time as dispassionately as possible. Such an assessment may also help in forming a correct judgment on my reaction to events at that critical period.

To begin with, I do not accept that my departure from Northern Ireland at that moment and my absence from the Sunningdale Conference was a mistake from the purely Northern Ireland point of view. I had the utmost confidence in Francis Pym: we were great friends and had worked closely together in the Opposition Whips' Office between 1964 and 1970. He knew my ways and totally understood my mind. I believe that if the Conservatives had won the February election he would have successfully resisted the Ulster Workers' Council strike and would have done everything in his power to support Brian Faulkner and the power-sharing executive. Furthermore, I suspect that in the phase after Sunningdale a fresh Secretary of State with new ideas was a sensible move.

I have, however, far more reservations about my suitability for my new job at Westminster as Secretary of State for Employment. First, as a result of the Press euphoria after the establishment of the power-sharing executive, too much was expected of me. I was credited with powers that even at that moment I knew I did not possess. I have learnt since that it is dangerous to be described as a born conciliator because it implies a tendency to compromise too easily. This in turn weakens one's negotiating position especially, as is true in my case, when one's instincts lead in the direction of compromise. Second, I was physically and mentally exhausted after my traumatic time in Northern Ireland. Third, I had been so engrossed in Northern Ireland affairs that I was inevitably out of touch with the events and moods of Whitehall and Westminster. Fourth, although I did not realize it at the time, apparent success in politics at any moment leads inevitably to feelings of jealousy and suspicion among one's colleagues. Taken together these factors combined to make me somewhat unsuitable for the centre of the stage which I had to occupy in the middle of a major industrial and political upheaval.

As the events which I shall now describe turned out, I probably fell between two stools in that I was still committed to Northern Ireland and not yet committed to my new position as Secretary of State for Employment. Just as my state of mind needs to be taken into account as I write about these events, so too does the prevailing mood at Westminster.

Part of the background to the dispute was the earlier confrontation between the Government and the NUM in 1972. In January of that year for the first time in its history the NUM had voted for an all-out national strike for higher pay. The Government had become involved. At first Ted Heath had attempted to stand firm, but from the end of January there were major power cuts. Pressure mounted on the Government to find a way out. On 11 February Robert Carr announced that the distinguished judge, Lord Wilberforce, would chair an independent inquiry into the level of miners' pay. Within a week Lord Wilberforce recommended a huge (by the standards of the day) pay award of more than 20 per cent, which the Government had little option but to accept. Even then further concessions were exacted by the NUM in Downing Street talks before a settlement was concluded.

The 1972 strike was a severe blow both to the authority and to the economic policy of the Government, although there was no doubt that the miners had some justification in feeling that their pay had been badly eroded over recent years. The settlement gave a further stimulus to other unions to press equally inflationary – but less defensible – wage claims. By the autumn the Cabinet agreed that the upward pressure on wages was such that it could only be met by a prices and incomes policy. Phase 1 of that policy was announced on 26 September. After an abortive attempt to agree a voluntary policy with the CBI and TUC, the policy was made statutory as from 6 November 1972. As has frequently been pointed out, this was a complete reversal of the declared policies of the 1970 manifesto.

The 1972 dispute and its consequences were the inescapable background to the renewed dispute of 1973–4. Inside and outside the Conservative Party the defeat was seen as a humiliation for the Government. There was a feeling in many quarters that the organized power of the miners was too strong to resist. However, it was just as strongly held that the authority of Government must in future be upheld and that, in view of the pressure on wages, a firm policy on prices and incomes was essential. It was a recipe for the adoption of tough, entrenched positions in any future dispute.

Phase 3 of the prices and incomes policy was announced on 8 October 1973. It allowed for a 7 per cent norm in wage increases -- below the rate of inflation at the time. Pressure on the Government had been increased by the outbreak on 6 October of the 1973 Middle East war. That soon led to fears over the security of oil supplies and in turn to a huge increase in the price of oil. With this uncertainty, a dispute over coal could be ill-afforded. Yet it was clear from motions already passed by the NUM that the limits of Phase 3 would be well below their 1974 pay claim, which amounted to 35 per cent. The chaos over the price of oil could only strengthen the confidence of the NUM, should it come to a dispute. At the first meeting with the NUM on the 1974 pay award on 10 October, the Coal Board offered the full Phase 3 maximum. They also added an element to cover something which had deliberately been put into the incomes policy to allow some flexibility – a payment for 'unsocial hours'. When the NUM predictably rejected this opening offer there was no significant room for negotiation. Conflict became inevitable.

On 8 November the Government lost a by-election to the Liberals at Berwick; however, Labour did even worse and also lost a seat in Glasgow to the Scottish Nationalist Party on the same day. Also on 8 November the NUM executive voted for an overtime ban to start from 12 November. The Government responded far more quickly than in 1972. On 13 November a state of emergency was declared and controls on electricity supplies were ordered. Street lighting was cut back and television was ordered to close down at

10.30 p.m. Already the country felt on the brink of a major crisis; at the same time fears of petrol rationing rose as the oil producers cut back production by one-quarter.

The Government again became involved in the substance of the pay claim as the statutory limits of Phase 3 provided the framework for talks. On 28 November the NUM executive was invited to No. 10 for discussions. Ted Heath appealed to the NUM to recognize the critical position of the economy and urged them to take advantage of the impending report on pay relativities, which might allow some adjustment of miners' pay even within the limits of an incomes policy. A further examination of pay in the coal industry was also offered. But the meeting was abortive. Indeed, further hardening of attitudes in the Conservative Party and among the public followed the alleged threat made by Mick McGahey that he would do anything to get the Government out of office. It was against this bleak background that I returned from Northern Ireland on 2 December.

Soon after taking office I decided that I ought to have a confidential talk with Joe Gormley, the President of the NUM, in order to understand his position. He made it clear to me that he could not accept the settlement for the miners within the Government's pay guide-lines. On the other hand, he did believe that he could persuade them to accept an increase which was only narrowly in excess of this. Privately I felt that such an approach had few objections, for the Government had power under the Act to sanction a higher settlement under exceptional circumstances. Further, it seemed to me that the increase in oil prices could be used to justify such action in the miners' case. However, I simply told Joe Gormley that I did not believe that my colleagues would be prepared to make any such exception and, indeed, so it proved.

Joe Gormley very fairly describes the conversation which took place between us in his book, *Battered Cherub*, in which he states that he outlined the NUM position and that I listened, he thought, with sympathy. This comment probably underlined the danger of my new position. In any event, I would not have been human if I had not felt it essential to seek a good working relationship with him.

These early exploratory talks did not lead to any immediate prospect of progress. With the long winter ahead the Government was determined not to weaken its hand by allowing the erosion of coal stocks. On 13 December Ted Heath broadcast on television to say that the country would go on to a three-day week from 1 January 1974 in order to cut back electricity consumption. On 17 December the Government announced a major package of expenditure cuts in response to the changed economic circumstances of the oil crisis and the rise in commodity prices generally. Some writers have said in retrospect that these moves were already calculated with an election in mind.

Certainly I cannot remember any of my colleagues discussing an election with me at that time. But I suppose in the circumstances I would probably have been the last person in whom they would have confided. After all, I had been brought back from Northern Ireland to help in settling a dispute, not in precipitating a general election. I only remember the start of election speculation in early January.

Throughout this time I simply continued to seek a settlement. On 20 December I had a meeting at my headquarters in St James's Square with Joe Gormley, Lawrence Daly and Mick McGahey. There was an IRA Christmas bombing campaign going on, and in the middle of the meeting we were warned that we should leave the building. To the delight of the assembled media we walked into the street outside and then into a neighbouring Italian restaurant for a drink together. At such informal meetings one has more chance of getting to know the personalities involved than on formal occasions. I had already had such an opportunity to gain a little mutual understanding with Joe Gormley. I admired his forthrightness, his honesty and his loyalty not only to the NUM membership but to the country as a whole. I believed then that he genuinely wanted a settlement for which he had a chance of gaining acceptance from his members. Nor did he want to press their claims to unreasonable lengths when they would clearly damage the nation's economy. I have never had any reason to change my mind on this assessment. Lawrence Daly was a mercurial personality whom I personally found agreeable. Despite some of his wild outbursts I felt he would be loyal to Joe Gormley over any possible settlement. Mick McGahey and I had a strange background link. He had worked in a pit close to my old family home in Lanarkshire. He knew that I had a strong family connection with William Baird & Co., the coal and steel company in the West of Scotland. As a result he regarded me as a representative of the wicked coal owners and treated me as such in any formal discussions. But behind this rough public approach we were able to talk amicably about his early days in Lanarkshire pits. I felt, perhaps unfairly, that he would be the hardest to bring to agreement.

On the other side of the coin, I became increasingly convinced that they tended to regard me as a soft touch because of my Press reputation. Obviously they also believed that Ted Heath had brought me back to find a settlement to the dispute. This was a disadvantage which I had constantly to remember. But perhaps it did have some value, for our discussions were consequently always constructive and frank, probably because they felt that I genuinely wanted a settlement and was strongly opposed to a confrontation, on which there was much media comment at the time.

In the restaurant Joe Gormley raised the question of a formula for settlement based on miners' working and bathing time. They explained that miners were different from other workers in two respects. At the start of their shift they had to spend a long time after changing into working clothes waiting for the lifts which would take them down to the pit-face. At the end of the shift there was the question of bathing, because of the exceptionally dirty nature of a miner's job. If they were to obtain some proper time allowance as compensation, then that could surely be applied exceptionally to miners in their special circumstances. I remember saying that this did seem a possible way forward if they could obtain agreement from the Coal Board and from the Pay Board, which was necessary under the Phase 3 prices and incomes legislation in force at the time. In his book Joe Gormley describes how he believed that Harold Wilson, as Leader of the Opposition, destroyed this possible plan by revealing it publicly in the House of Commons as his own idea. In fact Joe Gormley had informed him about it on a purely confidential basis. I have no reason to dispute Joe Gormley's account and I was furious at the time. It may be that the bathing and waiting time solution would never have worked, but certainly any hope of its success was utterly destroyed when it was publicly raised within a few hours in the House of Commons, rather than being the subject of careful consideration in confidential negotiations.

This episode only convinced me more firmly than ever that the principle of not discussing the details of industrial disputes publicly in Parliament during negotiations is most wise. Alas, it will only be respected if the old conventions of confidentiality within parties and between leaders of parties in Parliament are preserved. I fear that this is now increasingly unlikely, for relations between parties in Parliament appear to be deteriorating.

On 8 January 1974 the Pay Board ruled out the prospect of a realistic settlement on the basis of bathing and waiting time. In the debate in the Commons on 9 and 10 January we suggested that if the NUM went back to work on the basis of the present offer there would be an immediate inquiry into the future of the industry and into the pay of miners. I made this offer directly to the NUM in further talks on 9 January. This approach too was rejected by the NUM. At the same time the TUC was active in trying to promote a settlement. At an NEDC meeting on the morning of 9 January, TUC leaders claimed that if the Government would sanction an exceptional settlement to the miners' dispute, then the TUC would ensure that no other union would seek to take advantage of the precedent. Ted Heath and I believed that we must consider this suggestion, although there was serious doubt about the TUC's ability to influence the miners in any settlement or to contain other unions. We held talks at Downing Street with the economic committee of the TUC on 10, 14 and 21 January amid intense speculation about an election on 7 February on the old register that would have favoured the Conservative Party. Some felt that the TUC move was simply a political ploy to stave off an election. Whatever the truth, the talks themselves proved fruitless. At the end of the day the TUC could not formally accept the constraints of Phase 3 and could not convince us that they were capable of delivering the promise that was made.

After the last meeting on 21 January I felt deeply

depressed. I could not disagree with Ted Heath and my colleagues' assessment of the TUC. Yet, perhaps mistakenly, I still obstinately held to the view that the TUC leaders at the meetings were totally genuine in their determination to make a real effort to hold the line. I did not accept the argument that their proposal was just a ploy to delay the date of a general election, because I was sure that they did not want an election at all at that time. On the contrary, I believed what they told me privately: that they were convinced that the Labour Party would lose an election. This would give the Tories another period in Government which was the last thing they desired. Personally I was also strongly opposed to a general election, although I knew one would be inevitable if a miners' settlement was not reached, since coal stocks were running down fast. I did not accept the view that our party would win an election at a time of industrial dispute which was inevitably causing economic problems and personal inconvenience. I have never underestimated the British dislike of internal industrial conflict. I also felt that whichever party won the election, the settlement of the miners' dispute was bound to be more expensive in national economic terms after an election period of several weeks, because by then coal stocks would be close to exhaustion. Lastly, I was never clear what answer we would give during an election when asked how we would settle the miners' strike if we won. And so I found myself driven to accepting an election while dreading the whole prospect. But these views may well have been due to my state of mind and may provide further evidence as to why I was not the best person to be Employment Secretary at that time.

One final strand of potential settlement remained – the issue of 'relativities'. In the world of incomes policies, where market forces are allowed little play, a dominant issue is the question of rates of pay of one group of workers in relation to another. When all incomes move broadly in line, there is no scope for recognizing a particular extra demand for certain forms of labour. The miners contended that the oil crisis had greatly enhanced the value of mining activity to the country as a whole, and that this should be recognized in their pay packets. We asked the Pay Board to produce a report on this issue. It was published on 19 January and set out ways in which special cases could be examined for special treatment even under Phase 3. Although at first we were at pains to state publicly that there could be no guarantee that this system would produce a compromise over miners' pay, we did indicate to the NUM that were they to resume normal working we would refer their case for examination to the new Relativities Board.

By this stage, however, the NUM was not prepared to accept anything but a cash on the table deal. Their members were balloted for a strike, which was backed by 81 per cent in a result declared on 4 February. I made one final attempt to engage the NUM in talks on the morning of 7 February before the actual strike was called. They were unwilling to meet me. Later that same day the Government therefore asked the Queen to dissolve Parliament and went to the country.

And so, still feeling unhappy and reluctant, I found myself swept into an election campaign which I dreaded. I had to accept that by this time I could not offer any alternative other than surrender to the miners. Surrender was unthinkable and would have left Ted Heath and our whole Conservative Government in a hopelessly weak position. As I consider the situation today I realize that throughout all this time we had only one alternative: we could have accepted the TUC offer at the meeting in January and given them the opportunity to prove their capacity to restrain other unions following an exceptional settlement to the miners. Most of my colleagues were completely convinced that the TUC leaders could not deliver, even if they were genuine. I suspect that a large majority of our Conservative Members also doubted the authenticity of the TUC leaders' motives, which frankly I did not. But I could not advance any convincing arguments in favour of their capacity and power to deliver. Indeed, on considering subsequent trade union history, few would believe the likelihood of their success for a moment. But in 1974 TUC leaders were much stronger than they are today, and it has to be accepted that the existence of a prices and incomes policy certainly gave them considerable increased power.

Such reflections only bring me back to my own position and state of mind. My feelings at this time were out of tune with my Cabinet colleagues and our Parliamentary Party. On the whole they wanted an election and believed that we would win it. They felt that efforts like mine at conciliation only frustrated them and prevented an earlier election. And up to this day they believe that if we had gone to the country sooner, we would certainly have won. I, on the other hand, never wanted a general election and, given my position, I could not have been expected to do so. After all, I had been brought back from Ireland for the specific purpose of seeking a solution to the miners' dispute. I was bound to dislike a confrontation which resulted from a failure to find a settlement.

However, as with all general elections, there was no time for doubt as soon as the battle began. I thus launched myself wholeheartedly into a massive speaking campaign all over the country, with only infrequent visits to my own constituency. In the middle of the campaign I found myself involved as Secretary of State for Employment in a controversy which I believe very unfairly did the Conservative Party substantial damage. On 18 February the Pay Board began taking relativities evidence on the level of miners' pay. At a Press conference on the evening of 21 February the Pay Board was interpreted – incorrectly as it proved – as saying that the level of miners' pay against those in other manual manufacturing sectors had been miscalculated and that their pay was 8 per cent below the national average, not above it. Headlined in the *Daily Mirror* as 'The Great Pit Blunder', this suggested that the miners had been right all along and that the agony of the three-day week had been endured for nothing. Great embarrassment was caused until the reason for the discrepancy in the figures was explained, and Labour and the Liberals made havoc for a day or two.

There was no doubt in the end that there was no substance to the story, which only added to the suspicion that someone on the Pay Board had leaked the figures in a deliberately misleading way in order to damage the Conservative Party. I remember the day after the leak only too well. I left the Birmingham area early in the morning by train having learnt the news late the previous night. I travelled all morning up to Lanark in Scotland with my PA, Robert Jackson, now a most able junior Minister. He got out at every station to telephone for news on the crisis. Nearly always he had to rush back on to the train as it was leaving before he got through. I then did a tour of daytime and evening meetings right across the Scottish Borders from Lanark to East Lothian and back, finishing late at night in Selkirk. Then I motored the eighty miles home to Penrith, where I arrived exhausted and utterly miserable, for I felt responsible for the damaging incident arising from a misunderstanding for which I knew I was not to blame. Such is the fate of leading politicians during elections.

This incident depressed me still further. I felt that the 'relativities' approach, which I had believed to be the best answer to the question of our Government action if we won the election, had been rendered useless. Worse still, the apparently deliberate leaking of Pay Board evidence gave further ammunition to the critics in my own party of my conciliatory approach. And worst of all, it simply underlined my fears of fighting a general election during a major industrial dispute. But I knew that at the time I had to fight against all these feelings and maintain an outward impression of high morale and confidence in victory. I hope, and believe, that I succeeded, although the effort involved put an increased strain on my already depleted physical resources. Finally I collapsed, after my long constituency tour, on polling day.

In those days the Penrith and Border count was held the following morning. When I woke up I felt desperately ill and my wife found that I had a high temperature. The doctor was summoned and I insisted on him giving me some medicine to carry me through the count, which I felt I must attend. This had a bizarre result. My own constituency figures gave me a much increased majority and a greater share of the votes. Presumably, coming so soon after my apparent success in Northern Ireland, many uncommitted people voted for me. Sadly I knew nothing of this, for the medicine I had taken calmed my feverish temperature but also completely dulled my memory and my senses. I am told that I looked desperately ill but acted quite naturally and made a perfectly rational speech on the declaration of the result. So much so that nobody thought it necessary to stop me going on television.

I had absolutely no subsequent recollection of my interview with Robin Day, nor of the somewhat controversial remark I made at the time. It appeared then that the Labour Party had won more seats by a very narrow margin, but in fact with fewer total votes. I stated that if Labour seemed to have won most seats, then they had in my judgment effectively won the election. This certainly represented my actual view, which is that the British people have a simple and reasonable attitude to election results just as they do to football results. They consider that the side with the most seats, or goals, wins the match. For this reason I believed that any effort in 1974 by the Conservatives and Liberals to form a coalition together against Labour would have been very unpopular and thus doomed to early failure. If I had been in normal control of my senses I would probably have realized that such an honest expression of my views was unwise at that particular moment, when I had not spoken to Ted Heath or any of my other colleagues. I was naturally both praised and blamed for this remark. Perhaps happily for me I was taken home, put to bed and knew nothing of the controversy until the following morning. By then Ted Heath wanted me to join him and my Cabinet colleagues in London to discuss the future. But my doctor was properly determined that I was quite unfit to travel.

Only later did I discover that this whole incident had aroused some suspicion over my attitude. The mischief-makers' case was as follows. I was too pleased with myself. Personally I had experienced a remarkable increase in my own majority and had received too much support in the Press. I therefore now believed that I should set myself up as a challenge to Ted Heath's leadership. In fact, as I was able to prove conclusively within the year, nothing was further from my thoughts.

During the weekend I recovered from the collapse, which was simply caused by exhaustion and was soon cured by a little rest. Meanwhile the election result was that the Conservatives won most of the popular vote but that Labour had most seats: 301 to 296. The Liberals did well, winning nearly 20 per cent of the vote although only fourteen seats. There was a Cabinet meeting on the evening of Friday 1 March. Ted Heath then went to the Palace to report on the situation. On Saturday 2 March he met Jeremy Thorpe and offered the Liberals seats in a coalition Government. He also offered that the Cabinet would support the establishment of a Speaker's Conference on electoral reform. After discussions between Thorpe and his colleagues on Sunday and on Monday morning the offer was rejected. A telegram was sent to the Ulster Unionists, led by Harry West, on Sunday 3 March, offering the Conservative Whip. There was a non-committal response. After the rejection of the coalition offer by the Liberals the Cabinet met twice in the course of 4 March. Ted Heath went to the Palace again to resign at 6.30 p.m.

As I held strongly to the views that I had already expressed in such extraordinary circumstances on television, I believed that this was the correct outcome. Certainly the immediate result was bad: a weak minority Labour Government; probably another general election within a year or so; and traumatic consequences for the Conservative Party and Ted Heath's leadership in particular. But if, as I maintained, the proposed coalition would have been regarded as wrong in principle by the British people, then it would have been most unpopular. It would therefore have been most unlikely to work in practice, even if – improbably – it held together when faced with contentious issues. If, as seemed likely, it ended in chaos, it would have had disastrous long-term consequences for the Conservative and Liberal Parties. As I reconsider these events today I remain profoundly of the same opinion.

A New Leader is Elected

In the Conservative Party we now had to settle down to the depressing prospect of a term in Opposition. We had lost an election which many of our MPs and supporters in the country believed we were going to win. Worse still, the position of the Labour Government was so weak that it would be bound to call another general election at the next favourable moment. Even worse, in such circumstances it was likely, judging from past experience, that the British people would give Labour a further chance with a better majority on that occasion. All this ensured that there were recriminations in our party and major criticisms of the leadership, not a good basis on which to prepare for an early general election.

Understandably, Peter Carrington felt that someone else should take on the unenviable task of Chairman of the Party. In the spring Ted Heath asked me to succeed him. I cannot say that I relished the opportunity, but on my principle of always accepting any position offered I agreed to take on what was clearly a fairly poisoned chalice. I knew that we had to prepare for an early general election and that we would be doing so in a mood of defeatism in the Party as a whole, and particularly in Conservative Central Office. I realized at once that in my approach to the task I must separate completely my private thoughts and fears from my public attitude. Privately I believed that our objective must be to fight a successful rearguard action and so limit any subsequent Labour majority. I was only too well aware of the risk that we might be substantially defeated to an extent which was bound to delay the future return of a Conservative Government. But I reckoned that even a success in limiting the size of a Labour majority demanded a clear public position of confidence in our ability to overturn such a narrow defeat in February.

I appreciated that this was going to be a particularly difficult role for me, since I have never been renowned among my friends for being able to disguise my real feelings. I did have one advantage: my six years as Opposition Chief Whip had brought me into close contact with the leading figures in Conservative Central Office. I knew them well and admired their total dedication to the Party in good times and bad. I also understood the intricacies of the relationship between the professionals and the voluntary side of the Party which, as in all such organizations, is a study in itself.

The Chairman of the Party is responsible for the running of the Party Organization and the Area Offices throughout the country. But both at the Party's Central Office and in the Areas, the officials concerned have to work closely with the leaders of the voluntary side of the Party, the National Union. The Chairman therefore has to be careful not to interfere with the National Union's voluntary Officers but must, at the same time, establish a good working relationship with them; nor must he ever forget that they *are* volunteers, on whose good will he utterly depends. The National Union in turn exercises influence in the constituencies throughout the Areas, but the Constituency Associations have the last word, for they are wholly responsible for the running of their own organizations and offices. Some of the richer constituencies not only provide for their own finances but also contribute to the running of the Central Office. Certainly, some of the poorer Associations in the Labour areas do need help from the Central Office. Overall, as is quite proper, the voluntary side calls the tune and the Chairman of the Party will get great support from it, for it is the most loyal and hard-working body of people. Inside the Central Office the Party Chairman controls, *inter alia*, the activities of the Organization, Public Relations and Candidates' Departments. In recent years he has also become responsible for the Research Department. The financial side is run by the Party Treasurers, who are in turn responsible directly to the Leader of the Party, but naturally they work closely with the Chairman. All this means that the Chairman of the Party has a major task of co-ordination and reconciliation of many different interests. He needs tact and understanding, together with a capacity for sorting out problems quickly as they arise.

As Deputy Chairman I had Michael Fraser, a great and long-standing servant of the Party who had been head of the Research Department for many years. He was the leading thinker and intellectual in the Party and had been a considerable power in the formulation of party policy over the years. On the organizational side Richard Webster was the leading agent, with long experience of constituency work. In addition, Peter Carrington had recently introduced as a new Chief of Staff appointment Michael Wolff, who had great ability and considerable experience of journalism and a good relationship with the Press. I am convinced that if he had been given the chance to develop the influence and importance of his job, he would have been invaluable to the Party. He was certainly an enormous help to me, even in those early days when his position was the object of suspicion inside Central Office. His sudden tragic death at the age of forty-five in 1976 deprived political life in general of a potentially outstanding figure and a most delightful personality and companion.

As Vice-Chairman on the women's side I had Sarah Morrison, who has shown her forceful and dynamic personality in many fields since then. I suppose we were all contrasting personalities, but we were united in our determination to face up to what was an unenviable task. During the summer months I spent much time going round the constituencies trying to restore morale shattered by the February defeat. I persuaded myself that on the whole this feeling was not as bad as I had expected and that our troops were in reasonably good heart. Of course I did not allow myself to scratch below the surface, as that would have betrayed my inner anxieties. As a result I probably deluded myself but it did at least help my own morale. As my family and friends would tell me, there is no doubt that my constituency appearances were full of my well-known phrases such as, 'Splendid! Carry on the good work!' Over the years these have proved valuable in denying opportunities for difficult questions and criticism.

At the same time inside Central Office we were trying to establish an organization and prepare a strategy for an autumn general election while laying plans for what promised to be an unpleasant party conference. I often speculated to myself as to which of the two would be the worse. However, we did not have long to wait. Harold Wilson called the general election on 18 September 1974. I cannot say that I enjoyed the next three weeks.

At the start the opinion polls were against us, just as they were steadily throughout the campaign. So, naturally, was Press comment. It is not easy to keep up one's spirits in such circumstances, but a successful rearguard action such as I envisaged demanded an optimistic outlook. Accordingly at the start I made clear in a speech to the staff at Central Office that I would not tolerate pessimistic comments from anyone. This certainly had some effect, although I had no illusions about my inability to take action if I did hear of any. A Chairman of the Party has to stay at Central Office each morning during an election campaign and deal with all the problems before and after the many Press conferences. He has also to recognize, however, that the longer he stays in the building, the more tiresome and trivial become the issues put before him. Therefore – not least for his sanity – he must get out on to the hustings in the afternoons and evenings. Throughout this period I was mercifully sustained by two excellent PAs, Tim Eggar, now to my delight a very successful junior Minister, and James Loudon. Together with Stewart Newman, who organized my tours, they knew exactly how to maintain my morale.

As was inevitable in the second general election in a year, the campaign was quiet and uneventful. My main memory is of polling day. I travelled south from Cumbria in the evening in order to be at Conservative Central Office as the night results came in. Most forecasters and opinion polls had given Labour a comfortable working majority. When I arrived at Euston my worst fears appeared to be confirmed. A BBC exit poll, one of the first of its kind, had given Labour a majority of 150. At that time I had not experienced the dangers of relying on BBC exit polls, so clearly demonstrated in 1987, and so I believed it. I was therefore greatly relieved as the actual results came in.

In the end Labour gained just eighteen seats from us,

although we also lost to the Scottish National Party. Most important, Labour's overall majority was only four and their majority over the Conservatives just forty-three, far fewer than I had expected at best. I felt greatly relieved at this result, for we had achieved my reasonable expectation of a good rearguard action. I knew that it could only increase the pressure inside the Conservative Party against Ted Heath's leadership. But as the subsequent Parliament proved, we had severely restricted Labour's room for manoeuvre.

Socialist measures, such as the aircraft and shipbuilding legislation, were emasculated as Labour's slender overall majority was eroded at by-elections. In Jim Callaghan's premiership they were driven to rely on the obvious farce of the Lib/Lab Pact, which did neither party any good. Finally after the fiasco of their devolution proposals in 1979 the Government was defeated in the House of Commons and had to go to the country.

I am convinced that the limitation of Labour's victory in 1974 was an important prerequisite for the return of a Conservative Government in 1979. I am also sure that the success of our efforts to maintain morale under adverse circumstances helped us. In planning our strategy for the campaign we were all too aware that in February the country had shown that it was not yet ready to face up to the key question of the reform of the trade unions. Equally, we were conscious that there was growing concern that Labour's handling of the economy since February was stoking up inflationary pressures already inherent in the economy. Even at the time, Denis Healey's rather foolish election boast that inflation was running at only 8.4 per cent did not ring true.

Our aim was to respond to these underlying popular

feelings, while not alarming those who were worried that another Conservative Government would mean more confrontation with the unions and another three-day week. Our manifesto therefore floated the concept of a Government of 'national unity' in the face of the growing economic crisis. We said that Britain's problems 'should transcend party differences'. We were not suggesting that there should be a political coalition Government. The idea was that, given the exceptional problems of the day, a Conservative Government would be prepared to invite people from outside party ranks to try to form a common economic programme to solve Britain's difficulties. This was a rather vague concept, but it undoubtedly fitted the nervous mood of the time. Even the astute Harold Wilson admitted, in his book *Final Term*, that it was a 'difficult argument to repudiate'. Our main strategic aim was to limit Labour's margin of success, and that we achieved.

Additionally, our campaign on the cost of mortgages and on rates, publicized by Margaret Thatcher, clearly saved us both votes and seats, particularly in London and the South-East. All in all, it would be absurd to claim a success when the election results indicated a substantial defeat. Nevertheless, I have always derived some satisfaction from the October 1974 Election and from the part that Central Office played in it. We had gained my certainly modest objective and had left a solid base for our party at a time when a disaster with serious repercussions for the future was a real possibility.

The period following the second 1974 Election was an unhappy one inside the Conservative Party. It was certainly the worst time in my political life. I remained Chairman of the Party and so observed from one particular vantage point the bitterness, dissension and general bad feeling in the Parliamentary Party. It was only then that for the first time I appreciated the strong feeling against Ted Heath. I considered it most unfair. But even at that time I did not realize how widespread it was. I tended to regard it as the usual grumbling of malcontents who, for one reason or another, had a grudge against the Leader and were using the unhappy occasion of a second electoral defeat in one year as an excuse to campaign against him. For this reason I did not believe that the executive of the 1922 Committee accurately reflected the feelings of the Parliamentary Party, particularly since the Chairman, Edward du Cann, had never forgiven Ted Heath after their disagreement during his period as Chairman of the Party in the 1960s. It was probably also true that for much the same reason I did not have the close personal relationship with Edward du Cann which should exist between the Chairman of the 1922 Committee and the Chairman of the Party.

As a result, when it became clear that Margaret Thatcher intended to stand in a leadership election against Ted Heath, I simply thought such a challenge was good, in that it would clear the air and that Ted Heath would win. I was even unwise enough to ignore the warnings of my friends that all was not going well with the Heath campaign during the election period itself. I was therefore deeply dismayed when I heard that Ted Heath had trailed by eleven votes on the first ballot, for I realized that it marked the end of his time as Leader of the Conservative Party. I also recognized that almost certainly it meant that Margaret Thatcher would be the next Leader.

Until that moment, despite the usual gossip in the Press about my prospects of becoming Leader, I had never even contemplated the possibility. I was in fact wholly loyal to Ted Heath, with whom I had worked closely over the years, and I firmly believed that it would be in the best interests of the Party that he should remain Leader. Suddenly, however, I had to consider my own position. There was a procedure for a second ballot and many of my friends suggested that I should stand to represent the moderate wing of the Party against what many of them perceived to be the right-wing stance of Margaret Thatcher and her friends.

There was clearly no time to lose and so, almost on the spur of the moment, I decided that I would stand. In the event, Geoffrey Howe, Jim Prior and John Peyton also stood. Despite my decision, I never felt particularly enthusiastic in the circumstances, especially since Margaret Thatcher, having had the courage to stand against the existing Leader and defeat him, clearly had a strong bandwagon rolling for her. Nor did I get much encouragement from some of my best friends outside politics. They told me privately that they did not really want me to win, because they thought I would not be a good Leader of a party in Opposition and would be unhappy in the job. I had a nasty feeling that they were right; but I decided – following the old principle of 'in for a penny, in for a pound' – that I must campaign as hard as I could.

I did so and received much help from my friends and indeed, to my delight, particularly from many of those who had been close to me both in the Whips' Office and in various Government departments. However, I felt highly relieved when the election period was over, for I found the internal divisions and bad feeling among one's own parliamentary colleagues most disagreeable.

When I heard the result on 11 February I was not downhearted. I had hoped that I might get a few more votes, but seventy-nine out of 274 cast represented a substantial voice in the Party. I soon realized that the situation required an immediate decision from me about the future. There were those who suggested that I should wait a few days before committing myself to serving under Margaret Thatcher. But I knew almost at once that such a reaction was simply out of character. I know that some people regard my strong natural feelings of loyalty to causes and to people as old-fashioned and too extreme. My reaction is that there are worse faults in life and that I happen to be made that way. Such an attitude also has the advantage that I can expect, and usually receive, reciprocal feelings in return.

I decided that same night that in the interests of the Party I would serve Margaret Thatcher in any capacity she wanted, and that I would give my undivided loyalty to her as Leader. On that basis I made up my mind that I would do my utmost to work with her. I recognized that this might create problems for me, as I did not know her well at the time and we had never been close friends. I also appreciated that we were very different personalities with contrasting backgrounds and interests, and held rather dissimilar political positions on some issues. I had to accept that she might find me impossible to work with, even if I did my best to help her and subordinated myself to her as Leader. Fortunately I understood something about the problems of such a relationship, for I had been second-in-command of a battalion towards the end of the war and had got on well with a Commanding Officer with a different personality and outlook from my own.

I need never have had any of these anxieties. When I met her for the first time after the election the next morning Margaret Thatcher asked me to be her deputy. From that moment on she did everything in her power to make my position easy. And so started a relationship which I, at any rate, have enormously appreciated. She has always treated me with a kindness and understanding which have meant much to me and which have enabled me to feel that I have played some part in her remarkable achievements as Prime Minister and Leader of our Conservative Party.

In 1975, however, we were confronted by the realities of the present rather than by such hopes for the future. We were a divided Party under an unknown Leader who was also the first woman in British politics to hold such a position. I have to admit that I was among those who at the time still had reservations about the capacity of women to stand the immense physical and mental strains of leadership. Of course today Margaret Thatcher has proved that all such fears were founded merely on male chauvinism of the worst order. At the same time they also underlined the nature of the challenge that she faced.

She was also surrounded at the top of the Conservative Party by those who had served under Ted Heath and were dismayed by his defeat. In turn the divisions of the Party were underlined by the distrust which Margaret Thatcher's supporters still felt for those of us who had served with Ted Heath. I know that many of them were suspicious of me and my motives. My only hope was to show them that I was determined to put the interests of our Conservative Party above all personal feelings. In this I was greatly assisted by Airey Neave, who had been the main organizer of Margaret Thatcher's campaign for the leadership. He and I worked closely together and by the time of his tragic assassination just before the 1979 Election I believe that we had become great friends.

It must also be said that Peter Carrington's immense influence did much for Margaret Thatcher and the whole Party during those difficult times, both in Parliament and in the country. But of course none of this healing of wounds could have happened without Margaret Thatcher's leadership and enormous understanding. We had many difficulties and some crises, but the period of Opposition between 1975 and 1979 was a great triumph for her. When one considers the difficulties of parties in Opposition, and the problems that face Leaders of the Opposition with no power or patronage, her time as Opposition Leader must be counted an immense achievement. As a result she led the Conservative Party in the 1979 Election as a unified fighting force with the capacity to win. Not only did we have the capacity to win – but we actually won.

Immediately after the 1974 Election, Labour's internal divisions over Europe, which had been papered over during the campaign by the promise of renegotiation and a referendum, became a major issue. On the whole subsequent experience has shown that Labour's renegotiation procedure was simply a clever Harold Wilson political manoeuvre to keep Britain in Europe, despite the doubts and opposition inside his own party. In March 1975 Harold Wilson recommended agreed terms to the electorate, but five Cabinet Ministers were given the right to differ and issued a statement opposing the recommendation. This relaxation of collective responsibility on such a major issue has only one parallel in modern times: on Free Trade in 1931 and then under a national Government. It may have been the only course open to the Labour Government at the time, but I believe that their party has paid dearly for it since. Perhaps that is just retribution, for I do not believe that any Government can hope to govern successfully except on a basis of collective responsibility.

This arrangement set the scene for the referendum

campaign, which was a strange experience for party politicians, for we found ourselves working with our normal opponents against members of our own parties. I have to admit that I found the experience both enjoyable and rewarding. I became the Conservative Vice-President under the leadership of Roy Jenkins in the Britain in Europe Campaign. Harold Wilson and Margaret Thatcher, as Prime Minister and Leader of the Opposition, both campaigned in favour of Britain staying in Europe but obviously did not join the main group. Ted Heath, as the Prime Minister responsible for taking Britain into Europe, also campaigned most forcefully and effectively for European membership. In the Britain in Europe Campaign Roy Jenkins proved himself a most admirable leader in every way. Naturally as members of different political parties he and I have disagreed from time to time, but I must record that throughout the referendum campaign I greatly enjoyed working under his leadership.

The referendum on 5 June proved to be a conclusive endorsement of Britain's place as a member of the European Community. This turned out to be a most necessary safeguard in overcoming the political difficulties which are bound to face any multinational organization. Personally I do not pretend to be a great European, for by nature and outlook I share all the insular qualities of the British people. But having seen the suffering of war arising from past animosities between Western European nations, I am enthusiastic about the cause of European unity, which I trust will make such conflicts impossible in future. I look forward also to the plans for closer economic union, but I cannot share the extreme position of those who appear to contemplate scrapping national identities altogether. I shall always remain British first, just as I suspect people in

France or Germany and the other nations in the Community will also keep their identities.

For the rest of the Parliament I spent most of my time as Deputy Leader of the Opposition helping Margaret Thatcher in promoting the unity and cohesion of the Conservative Party. It ought to be recorded that during this time Peter Thorneycroft did a remarkable job as Chairman of the Party. His long ministerial experience and position as a much-respected elder statesman gave him just the authority and prestige needed at that difficult time. He made full use of them all to the great benefit of the Conservative cause.

During these years I also made two official visits abroad, one to India in 1977 as Deputy Leader of the British delegation to the Commonwealth Parliamentary Association Conference in Delhi in October of that year; the other to Israel in 1978. I had never been to an Inter-Parliamentary Conference before, as my ministerial and Chief Whip work over the years had made it difficult to get away. But I thoroughly enjoyed the atmosphere of the CPA Conference in Delhi, where we had the advantage of a friendly British delegation admirably led by Malcolm Shepherd, Leader of the House of Lords in the Labour Government.

At that time Mrs Gandhi was ruling under the emergency powers which she imposed earlier that year. She had recently detained some politicians and imposed Press censorship. I had the opportunity of a private meeting with her. She immediately impressed me as a powerful personality, with piercing eyes, who spoke quietly but forcefully and used the whole period of the interview to set out her case for the emergency in great detail. She was at pains to stress that she was not being autocratic but, frankly, as far as I was concerned, her words failed to carry conviction. She claimed that she had had to act in order to preserve democracy, and to prevent an outbreak of violence resulting in chaos. She told me that she was determined to maintain parliamentary democracy. In the event, Mrs Gandhi proved as good as her word. My impression at the time was that if she did relax the emergency powers she would face the difficulty of maintaining her aim of fostering a new spirit of national resolve. Subsequent events show that she did not succeed in that, and that India remains as difficult to govern as ever. This is not surprising when one reflects on the vast size of the country, the pressures of an ever-growing population and the stark contrasts in living standards.

Any British visitor going to India for the first time must be struck by the strangely ambivalent attitude towards Britain and the age of the British Raj. On the one hand, many of our traditions, particularly military, survive virtually intact. On the other hand, much public comment underlines the wickedness of British rule and the great moment for India when they freed themselves from the British yoke at the time of independence. It seems to me that considering the appalling problems of running the huge country with its amazingly diverse population, British administrative skill must have been remarkable. Clearly British rule had to come to an end, but despite some of the insults which may be difficult for us to bear from time to time, we should always remember that on the whole the Indian people retain a strange respect for Britain. We should never forget that in our future relations with their country.

Then, in 1978, I went to Israel with my wife at the invitation of the Israeli Government. This was interesting for me because I was to revisit many of the places which I had last seen when I was in the Army in 1945–6. At that time the State of Palestine was still in existence under the British mandate and we were trying to deal with the Jewish terrorist campaign. It was therefore fascinating to appreciate the amazing transformation of the country under the State of Israel in the intervening thirty years.

I remembered that in 1946 we were amazed to see the recently arrived Jewish immigrants from Europe literally slaving in the fields at the new Jewish kibbutzim throughout the heat of the day. In 1978 I saw some of the results, which were truly remarkable. We stayed in one such settlement in northern Israel close to the Syrian border. I remembered the area as Lake Hule, a vast swampy district at the head of the River Jordan. In thirty years it had become a prosperous farming area. The settlement itself had all modern amenities and was surrounded by excellent crops. The dedication of the inhabitants and their pride in their achievement was most impressive. I convinced myself that our bedroom in the guest house was close to the spot where on my last visit I had to be pulled out of the swamp into which I was sinking during a duck shoot. I suspect that this reminiscence was more than a little fanciful. The story, however, underlines the amazing achievement of the Israeli nation and the total dedication of their people. That dedication was most evident when one appreciated the extent of their defence effort, including three years' compulsory military service for men and two years' for women, as well as an annual call-up of five weeks for reservists up to the age of fifty.

At the same time the intractable nature of the Israeli problem and the fragile state of the area are underlined by the poverty of some of the Arabs on the West Bank, and by the hostile frontiers on all sides so close to Israel's inhabited areas. And there is the sharp contrast in living standards between the modern Jewish towns and their settlements and traditional Arab standards in their areas.

Then for any Christian there is, in some ways, an even more tragic impression. On the one hand, there remains from the distant past the traditional religious feeling of peace and understanding in the holy places round the Sea of Galilee, in Nazareth and in Bethlehem. But side by side there is the bustle and obvious conflict of the present-day situation. Perhaps Jerusalem itself presents these contrasts more clearly than anywhere else because the holy places and the frenzy of modern life there are so closely connected.

In addition to travelling round the country I met some of the country's leaders, including the Prime Minister Mr Begin, the present Prime Minister Mr Shamir, and Mr Shimon Peres, then Leader of the Opposition, since Prime Minister and Foreign Secretary. In particular it was strange to meet Mr Begin and Mr Shamir in friendly discussion when, as a soldier thirty years earlier, I had feared and pursued them as leaders of the Jewish resistance. As a result I felt uneasy talking to them, particularly since I suspected that they were well briefed about my Army past. Despite their politeness, I came away with the feeling that they were both much influenced by their hard and bitter battles for the Jewish cause earlier in their lives. I certainly formed the impression that they were both formidable advocates of the Israeli Government's position in the Middle East and would be hard bargainers in any discussion of the Jewish/Arab problems. Mr Peres was clearly different in his approach. He was quietly charming and persuasive. I felt that he would certainly be amenable to reasoned argument, but I also concluded that he had little room for manoeuvre over Israel's basic position in the circumstances of the day.

In general, even as a soldier in 1945, I could not help admiring the passionate dedication of the Jewish people in Israel to their State. Then I believed that, however difficult its formation was going to be, Israel would be a powerful State and the sooner we in Britain recognized this the better. Thirty years later my views and admiration for the Israeli people were simply reinforced, with one qualification. Now that the State of Israel has been established for good I can only trust that its leaders will seek to forget their bitter conflicts of the past and to promote reconciliation with their Arab neighbours. Of course Arab antagonism may make this difficult, but in the end there is no other way forward for a successful State of Israel.

As well as honouring me by inviting me to be Deputy Leader of the Party, a post held only once before, Margaret Thatcher asked me to act as Shadow Home Secretary. I took up this portfolio in 1976. While to become Home Secretary in 1979 was to fulfil one of my greatest ambitions, the prospect was a heavy responsibility at this time. In 1976, as so often in recent years, the level of crime was rising. An added problem was the abrupt decline in morale among law enforcement officers. I knew well, too, that my policies would come under severe scrutiny from my friends. Whereas the other political parties have taken a relaxed – some might say negligent – attitude to law and order issues, the Conservative Party has always thrown itself passionately into debate on crime and immigration.

I was determined to set about a systematic revision of the Party's policies in the main areas of Home Office concern – police, prisons, crime, broadcasting, race relations and immigration. In doing so, I was greatly assisted by the generous help of a number of my parliamentary colleagues.

My most immediate area of concern was the police. Despite strenuous efforts by Labour's Home Secretary, Merlyn Rees, relations between the Labour Government and the police were not good. Police recruitment was poor. Many forces, particularly in the major cities, were well below establishment. Furthermore, police pay at that time of soaring inflation was not high enough to attract recruits of sufficient calibre.

In 1976 the Police Federations withdrew from the Police Council, the negotiating council on police pay, in protest at Labour's attitude. In 1977 alone over 1,000 police officers retired prior to pension from the Metropolitan Police. Throughout the country as a whole staff losses exceeded recruitment. Most seriously of all, the force was losing large numbers of its ablest, most experienced officers. There were even the beginnings of talk in police ranks of seeking the right to strike. I was very concerned about that threat and warned of the dangers in both private meetings and public speeches.

It was against this background that in July 1977 I urged the Government to set up an independent inquiry into police pay. The Shadow Cabinet was unanimous in support of my view that the situation in the police force was so serious that the police should be treated as a special case outside any of the prevailing guidelines of Labour's pay control policy. My arguments for an exceptional increase in public expenditure on the police were also accepted by my colleagues; our views were enthusiastically endorsed by the Party as a whole at the 1977 party conference. I was not therefore surprised that within days of that conference, on 27 October 1977, Merlyn Rees announced that the inquiry into police negotiating procedures under Lord Justice Edmund-Davies would be widened to investigate police pay.

The Edmund-Davies inquiry reported in July 1978. It fully endorsed my view that pay improvements were essential to staunch the outflow of good officers. It asked for *full* implementation of its substantial awards on 1 September 1978 and advised on a new mandatory formula for establishing police pay in the future. Regrettably, the Labour Government was then locked in agonizing over the next stage of its incomes policy, the issue which led directly to the Winter of Discontent. Labour therefore decided to hold back half the Edmund-Davies award until September 1979. I condemned that decision. There was no doubt that the police force had been going through an exceptional crisis of morale. Nor was there any question that the police, one of the few groups in that strike-torn era never to strike, had suffered in pay terms and deserved special treatment. I therefore gave a clear pledge that we would implement the award in full as soon as we came to power.

Our plans for a larger, better paid police force were thus clearly laid out. In my view the fear of being caught by an effective police force is the most effective deterrent against serious crime. That was why in Opposition I also set out proposals to reverse Labour cuts in the civilian back-up to police operations and to dispense with unnecessary bureaucratic checks on the police, wherever their removal did not threaten essential civil liberties. No one could guarantee police success in fighting crime; however, my aim was that no police officer and no citizen should be able to say that lack of success was the result of lack of resources or a failure of support from a Conservative Government.

Another key area for consideration was the criminal justice system. Better by far, it seemed to me, to prevent people from committing crime; but when crime occurred we needed a more flexible range of penalties to fit both crime and offender, and a modern penal system that could cope in a more civilized way with the demands of the courts. Over my first year as Shadow Home Secretary I was grateful for the opportunity given to me to meet many people concerned with policy in these areas and to visit a number of establishments. The co-operation that is given to an Opposition party in policy-making has always been a distinguishing mark of our democracy. Any party which tried to develop policy in cells of party members without drawing on outside advice and the experience of others would make a serious error.

After this process of consultation was complete, I gave details of our proposals in a major speech in the House of Commons on 7 November 1977. I believe that it is important for an Opposition to reveal details of its policy-thinking as early as possible in the Parliament. This does expose the programme to criticism by Government, but it has the advantage of allowing the ideas to be discussed and refined well in advance of taking office. It also gives time for the public to take on board the ideas of the Opposition, whose policies will always need to fight harder for Press attention than those of the Government.

It is therefore not surprising that many of the points of my 1977 programme became key features of our policy in Government. These included closer attention to the problems of younger offenders; an end to the policy of closing down attendance centres where offenders could be sent in spare time; use of more imaginative alternatives to custody; tougher detention centres for violent young offenders – the so-called 'short, sharp shock' – and, for the prison service, greater independence from the Home Office, which would give a better corporate identity and more pride to the service. This proposal was one of a number which were suggested by

197

a small study group I had established, which was ably led by Edward Gardner, a prominent Conservative lawyer and Member of Parliament for South Fylde. It also included a number of my other parliamentary colleagues, as well as outside advisers with experience of the prison and probation services, the Parole Board, magistrates and higher courts.

I went on to propose that there should be a significant programme of prison building in order to reverse the cumulative neglect of decades. At first the reaction of the Government to all this was one of masterly inactivity. Inevitably, however, the problems inside the prison service worsened throughout 1978. By October of that year the prison governors were driven collectively to send an open letter to the Home Secretary saying that 'total breakdown' was imminent in the prison service. This, added to the pressure that we had been exerting inside and outside Parliament for months, finally persuaded Labour to set up an independent inquiry into the service under Mr Justice May. I welcomed this decision, overdue though it was; indeed, as Home Secretary I was to profit greatly from the splendid work that was done by the May inquiry over the succeeding year.

A third major area of policy development was that of race relations. Here I began from two basic positions – first, total hostility to racial discrimination of any kind but, second, a recognition that there were real social problems in many of our major cities and genuine concern over continuing high levels of immigration. No policy of integration could succeed unless it was pursued against the background of strict immigration control.

As far as improving race relations were concerned, my proposals were set out early in 1977. These were linked to the Party's other policies for improving the economic position of inner cities and for lifting many of the barriers that then stood in the way of small businesses. I also made it clear that we supported the work of the Commission for Racial Equality and that we accepted a role for the law where discrimination, particularly in work or housing, was serious and persistent. I also suggested an expansion of provision for English-language training, in the workplace as well as in schools, and special attention to the educational performance of ethnic minority children.

All of this was common ground between the parties. More controversial was the development of our plans on immigration. This took place at a time of surging immigration under the Labour Government. The numbers of new Commonwealth and Pakistani immigrants rose from only 32,000 in 1973 to over 55,000 in 1976. Immigration from Pakistan alone tripled in those years. Partly this was related to the way in which applications for entry were processed. I sent my assistant spokesman, Keith Speed, to the Indian subcontinent to look at the way matters were handled. There was no case for those with a genuine claim to entry being treated inconsiderately. However, it was clear that the rise in overall numbers of new entrants must be reduced if race relations were not to suffer. A further damaging decision was that of the Callaghan Government in November 1977 to grant an amnesty and the right to stay to illegal immigrants who had broken the law in getting into, or over-staying their visit in, the UK.

By early 1978 we were almost ready to announce our plans. At that stage Press interest in the issue was at its height; an interview given by Margaret Thatcher on 30 January, in which she frankly and correctly pointed out that many people were worried by the levels of immigration, was seized on by the media as a stick with which to beat us. At one and the same time our critics said that we were planning draconian controls and that we had no effective policy at all. Over many years in politics I have never found that this kind of illogical contrast in views deters those who are looking for a story. The Labour Government too claimed that we would be able to do nothing to reduce numbers. As it proved, all those commentators were wrong. We had to do some swift work to put the final details to our proposals; but in March I announced our plans to the Conservative Central Council in Leicester. The comprehensive and practical nature of the programme surprised most of the critics. It included not only a series of specific ideas for checking the rate of immigration, but also a pledge that our Government would introduce a new British Nationality Act in order to bring the law on this subject up to date with the realities of the post-imperial world. All the items detailed in my Leicester speech were incorporated in our general election manifesto a year later. I believe that the improvement in race relations and the decline in immigration in the last ten years fully justified our policy.

All this work in preparing and publicizing our policies took a great deal of time. Other members of the Shadow Cabinet were equally heavily engaged in helping Margaret Thatcher put together our election platform. When the election would come remained uncertain. However, since 1976 the Labour Government had limped along without an overall majority.

By the time Parliament rose for the summer recess in 1978 most of us were convinced that Jim Callaghan would call a general election in the autumn. As far as could be judged from by-elections and opinion polls, the Conservatives and the Labour Government were fairly evenly matched. But I for one felt that Labour would have a reasonable chance of re-election in the autumn after four years in power and that it would be dangerous for them to soldier on through the winter into the fifth year of the Parliament. It was therefore with a mixture of anticipation of a return to power and a nagging fear of a further period in Opposition that I waited to hear Jim Callaghan's promised broadcast to the nation in September.

I was on a party tour in the north-west and was staying the night with one of our party stalwarts, Oulton Wade, near Chester. We both presumed that the election date was to be announced and therefore heard the curiously negative message that there would be no autumn election with incredulity and some relief. I remember ringing up Margaret Thatcher, who was on a tour elsewhere, and saying that I believed that we had got him now. Jim Callaghan had missed his chance. Characteristically she was disappointed because she was, as always, ready for battle and full of fight. Moreover she feared, probably correctly, that the Party was geared up for the battle and that there would be a risk of a difficult party conference instead, which would be something of an anti-climax. Still I remained relieved, convinced that we had nothing to lose from delay as the Government's prospects did not look good. Ironically it was the action of the trade unions during the subsequent Winter of Discontent that undermined their own Government and proved my views correct in the final event.

The last six months of the Labour Government were dominated by industrial strife and increasing troubles over their devolution proposals, which occupied considerable parliamentary attention. Partly I suppose in response to the Lib/Lab Pact, Labour had introduced the Scotland and

Wales Act in 1977 which paved the way for directly elected assemblies. There was considerable opposition inside the Labour Party in Parliament and when the promised referenda were held in 1978 the results were very damaging for the Government. In Wales – home of the Labour Party – the proposals were humiliatingly defeated. In Scotland there was a vote in favour but the requisite majority was not achieved. Therefore, beaten in their devolution proposals and undermined by their supporters in the trade unions, the Government looked increasingly beleaguered in the early months of 1979.

By the end of March it was increasingly clear that an early general election had to take place. The Government had lost the initiative and, more damaging, the will to act. Their supporters were increasingly demoralized. The House of Commons was obviously bored with the Government and indeed with itself. Everybody and everything was waiting for the election. That was the mood in which the House of Commons entered into a vote of confidence on 28 March. In the build-up to the debate it became clear that the Liberals and minor parties were likely to vote against the Government. This meant that there was clearly a possibility of a Government defeat. The atmosphere was one of rumour and counter-rumour. Would all the members of the minor parties vote against the Government? Would some of them vote at all? How many might abstain? Clearly it was going to be a very close vote.

In these circumstances I did not relish my responsibility for winding up the debate on behalf of the Opposition. During the day our Chief Whip, Humphrey Atkins, who was mustering our troops with great skill and was in close touch with the Opposition parties, kept on telling me what I must not say. He feared that some words of mine might offend members of minor parties and indeed change their voting position. Increasingly I dreaded my allotted thirty minutes which, after all, I had to fill if I was to avoid accusations of having no case. What was more, I was to be followed by that great parliamentary orator, Michael Foot, whom I could never match on such an occasion. I kept on comforting myself with the knowledge that it was the vote which mattered.

I have reread my speech recently. Clearly it could not have offended anyone but equally it certainly would not have convinced any doubters. It was by any standards a dull speech but at least I escaped without derision. Michael Foot followed with a speech that was brilliant even by his high standards. Still, I had obeyed my instructions and we won by one vote, 312 to 311. Immediately after the vote Jim Callaghan announced that he would propose to the Queen that Parliament should be dissolved and a general election held.

Two days later on Friday 30 March came the tragic death of Airey Neave, cruelly murdered by an Irish National Liberation Army bomb in his car at the House of Commons. Margaret Thatcher particularly, and indeed our whole party, had suffered a grave loss. The further irony was that he was struck down just at the moment when all his work was to be rewarded by the return of a Conservative Government under Margaret Thatcher whom he had especially championed. Naturally the general election which was called for 3 May was fought under strict security arrangements after this.

This time the Conservatives were ahead in the polls throughout the campaign, except in what turned out to be a rogue poll in the *Daily Mail* two days before polling day. I remember this occasion only too well because of the effect that such poll reverses have on leading politicians already overtired and overwrought by a strenuous campaign. I was in the North-East on one of my extensive and gruelling daytime tours. As I drove between meetings of supporters, who were also rather shattered by this apparent blow to our prospects, I found myself thinking seriously in terms of losing. I began to contemplate the miserable possibility of four or five more years in Opposition. I have often envied the politicians in those countries where polls are banned for some days before the election date, but I suppose that only leads to a mass of unofficial polls being published. Yet there is a serious point here. Opinion polls certainly affect the morale of politicians, and indeed the media do not believe those politicians who pretend that they do not read much into the polls. But do polls have too much influence on actual voting and thus on the result? No one can be sure. I have fought eleven general elections, some with my party ahead in optimistic frame of mind, and others dreading the publication of each poll showing the Party well behind. I know how much they affect party confidence. And this in itself must contribute towards the result. But on balance I would prefer to grin and bear all this, as I fear that some sort of regulation on this issue would turn out to cause more problems than it would solve.

On this occasion I did the most extensive election tour of my career. It was planned that I should visit marginal seats all over the country in the remoter areas while Margaret Thatcher herself concentrated on the major centres of population. In my constituency once again my wife, my excellent agent, Norman Dent, and my party organization provided me with a good majority.

In the end we gained a Commons majority of forty-three with a lead of some two million votes over Labour. It was indeed the biggest swing since 1945, which was a triumph, particularly for Margaret Thatcher. We won, I believe, mainly on our proposals for trade union reform after the Winter of Discontent and on the old argument of time for a change at a moment when the Government was unpopular.

In the Conservative Party we were naturally excited by our victory with a solid working majority, but at the time we were far too absorbed in our new tasks to take stock of the general political situation. Even if we had, we could have had no appreciation that in ten years' time there would still be a Thatcher Conservative Government which had transformed our country's position at home and abroad. Nor could we have foretold that it would have changed the whole face of British politics in that period.

Now it is possible to look back and consider the previous years of Labour rule. By 1979 I had spent twenty-four years in the House of Commons, thirteen under Conservative Governments and eleven under Labour. Much of the time under Labour rule was dominated by Harold Wilson as their Prime Minister. Many people believed that if Hugh Gaitskell had lived, Labour would have won a decisive victory in 1964 rather than winning by a whisker under Harold Wilson. However that may be, Harold Wilson took full advantage of his position as Prime Minister in 1964 and followed up with a substantial election victory in 1966. At that time he certainly dominated the British political scene. At his best he was an outstanding House of Commons figure, an astute Prime Minister and a most cunning Leader of his party. He was therefore both feared and hated by our party in Parliament. We were right to fear him because for a time he appeared invulnerable. But I could never subscribe to the feelings of dislike, for I found him a kind and considerate man in personal terms.

Even in his first term his greatest strength was as a party Leader closely attuned to the shifting sands and intrigues of the Labour Party, rather than as a national figure as Prime Minister. Yet subsequently history has shown that making Labour appear for a time as the natural party of Government was in itself a remarkable achievement. Curiously his political skill deserted him in 1970, for he chose an early date for a general election on a sudden improvement for his party in the opinion polls which turned out to be short-lived. He then conducted a complacent election campaign which surely must be a grave error for a party in power, as there are always difficulties to face and problems to be solved. His subsequent defeat always seemed to me to have taken the political stuffing out of him. In the general election of February 1974 he was clearly surprised by his narrow victory and never quite regained his old political skill and guile. His resignation in 1976 came as a great surprise, but I suspect that the reason was simple enough. He was exhausted after many trying years and had lost his zest for the political battles, perhaps particularly inside his own party.

His successor Jim Callaghan always seemed to represent a very different danger for the Conservative Party. He came across to the public as a straightforward, honest national leader. Like all of us in politics, he undoubtedly had his own party political skills but he appeared far more a national than a party Leader. At the time this presented a problem for his opponents, for many of his views and actions appealed to members of our party. But in retrospect I suppose this same national stance eventually undermined him in sections of the Labour Party and thus led in some measure to his defeat in 1979. Had he won that election I believe he would have become a formidable Prime Minister and political opponent. He probably lost his best opportunity of such a victory by his own decision not to go to the country in October 1978.

'Box In, Box Out'

I remember Friday 4 May 1979 as one of the most exciting days of my life. My Penrith and Border count that morning prevented my early return to London, but I had promised Margaret Thatcher to fly down as soon as I could in the afternoon to help her in forming her Government.

My initial reaction to our party's victory was one of considerable excitement and relief. I felt we were lucky to have been given an opportunity to govern again only four years after the Party's troubles in 1974–5. I was also, by that stage, confident that Margaret Thatcher would make an excellent Prime Minister in home affairs. Surprising as it may seem now, when she is recognized as an outstanding world leader, there were the obvious doubts about her experience of foreign affairs. But I was reassured on this score by the knowledge that she intended to have Peter Carrington as her Foreign Secretary. I knew he would be first-class in the job, for he certainly inspired confidence both at home and abroad and was universally highly regarded. This was all the more welcome to me as we had long been strong friends and political allies.

On my own future I had mixed emotions. I knew that Margaret Thatcher was likely to make me Home Secretary. That was certainly my ambition, because the Home Office is a great department of State and I had studied many of its functions in Opposition. At the same time I knew that a Home Secretary has daunting responsibilities and is bound from time to time to be subject to considerable criticism. Worse still, a Home Secretary is particularly exposed to sudden and totally unexpected storms. It is truly said that he can go to bed at night with a clear sky as far as Home Affairs are concerned and wake up the next morning with a major crisis on his hands. Worst of all, many of these particular events permit no simple solution and provide the Press with marvellous copy. The unfortunate Home Secretary then receives much advice of a totally impractical nature for the solution of the problem. At the same time he is blamed for allowing the incident to arise when it is usually inconceivable that he could have prevented it. On crime and immigration he usually cannot win. Indeed, Conservative and Labour Home Secretaries inevitably face harsh criticism from their own parties of an almost entirely opposing kind. Labour Home Secretaries are blamed by their left-wingers for harsh and authoritarian actions, whereas the alleged weaknesses and inadequacies of Conservative Home Secretaries are annually paraded at their party conference, in what has become an almost traditional right-wing exercise. These emotional reactions are nevertheless justified, for Home Office responsibilities impinge directly on individuals and their families. They also concern cherished rights to freedom and protection where feelings naturally run high.

Home Secretaries are fair game, for they are politicians responsible directly to the electorate and so must be prepared to accept Press and parliamentary criticism, whether fair or unfair. On the other hand, I regard some of the blame attributed to the Home Office itself and its officials

as both unjust and wholly misplaced. In my four years as
Home Secretary I came to admire greatly the understanding
and care with which they handled all the intricate personal
problems that faced them. The Home Office has to be a
human department and, contrary to some comments, it
certainly is. Furthermore, that humanity and fairness are
founded on a long and honourable tradition throughout
our nation's history.

With all these thoughts in my mind I went to the Home
Office in a mood of keen anticipation tempered by considerable anxiety. The account of my four years there which
follows will show that I was wise to be apprehensive, particularly about the dangers from sudden dramatic events. I
was, however, powerfully reinforced by the Ministers who
were assigned to me. My two Ministers of State were Leon
Brittan and Tim Raison, and my Minister in the Lords was
John Belstead.

I was also fortunate as I knew and respected many of my
senior officials. Robert Armstrong, my Permanent Secretary, had been Ted Heath's Private Secretary in the 1970
administration and was therefore an old friend. All too
soon, from my Home Office point of view, he became
Secretary to the Cabinet, where he has been a tower of
strength in recent years. He was succeeded by Brian
Cubbon, whom I had also previously known, and who was
a most trusted adviser and staunch ally throughout all the
traumatic experiences of my time as Home Secretary. No
one could have been luckier in his principal advisers.

The breadth of Home Office responsibilities requires a
Home Secretary to give thought to the manner in which he
will approach his task. He must first choose the subjects in
which he will involve himself personally and must decide
how best to keep his finger on the pulse in those areas where

he has delegated day-to-day responsibility to his Ministers. At the same time he must never forget that he bears the ultimate responsibility and has to be ready personally to present and defend his department's case in Cabinet and Cabinet Committees.

As far as delegation is concerned, in my case there were two obvious areas. The criminal justice side of the Home Office responsibilities requires a legally trained and qualified Minister. I was lucky enough in my time to have two outstanding lawyers, Leon Brittan and Patrick Mayhew. I knew that I could leave the detailed planning and handling of criminal justice legislation in their hands. Each in their turn carried through Parliament highly complicated and most important Bills with great success.

Immigration inevitably was a subject in itself. It involved a vast number of individual cases, many of them highly complicated and frequently of an emotional nature. The handling of Members of Parliament's representations and correspondence was also a major task. Again I was fortunate in having Tim Raison, whose sensitivity and understanding were an enormous asset. In addition, he carried through the British Nationality Bill, which I believe will be a measure of lasting value. He was succeeded towards the end of my time at the Home Office by David Waddington, whose qualifications and standing in Government as Chief Whip are showing his genuine worth. He was a great asset to me.

Prisons also require a Minister of their own. John Belstead, in addition to his overall House of Lords duties, was ideal for this task. He was succeeded by Rodney Elton, and David Mellor joined me as well. I owe much to them both.

Each Home Secretary will have his own particular interest

in other and smaller areas of responsibility. I had always been interested in broadcasting, from my Opposition Chief Whip days, and so largely dealt with this myself. I also dealt with racing, having many friends in the racing world and appreciating the importance of a sport which provided considerable employment, gave much pleasure to many people in the country and indeed also supported a valuable bloodstock industry.

On the negative side, I was well known for my reluctance to become involved in legislation over Sundays, alcohol, animals and sex – subjects which tended to arouse fierce passions and cause immense parliamentary difficulties, usually without solving the problems. Subsequent experience in these areas at least provides some evidence in favour of my attitude. However, my reluctance denied me the reputation of a social reformer, one which, in any event, I did not particularly seek.

Once the delegation of subjects to Ministers had been settled, I had to decide how to exercise my general supervision of the Home Office and keep in touch with any major problems and, indeed, with areas of potential difficulty. A Minister in charge of a department has two important figures available to help him in this task. They are his Permanent Secretary and his Principal Private Secretary. They, in turn, also have the problem of knowing what is going on in many diverse areas. However, I found it immensely valuable to treat them as complete confidants and to ensure that time was made available as often as possible for a relaxed discussion with them, either together or on their own. This in itself requires planning, which could easily be upset by sudden emergencies involving all or any one of us at the Home Office.

For wider consultation I believed in a meeting every

morning. This was attended by all the Ministers, Parliamentary Private Secretaries, the Permanent Secretary, my Principal Private Secretary, any senior officials whose responsibility happened to be in the news at that moment and the Chief Information Officer. I believe such meetings should be brief, business-like, relaxed and informal. I wanted my colleagues to share each other's difficulties and, even more important, their anxieties. Above all, I wanted to feel that, whatever the problems, we were a team and, better still, a happy team. I was never more pleased than when I heard the following story about one of these meetings.

An agitated official from the department entered my Private Office next door to my room and heard what he thought to be a considerable commotion next door. 'Is anything wrong?' he inquired anxiously, 'or is everything all right?'

'Very much all right,' replied one of my Private Secretaries. 'That bellowing and laughter means that the Secretary of State is enjoying his morning meeting!'

Alas, there were other serious and anxious occasions when laughter was certainly not the order of the day. Yet I like to feel that such meetings were as valuable, and indeed perhaps as enjoyable at times, to the Ministers and officials as they were to the Secretary of State himself.

The rest of my working day was usually occupied by meetings of all kinds – Cabinet and Cabinet Committees, meetings with various delegations, together with internal departmental meetings to discuss policies, details of legislation and any other particular problems. A senior Cabinet Minister has to learn to address his mind to many difficult subjects in one day, and must ensure that he has read the essential features of the numerous briefs which are put before him. In addition he must be ready to use lunches and dinners as a means of keeping in touch with the world outside Westminster and Whitehall. Nor must he neglect the House of Commons. Having been a Chief Whip for six years, I was accustomed to appearing regularly in the Members' Smoking Room at a particular time every evening, and also to eating regularly in the Members' Dining Rooms.

One essential requirement is, of course, personal contact with one's parliamentary colleagues. A good Parliamentary Private Secretary is essential for this part of a Minister's life, as he can keep in touch with friends and critics alike. I was very lucky to have Roger Sims, who remained with me all my time at the Home Office. He was immensely conscientious and loyal and, also important, he came from a different parliamentary generation. He had different friends and interests and was a London Member, whereas I was firmly based in a North of England constituency. I suppose we were rather an unlikely combination, but perhaps all the better for that.

This sketch of the day ends with the inevitable despatch boxes, with which of course it had also begun. Between 10.30 p.m. and 8 a.m. I found I required three, and at times four, hours' work on these boxes if I was to complete the routine work and prepare myself properly for the following day's meetings. My trouble was always that, unlike Margaret Thatcher, I liked – and felt I required – eight hours' sleep a night. As Home Secretary I had to get used to less. I had always had difficulty in keeping myself awake late at night and, as my wife would say, 'not only late at night'. I therefore never worked much after midnight for there was always the danger thereafter that I would simply fall asleep over the brief – needless to say, not the best way of absorbing it. I made up the necessary hours by waking myself up for two hours' work between 5.30 and 8. a.m. as required.

From my first meeting I was determined to impress my

own personality – and through it the personality of the new Government – on the department. I knew that this was a major task in view of its size and diversity, but I also appreciated that what happens at the top soon filters down. In the general conduct of business Ministers must set an example of urgency. Early on in my ministerial career Lord Swinton, probably one of the best administrators of his generation of Ministers, gave me an excellent piece of advice. His principle was 'box in, box out'. By this he meant that all the despatch boxes given to a Minister when he leaves the office at night should be completed by the time he returns the next morning, except in very special circumstances. The reason for this is simple. Once it becomes known that decisions and correspondence are being delayed at the top, that same practice becomes accepted at all levels. I have found it a good rule and have always been a nuisance to my Ministers on its enforcement. It ultimately helps in the constant battle against delays in a ministry, particularly in replies to Members of Parliament, which are a running sore for all departments. And the bigger the department, the greater the problem.

This was certainly true of the Home Office, where officials have to rely on many outside organizations to give them the necessary facts and figures, and yet the reputation of a department in Parliament depends greatly on efficient arrangements for MPs' correspondence. This in turn affects Parliament's attitude to the department and to the Ministers concerned, which is crucial to their success. So too does courtesy from Ministers' Private Offices, and from the Minister himself, particularly on the telephone, a problem upon which I have always placed great emphasis. In this connection a good story is told of me, which will ring true to all those who have had the misfortune to talk to me on the telephone from time to time.

A new entrant into my Private Office was heard to say to one of his colleagues, 'Does the Secretary of State think it is courteous and polite to shout like that down the telephone?'

To which the reply came, 'He isn't shouting, that's him speaking perfectly normally.'

I stress these comparatively small matters in a Minister's attitude to his department because I believe that such personal relations are immensely important to the reputation of the Ministers themselves, and indeed of their ministry. So of course is a Minister's personal consideration for those who work closely for him. In such matters gossip travels fast and a good team spirit helps so much in the conduct of department business, particularly when the going is rough.

Exceptional days at the Home Office were those when the department had parliamentary questions, debates or legislation in the House of Commons. The Home Office came top for questions, and therefore for oral answers, once every four weeks. I liked to ensure, as far as possible, that all my Ministers had some questions to answer near the top of the list. I obviously kept the most important, and the most highly charged politically, for myself.

I found answering departmental questions the easiest of parliamentary activities – far easier than asking them in Opposition, because in answering you have the last word and of course are equipped with all the facts. Nor, in the quick cut-and-thrust of the House of Commons, is one required to answer in detail, as one is in the House of Lords, which is a far more difficult assignment altogether. It is therefore possible to use House of Commons Question Time to get across some parliamentary information, whatever the question actually asked.

When I was Home Secretary I also had to answer for the Prime Minister when she was away. I found this a daunting task and was always extremely nervous beforehand. I was just relieved that the Prime Minister's immense sense of parliamentary duty ensured that she only missed Question Time when her attendance abroad was absolutely essential. Having had the experience, I marvel at her skill in answering questions, which can be broadened out into almost any subject. Fortunately for me, when she was absent my appearance at the despatch box came to be regarded as a sort of school holiday with the headmistress absent. I have to admit that I rather encouraged this development, for after all it was my purpose not to score runs but to keep the political ball out of my wicket.

As for debates, my long years of silence as Chief Whip meant that I had never had the speaking experience necessary to become a good House of Commons orator. And so I concentrated on trying to be competent, polite, and aggressive in party political terms only if absolutely necessary. In opening debates I always stuck closely to a prepared speech as, in departmental terms, the Hansard record was all-important. I allowed myself more latitude in winding up, but was always nervous, since it was never a job I enjoyed.

I have to say that I found the Home Secretary's job easily the greatest strain of my political life, as far as workload is concerned. I suppose, for permanent stress, Northern Ireland came ahead of it. But in physical terms there was no doubt that the Home Office was the harder of the two, because of the extent of its responsibilities and the unpredictability of its crises. But I enjoyed the job so much that I realized the extent of the strain only when I left the office after four very happy years.

My time as Shadow Home Secretary had given me a reasonable insight into the responsibilities of the Home Office. I had also formed clear views about my priorities for early action. My previous period in Cabinet from 1970 to 1974 had taught me that the easiest time to get decisions out of one's colleagues is in the early days of a new Government. And I had a clear advantage by being given the same responsibilities in Government which I had been studying in Opposition. I therefore called a meeting at the earliest possible moment of all my Ministers and senior officials to draw up a preliminary agenda for action. I suspect that I surprised them by my determination for quick decisions on a variety of topics. In turn they certainly amazed me by the scope of the Home Office responsibilities. I soon learnt that all subjects could cause trouble and controversy, for each had its own group of devoted adherents and lobbyists.

The issues at my first meeting on 8 May concentrated mainly on law and order. This is, of course, a major responsibility of the Home Secretary. He must give a lead in the constant battle against rising crime in society, but at the same time he must realize, and make quite clear to the public, that he and the law and order services for which he is responsible cannot succeed on their own. They need the help and support of all responsible citizens. In turn the Home Office must appreciate that it will receive such backing only if it inspires confidence and trust throughout the public. This is of course particularly true of the police service, which certainly required my immediate attention in 1979.

I was determined that we should carry out our pledge to implement the Edmund-Davies award in full immediately on our return to office. At this meeting we therefore set in motion arrangements for making the increased pay award to the police. Later that afternoon the Cabinet agreed to this, thereby confirming my view of the value of instant action on return to power. The award was announced the following day, 9 May. As the years have gone by, the generosity of the Edmund-Davies formula linking annual police pay increases to movements in the index of average earnings during the previous twelve months has been questioned. My answer is that the action we took in 1979 was essential to boost both police morale and recruitment. I feel I am entitled to ask any critics where we would have been in the troubled years since had we not had 10,000 more police officers when I left office in 1983 than in 1979. At least I left a strong police service of well-paid policemen as a foundation for my successors. I accept that much remains to be done, but without this foundation we would certainly be in dire difficulties today.

At the same meeting we discussed some of the other major problems we faced and reached some tentative conclusions on the work which should be set in hand. It was clear that a new Criminal Justice Bill was urgently required to deal with the treatment of offenders and sentencing policy. The state of our prisons and the conditions in the prison service were deeply worrying. On the one hand, increasing numbers of offenders were being committed to prison. On the other hand, over many years as a nation we had failed to spend the necessary money on the building of new prisons. We had even gravely neglected the modernization and even the maintenance of our existing prisons, mostly built in the Victorian era. As a result prison overcrowding had increased to worrying levels.

I was deeply depressed about the prison situation in 1979 because I knew that whatever we did nothing could be done in time to prevent crises in the years immediately ahead. And so it proved. Our Conservative Governments during my period as Home Secretary and those of my successors have spent large sums of money on prison modernization. For the first time in generations large numbers of new prisons are under construction. But the years of neglect cannot be put right overnight. The further tragedy is that the consequent overcrowding and poor working conditions have inevitably undermined the morale of prison officers, which has in turn caused industrial relations problems in the prison service. Basically I know that we have a dedicated and trustworthy body of prison officers. But we cannot as a nation expect them to work contentedly in inevitably difficult circumstances when they have to face poor conditions at the same time.

As I found out in 1979, the problem facing any Home Secretary is that few people in our country care about such problems. As a nation we have dangerously turned our back on our prisons and those whom we are forced to send there. All too few people, even those in responsible positions in our Government and in society generally, have ever been inside a prison. Most people want to see criminals kept out of circulation in society, but do not stop to consider whether prison is likely to reform them. The small minority of citizens who do care carry out much dedicated work. Often they become convinced that our courts are sending too many people to prison. To an extent they are right and encouragement is indeed being given to schemes for non-custodial punishment. But at a time of rising crime, when the community generally fears for its safety and for its property, it is illusory to imagine that sending fewer people to prison will satisfy public opinion, even if it helps the prison problem.

As so often in life, there is no simple solution. I am convinced that we need both more and better prisons, together with constant encouragement for imaginative, non-custodial punishment. I am encouraged because I know that Douglas Hurd, the present Home Secretary, is energetically following that course. But I confess to considerable frustration at my own failure during the time of my responsibility to promote successfully interest and informed discussion even among my parliamentary colleagues, let alone among the media and the general public. Alas, 'get on with it and lock them up' is the one thought in all too many minds. Nevertheless I remain grateful to my Cabinet colleagues, and in particular to Geoffrey Howe, Chancellor of the Exchequer in 1979, for their support in spending considerable sums of money on new prison building, modernization and maintenance. At least we started to repair the damage to our prison system caused by many years of neglect.

Mr Justice May's excellent report, following his inquiry into the prison service, had been handed to me after the general election and gave me a foundation upon which to work. The inquiry reached many conclusions which were similar to my own. In particular, it argued for more imaginative alternatives to custody and shorter sentences for non-violent offenders. It called for a substantial prison building programme. Finally, it shared my own belief that general morale inside the prison service could be raised by establishing a more independent prison department under its own Director-General and with an independent Inspector of Prisons.

I was able to accept all these major conclusions. On 30 April 1980 I announced that we were reorganizing the prison department along more independent lines and establishing the inspectorate – innovations whose common sense has, I believe, been fully borne out in practice.

As a result of my colleagues' agreement to allocate more

money to the prison service, I also ordered the construction of a series of new prisons. Not only was it right to add to the prison stock when the courts required places, it was high time after some sixty years of political neglect to do something to improve the poor conditions which contributed to low morale and outbreaks of trouble in some of our older prisons.

As soon as I became Home Secretary I planned personal visits to a number of prisons, including some of the older ones in the London area. This enabled me to see conditions at first hand and to meet prison governors and staff. The conditions quite frankly appalled me, and the extent of the modernization required depressed me deeply. For example, I learnt that large sums of money and thus many years of work would be required to provide integral sanitation in all our prisons. I wonder how many members of the general public realize that it will still be some years before slopping-out of cells becomes a thing of the past? I suppose some people would argue that the prisoners deserve such squalor because they have brought it upon themselves. But do those who think like that then expect the prisoners to be reformed in custody under such conditions? If they don't expect that, then do they realize that they may be encouraging outbreaks of trouble in prison and further criminal acts on release? Of course it may be that some prisoners are so appalled by their conditions that they resolve never to risk any return to prison. I believe it is more likely that dreadful conditions brutalize human beings still further. On top of the effect on prisoners, it should also be realized that we are asking prison officers to spend their lives working in squalor. At the same time we expect from those same prison officers high standards of dedication and service. Do not let us be altogether surprised if they and the Prison Officers' Association can be difficult on occasions.

On the positive side, I found the prison catering service was highly efficient and produced on the whole good food, even where they were still working with poor kitchen facilities. Good food in a prison is important because it alone can do something to improve morale and thus make troubles and riots less likely. I never minded the tradition of an important visitor tasting the prison food. Indeed, I often enjoyed it, but I certainly would not have relished the experience of sampling a night in a cell and slopping it out in the morning.

The aim of my programme was to produce 3,400 new or refurbished places by 1985 and an additional 1,500 places by the end of the decade. I also doubled the amount of money available to fund the repair and maintenance of prisons. While in no sense popular, all these moves were absolutely essential to reverse years of decline.

The May inquiry also made specific recommendations on the pay and allowances of prison officers. These were, I believe, a fair assessment of what had been long-running difficulties between the Prison Officers' Association and the previous Labour Government. I accepted in full the independent recommendations. Sadly, the Prison Officers' Association was unable to agree with all the May inquiry's rulings on allowances. The main concern was over the Prison Officers' Association's claim for particular payments for meal breaks. The union resorted to quite unjustifiable industrial action; new prisoners sentenced by the courts, some violent, were to be refused entry to prisons. I was not prepared to give way in the face of this kind of challenge. I pressed the Prison Officers' Association to accept what had, in effect, been independent arbitration by the May inquiry. In view of their refusal to co-operate, I brought before Parliament special legislation – the Imprisonment (Temporary Provisions) Act 1980 – to allow prisoners to be held elsewhere than in prison. The Act was passed in October 1980. By that time some 3,500 prisoners were being held in police cells. We used the powers of the new Act to make available temporary accommodation which was staffed largely by the Armed Forces. The half-completed Frankland prison and Rollestone army camp were brought into use.

Once it became clear to the Prison Officers' Association that we were not prepared to be forced into making concessions by irresponsible pressure, the association decided to suspend action in January 1981. We were able relatively swiftly to reach agreement on a nationally recommended duty system common to all establishments. Frankland and Rollestone were closed in January and February 1981 respectively, although the latter did have to be used again temporarily when the prison population became exceptionally high in the summer.

Unfortunately the detailed negotiations on the implementation of this nationally recommended duty system have dragged on over the years. They have also become enmeshed in arguments about staffing levels as the total prison population has risen dramatically. I am bound to say that I consider the Prison Officers' Association to have been unreasonable recently in their arguments with Douglas Hurd and the prison department. I hope that the arguments for his fresh start proposals will eventually be fully accepted and implemented. I am certain that they represent a sensible arrangement for prison officers. At the same time, the nation as a whole must accept that if at a period of rising crime we insist on sending increasing numbers of people to prison, we shall have to find even more money to provide proper accommodation for them. It cannot be stressed too often that the prison officers will not work successfully in conditions of heavy overcrowding in poor and inadequate accommodation.

At the same time as we were tackling the problems in the prisons, we were taking action on the other element of my strategy – the search for more practical, appropriate and above all effective alternatives to custody. Our 1979 manifesto had set out my basic principles on sentencing policy. Broadly that meant tough deterrent action in serious cases, combined with a more flexible approach to less serious offenders. It would be fair to say that the first part of my strategy had rather more appeal to some people inside the Conservative Party itself than the second. However, I always made it abundantly clear that I wanted to see the courts deliver substantial terms in prison for violent offenders. In fact, in Britain there is a far higher proportion of lengthy sentences than in most comparable countries. Equally, I still strongly maintain that our development of alternative approaches to the sentencing of less serious offenders was right. Thanks to action taken by Conservative Governments since 1979, the courts now have available to them a range of remedies that simply were not available when we came into office. The old saying of 'let the punishment fit the crime' is truer today than ever before.

Soon after I became Home Secretary I put into effect an experimental move towards a firmer, more deterrent regime in detention centres, as we had proposed in Opposition. At the end of the experiment many of the principles of that regime were applied more widely in the service. In addition, we expanded the use of community service orders. In 1981 we toughened the law on financial reparation by criminals to their victims: it appeared quite wrong to me, for example, that until our legislation the payment of a fine to the State had precedence over financial compensation to the victim. We also reversed the contraction of attendance centres where young hooligans and others could be sent in their prime leisure time.

The main item of legislation in this area was, however, the Criminal Justice Act 1982, which was eventually to cause me some problems with elements of the Conservative Party rank and file. The proposals behind the Bill were undoubtedly a contributory factor to the difficult passage that I had at the Conservative party conference in 1981. In the event, some of the particular principles of the Bill in fact differed from what was anticipated at the time of that debate. The main provisions in the Act were intended to extend further the remedies available to the courts. They included the introduction of residential care orders, of so-called curfew orders on young offenders, the further extension and improvement of community service orders, and new duties by parents to discharge the payment of fines incurred by schoolchildren. Borstal training, which had become wholly outdated and ineffective, was abolished and replaced by detention centre orders and youth custody orders, depending on the length of the sentence incurred.

Siege, Riot and Capital Punishment

My first real parliamentary test as Home Secretary came in a debate on 19 July 1979 on the emotive and vexed question of capital punishment. During our time in Opposition we had promised a debate and a free vote on the subject if we were returned to power.

The traditional parliamentary division of opinion on capital punishment has always seemed curious to me. In the country as a whole, if opinion polls are to be believed, there is a strong and vociferous body of opinion in favour of its return. That is undoubtedly true of the Conservative Party, as debates at successive party conferences have made abundantly clear. The same situation must be reflected to some extent among Labour and Liberal supporters in general. But in Parliament on a free vote the Conservative Party is deeply divided while the Labour and Liberal Parties vote virtually unanimously against capital punishment. As a result the issue causes violent dissension and passionate argument within the Conservative Party, both in the country and in Parliament. Meanwhile, the other parties remain calmly united and apparently have no difficulty in their constituencies. This leads to the further irony that the Conservative MPs who are against reintroduction are bitterly criticized within the Party for Parliament's overall decision to vote for continued abolition. Yet, if the apparent countrywide view were reflected in all parties in Parliament, the restoration of the death penalty would be assured. Certainly I had only myself to blame for the hostility and, at times, vicious condemnation I received from my own supporters.

When I was first in Parliament in the 1950s and early 1960s I had been mildly in favour of capital punishment since it was the law of the land and clearly might on occasion be a deterrent. I never believed – as some passionate advocates do – that it was a unique deterrent which would have a dramatic effect on would-be murderers, and indeed on all potential criminals. But once it was suspended by Sydney Silverman's Bill in 1965 I became convinced that it should not be brought back and that we should fall in line with many other countries.

I was powerfully reinforced in my view when I became Secretary of State for Northern Ireland in 1972. I found that the death penalty was still in force in Northern Ireland for the murder of soldiers and policemen in particular. The Royal Prerogative of Mercy was exercised not by the Queen but by the Governor on the advice of the whole Stormont Cabinet. This collective responsibility had effectively ensured that throughout the Northern Ireland troubles no one had been executed. These powers had been vested in me as Secretary of State on the abolition of Stormont.

Certainly Northern Ireland affairs have a reputation for perverseness. But even there it was remarkable that the first case which came before me was that of a Protestant. Immediately Ian Paisley, the militant Protestant, demanded a reprieve for this 'good Protestant' and threatened dire consequences if I did not oblige. Fortunately, as it turned out in the violent turbulence at the time, there was a strong case for a reprieve, which I duly gave. But I knew that this case would in the near future be followed by some involving members of the IRA. I decided that if, surrounded by intolerable violence on all sides, I had to make decisions of that sort, which would certainly be represented as discrimination, I would only succeed in promoting the mayhem and killings which it was my purpose to stop. In the 1972–3 parliamentary session I therefore introduced in Part I of the Northern Ireland (Emergency Provisions) Bill provisions to bring Northern Ireland into line with the rest of the United Kingdom. That experience strengthened my general view against the death penalty and certainly my conviction against it in terrorist cases.

Capital punishment debates in the House of Commons provoke particular interest immediately after a general election, because the influence of new Members may sway the decision. New Conservative Members, for example, have come straight from the hustings and the pro-capital punishment views of many of their supporters. In 1979 there was the additional factor that Margaret Thatcher, as the new Prime Minister, was known to be a strong advocate of the reintroduction of the death penalty. There was the obvious speculation that she might, by her example, influence new MPs. Equally there was the spectacle – particularly attractive to the media – of the Prime Minister and her Home Secretary entrenched in opposing camps. In truth we had, and indeed have, never discussed the issue with each other. There was little point in doing so, I suppose, because we were unlikely to change each other's point of view. Anyway, there was a free vote and our votes would be clear proof of that.

Still, this background made my speech, as far as my position in the Party was concerned, an important occasion. I

231

had to be calm, and judicial in examining the conflicting arguments and in explaining the particular problems which reintroduction, after some twelve years, would present. Above all, at the end of the day I had to make my own position abundantly clear without prevarication.

In preparing my remarks I had the benefit for the first time of the Home Office's special knowledge of all the issues. This only increased my own conviction that reintroduction of the death penalty would present many difficult problems, some of which had arisen since abolition. Of course there are advocates who believe that the deterrent effect of having capital punishment on the statute book would be valuable in itself. Personally I can never accept that argument. If the reintroduction of capital punishment was not followed very quickly by its use, the public would feel duped and would consider the whole exercise a charade. Such an outcome, on an emotional issue where feelings run high, would be highly undesirable. Therefore if it was to be reintroduced the details were highly relevant and the problems they would create had to be taken into account in any decision of principle.

I discussed some of these problems in my speech. In Northern Ireland cases many of the terrorists would, in new circumstances, have to be tried in special courts by a judge without a jury. Would that be acceptable in capital cases and would the alternative of bringing back juries in a situation where intimidation is rife make any more sense? Since abolition of the death penalty in the United Kingdom as a whole, majority jury verdicts had been introduced. Could we justify the execution of someone about whose guilt two jury members, or even one, were not persuaded? But would the alternative of requiring a unanimous verdict in capital cases make any sense when, on past experience, juries were noticeably less inclined to convict while the death penalty was an issue? How would executions be carried out in future? The Gowers Committee twenty-five years ago had made a careful study of alternative methods to hanging. As I said in my speech, 'The relevant section of its report should be compulsory reading for anyone who supposes that there is some clear and easy manner of carrying out an execution.' What about the problems of television treatment of the emotional period prior to an execution? And what would be its effect on public opinion? What about the problems surrounding the exercise of the Royal Prerogative on the recommendation of one man alone, the Home Secretary?

I set out all these issues carefully and without emotion in my speech. At the end I made my personal position totally clear in these words: 'I shall therefore cast my vote against tonight's motion. In reaching that decision I recognize that I am going against the wishes probably of a majority of my constituents and of people in the country as a whole. Of course, I regret that. However, there are occasions when, whether as a Minister or as an Hon. Member, one has to have the courage of one's inner personal convictions.'

In the event there was a clear majority in the House of 119 against restoring the death penalty. I was reasonably well satisfied by the result and by the debate. My speech appeared to have been well received, although I appreciated that my remarks and the good parliamentary reception of them would only increase the antagonism of those who were so strongly in favour of the death penalty inside the Conservative Party. And so it has proved.

My first major incident as Home Secretary occurred on 30 April 1980. On that day I was informed that a group of armed Iranians, calling themselves the Group of the Mohieddin al-Nasser, had burst into the Iranian Embassy in Princes Gate, Kensington. They had overpowered the Embassy staff and seized twenty-six hostages, including four Britons. One of these was Constable Trevor Lock, a member of the Metropolitan Police Diplomatic Protection Group. Two others were BBC employees, one of whom was released the following day because of a stomach complaint. The gunmen demanded that attention be given to the demands of the Arab minority in Iran in the oil-rich province of Ikhuzistan. They called for the release of ninety-one Arabs held by the Iranian Government and demanded that the captives be flown to London where the British Government should provide an aeroplane to fly them to a destination of their choice. Failing that all the hostages would be killed and the Embassy blown up.

The international dimension of the problem presented a diplomatic, as well as a terrorist, challenge. Relations with Iran were difficult following the overthrow of the Shah in 1979. The new Islamic regime had still not fully stabilized. Forty-nine American diplomats were being held hostage in Tehran and earlier that same month President Carter had ordered an abortive helicopter-borne raid in an attempt to free them. The Cabinet had recently been considering American requests that we should impose economic sanctions on Iran in view of their refusal to release the US hostages; emergency powers to this end were taken by legislation in May. It was thus not surprising that the diplomatic response from Iran was frosty. The Foreign Minister made it clear that Iran, for its part, would meet none of the terrorists' demands. Iran declared that if any hostages died an equal number of Iranian Arabs would be 'tried and executed'. The Foreign Minister also warned on 1 May that Britain would be 'held responsible for everything that happens to our diplomats'.

The Home Secretary is responsible for the Government handling of such emergencies, while the primary responsibility for handling operations on the ground rests with the police. He therefore presides over a well-organized team, supported by the Cabinet Office machinery, which consists of Ministers and senior officials from the Government departments involved. On this occasion our emergency plans were immediately established and for the next few days I lived in this world of crisis management. My first impression was that I had to hand a first-class and highly efficient organization which appeared to have assembled at the drop of a hat. Once again I was struck by the immense administrative efficiency of our senior servants. Douglas Hurd, the present Home Secretary, was the most senior of my ministerial colleagues as Minister of State at the Foreign Office.

At first the responsibility rested on the police under David McNee, the Metropolitan Police Commissioner. His senior officer on the spot was Deputy Assistant Commissioner John Dellow, now Deputy Commissioner of the Metropolitan Police. He directed the operation, including the negotiations with the terrorists, under the now well-established police procedure for such incidents, and he proved to be both extremely skilful and calm, which was an immense comfort to us all.

My advisers and I at the Cabinet Office were initially concerned with longer-term contingency plans and with the international implications. It is essential to appreciate that the primary objective of such an operation is to secure the unconditional safe release of the hostages through peaceful persuasion. This was therefore the purpose of the long, painstaking and often frustrating exchanges between the police negotiators and the armed terrorists. It required considerable patience, but the procedure had been success-fully used on previous occasions and was well practised in police circles.

We had to make contingency plans against the possibility of the failure of these negotiations, leading to the subsequent commitment of troops to an assault. Fortunately we were able to bring the SAS secretly to the scene, so that they were able to carry out much necessary reconnaissance and planning without detection. This also meant that, despite the usual speculation, we were able to disguise all troop movements. This was most important for it must be remembered that in all such incidents the terrorists themselves are well-equipped to listen to news bulletins. In a free society, Press speculation – whether accurate or wildly inaccurate – cannot be avoided. But it can be very damaging. Almost worse, I have found, are the comments and opinions of former experts. Some of these were no doubt very knowledgeable in their day but they are invariably out of date and naturally not fully informed. I have always promised myself that I will never agree to be one of them. Now, as a very ex-Home Secretary, I have to be extremely careful.

The early days of the siege were full of activity with little tangible result. Indeed, I was reminded of a comment made to me during a Northern Ireland crisis: 'Secretary of State, much has happened but nothing has changed.' On Thursday 1 May the sick BBC man was released. On Saturday 3 May one pregnant woman and one Iranian were released, followed by a Syrian journalist the next day. On the Sunday the Foreign Office also arranged talks with Jordanian, Kuwaiti and Syrian diplomats in the hope of breaking the deadlock. By Monday it was clear that these efforts at mediation were not going to succeed.

Meanwhile I had of course cancelled my weekend

engagements and spent the time either in the Cabinet Office, at home in London or at my official residence, Dorneywood, near Slough. On Monday 5 May, which was the May bank holiday, I had arranged an official lunch party which it was important for me to attend if possible. In the morning the police talks with the terrorists appeared to be producing little reaction and everything seemed calm. After some discussion it appeared sensible that I should go to Dorneywood for the lunch, provided I could return quickly in an emergency. As it turned out, just before we went in to lunch I was summoned to the telephone to be told that one of the hostages appeared to have been shot. I agreed that I would be back in the Cabinet Office as soon as possible. My Private Secretary, John Chilcot, and my splendid driver, Jack Liddiard, were ready to move at any moment. We left at once and, met by a hurriedly summoned police escort on the way, Jack Liddiard drove us from Slough to Whitehall in nineteen minutes. During this exhibition of superb fast driving, John Chilcot and I remained permanently in telephone contact and so had little opportunity to savour the incredible experience. I did once look at the speedometer as we were going over Hammersmith Broadway and noticed that it showed well over a hundred. The assembled company at the Cabinet Office was obviously amazed to see us so soon. But there was no time for such customary comments as, 'You have been quick.' We had serious business on hand.

By then it had been established that two hostages had been shot and one of their bodies thrown out of the Embassy. Furthermore, the police reported that in their discussions the terrorists were becoming increasingly hysterical. Clearly the time was fast approaching for a major decision on the deployment of troops. Eventually David

McNee asked to speak to me on the highly secret telephone which, as is the custom on such occasions, failed to work. He then told me on the open line that he and his police team could do no more. It was a particularly strained moment for both of us, for we appreciated the risk of sending in the SAS to storm the building. And of course we had in mind that PC Trevor Lock was among the hostages and at grave risk. However, I had discussed the pros and cons of such a decision exhaustively with my team and I was in no doubt what I had to do. I had of course also been over the problem with the Prime Minister and she had authorized me to act if I felt it was necessary. At that moment of decision I felt very lonely and yet strangely calm. Curiously, I do not remember contemplating the appalling possibilities which might result. I suppose this was because I knew that there really was no alternative.

I gave authority for SAS action and there followed an odious period of waiting. Then, of course, I became increasingly aware of all the risks as they flitted through my mind. If the terrorists got a warning of SAS troops entering the building would they kill all the hostages, including PC Trevor Lock whose brave conduct had already gained such admiration? Perhaps they would single him out? Perhaps there would be a major shoot-out and all the hostages would perish with the SAS troops? Then I tried to comfort myself with the knowledge that the SAS were highly trained in such operations and that their instructions were to obtain the release of the hostages unharmed. I had indeed every confidence in them. Yet the nagging fear returned. And all the time I tried to appear outwardly calm in front of my team, since I knew that such an attitude was important to general morale. But in the end we all abandoned such pretence as we, like the rest of the country, saw the whole scene enacted on our television screens. For only a few minutes the tension was hard to bear. Then came the thrilling news. All the hostages, including PC Trevor Lock, were free, safe and unharmed. Four of the terrorist gunmen had been killed, one died on the way to hospital and the sixth was captured. The SAS operation had been a complete and dramatic success. This said much for their professional skill and courage.

I immediately tried to report to the Prime Minister, who was motoring back to London from Chequers. Once again I was temporarily thwarted by communications difficulties. Her car was in a valley and was briefly out of touch. Fortunately I was soon able to tell her of the successful outcome, as she was naturally as anxious as I was. On such occasions one is struck by the immense burden of responsibility imposed on a Prime Minister. Certainly I was the Minister directly in charge but she, as in all such crises at home and abroad, had to bear the ultimate responsibility.

I then drove straight up to Princes Gate in order to see and congratulate all those concerned. It was an exciting moment for all of us, and certainly one which I shall never forget. We in Britain had shown the world that we were prepared to take a stand against terrorists, and indeed to defeat them. There can be no greater deterrent to future action than that.

There were demands that David McNee and I should hold a Press conference. I believe we were right to do so, but in the event I found it a great disappointment. Perhaps the success had gone to my head and I appeared too pleased with myself. Nothing is more dangerous as far as cynical Press correspondents are concerned. They are so often obliged to report tragedies, difficulties and problems that they seem to become almost wary of apparent success.

'Where is the snag?' seems to be the main thought in their minds. It may be that on this occasion their main story had been dramatically scooped by the television cameras' on-the-spot recording. Whatever the reason, they concentrated on detailed questions about the incident itself, to which naturally we could not know the answers. Other questions directly concerning the deployment and composition of the SAS contingent we were not at liberty to answer. As a result, I feared that I had not answered well, and expected a hostile Press reaction. However, I should not have worried, for the Press reports the next day were very favourable. I soon discovered thereafter that success brings a Home Secretary little credit, whereas trouble soon heaps massive blame on his head.

Reflecting on this experience leads me to a conclusion which is topical today concerning the use of SAS and specially trained troops. During and after this incident the main criticism was that too much time was wasted in police conversations with the terrorists. The critics thought that the SAS should have been sent in much earlier. I believe that this criticism ignores the main objective in handling such incidents, which must always be the release of the hostages unharmed but without conceding the terrorists' demands. Therefore all efforts at peaceful persuasion must be exhausted. That is the task of the police negotiators. If they fail, and before force is used, all the possible consequences of action by the SAS or other troops must be accepted before the order for their deployment is given.

Those who give the orders have to recognize that troops have an immensely difficult role when used in the twilight area between peace and war, euphemistically described as action in support of the civil power. I accept at once that there is no alternative to the rules of engagement on opening fire when dealing with terrorist action in Northern Ireland or anywhere else. But when confronted with armed and ruthless men such limitations, imposed under a peacetime rule of law, present substantial problems for the defenders of the peace and also sometimes, alas, advantages for the terrorist. In this connection the long-term considerations cannot be neglected. All too often the immediate benefit of the troops' action is quickly forgotten. Then, after considerable delay, come the legal proceedings accompanied by accusations of excessive force and unnecessary loss of life. These in turn increasingly expose the Government, which has been protecting its citizens, and its troops to substantial criticism at the bar of the world media. As a result wicked and violent organizations achieve propaganda success and increased financial support. All these repercussions may seem tiresome to those who prefer the luxury of considering only one side of any complicated problem. 'Take the gloves off and set the troops free!' they shout. 'Crack down!' is their battle cry. But free nations do not have that option since they proclaim, rightly, that they are upholding freedom under the law. They cannot pick and choose when to do so themselves. Incidentally they would be the first to suffer from a complete breakdown in international law and in the code of behaviour among nations.

My firm conclusion, based on considerable experience, is that our present methods are the best available, but they must be pursued calmly and deliberately. After all, over the years they have earned us considerable international respect.

During the same month of April 1980 our police force faced another substantial challenge, but one very different in character from the Embassy siege. On 2 April serious riots broke out in Bristol. The ferocity of the outbreak in the St Paul's district was a surprise to the authorities and for a time, under the violence of the attack, police were withdrawn from the area. Hundreds of youths were involved in four hours of looting, arson and criminal destruction after a police raid on a club used predominantly by Bristol's minority black community. Thirty-one people were injured, including nineteen police and three firemen.

The St Paul's district of Bristol was known to be a difficult area from a policing point of view. But this very fact meant that we in the Home Office, and indeed in the police service as a whole, failed to recognize this disturbance for the warning signal of danger which it turned out to be. We did, however, realize that one aspect of the police response was unacceptable. Owing to the lack of available police reserves, the police had to be withdrawn from the area. The removal of police protection in this way could not be allowed to happen again. Arrangements were therefore immediately set in hand for co-operation between different police forces which would ensure adequate reserves for any such emergency in the future. These plans have frequently been put into practice in subsequent years in many differing circumstances. They have proved to be a vital element in policing the country as a whole.

Within a year we were to discover that our studies of police action in riots had been inadequate. This was understandable, for the police service naturally resisted a drift towards the riot police image so foreign to the tradition of the British bobby. We were all to learn that if there were to be riots in our streets they had to be met by changes in police equipment, development and training.

A year after the Bristol riots, over the weekend of 10–12 April 1981, violent clashes took place between the police and young people – mainly, but not exclusively, black – in

Brixton. This time there was certainly no question of withdrawing police protection and the necessary substantial reserves of manpower were available. Even so calls were made by a number of people on the Labour Left that the police should be withdrawn from the area in order to reduce tension and thus contain the violence. I was grateful at the time to Roy Hattersley, the Shadow Home Secretary, for condemning such suggestions.

Meanwhile the police and fire officers conducted themselves with the utmost bravery and professionalism in the face of appalling violence. Nevertheless, personal injuries, damage to property and financial loss to wholly innocent people were widespread and totally unacceptable. Over the worst two days of disturbances on 11 and 12 April almost 150 police officers were injured, as well as fifty-eight members of the public. Shops were looted; petrol bombs were thrown; private houses and cars were burnt out. The mob even attacked and damaged ambulances and destroyed a fire engine which was trying to contain the violence.

I toured the area on Sunday 12 April with the Metropolitan Police Commissioner. There were scenes of appalling damage and I felt that I was back in the war during the London blitz or fighting in a town in north-west Europe. The atmosphere was extremely tense, which the Commissioner and I of course made worse by our presence. Yet it was essential that we were there personally. I then visited some of the injured policemen in hospital. Throughout, I was greatly impressed by the courage and spirit of the young policemen.

During this visit, and watching the scenes on television, I had come to some clear conclusions about police equipment and tactics. First, we had to protect our policemen properly and must at once abandon any inhibition about British police in riot gear. I was particularly distressed by the number of policemen in hospital with head injuries – riot helmets were clearly an urgent necessity. There was now no dissension in the police service, certainly not among those who had been at the centre of the action. Riot shields and other equipment were also essential. In the following weeks I became impatient as supplies, particularly of helmets, were slow in coming forward. I could only reflect that committees, inquiries and studies are undoubtedly necessary but all too often they are overtaken by events. So it was on this occasion. However, better late than never. Such equipment is now regarded as commonplace. It was necessary for police morale but also as part of the new tactics which have since been developed with great success.

As one trained as a soldier, I was struck by the immobility of the police response on the Brixton streets. In this I was certainly not alone. Large groups of policemen were seen on television bravely standing their ground under a hail of missiles of all sorts. What about the outflanking movements, so much a part of military folklore? Should the rioters not be harried and kept on the move by such action? Of course, with the benefit of hindsight, the answer to both questions is yes. Again such police action is now effectively practised as normal routine in response to riots.

As I walked unhappily through Brixton I came to another firm conclusion. We needed an independent inquiry with a wider brief than investigation of police equipment, training and tactics in response to trouble. We needed to know more about the reasons behind the outbreak of violence for I did not then, and do not now, accept the easy solutions offered. They are usually part of the story but certainly not the whole answer. Furthermore, they are nearly always proposed by those who want to be convinced by their own prejudices. It is all a question of race and colour, some say. That will not do, because there were many white youths in the riot gangs at Brixton. It is all caused by social deprivation and unemployment, is the favourite cry of the Left. Again this will not do, for it was found in Brixton and in the more extensive riots which followed immediately afterwards that rioters often had steady jobs. Of course these reasons may be a contributory factor, as is the state of relations in any area between the police and the community. But none of them on their own provides the basis of a comprehensive, satisfactory response by authority.

At this time my Northern Ireland experience was valuable to me, for I knew exactly the man to head the inquiry. Lord Scarman, a most eminent judge, had proved by his work in similar circumstances in Northern Ireland that he had a feeling for, and understanding of, social problems in addition to his judicial experience. I knew that the right wing of the Conservative Party was suspicious of him as too Liberal and left-wing in outlook. However, I was delighted to find that the Prime Minister, when I approached her, fully supported my proposal. I also knew that I could not expect the Commissioner of the Metropolitan Police to be enthusiastic about a judicial inquiry. He was bound to feel that this was a matter for the police themselves. But I was convinced that the gravity of the disturbance required a full independent inquiry.

I was therefore pleased to be able to approach Lord Scarman the next day, Monday 13 April, and delighted when he accepted my proposal. Accordingly, I asked him to conduct an independent inquiry under the Police Act 1964 and gave him full authority to make recommendations. I subsequently announced the establishment of the inquiry in detail in the House of Commons that afternoon. I heard some private mutterings from my own supporters, but on the whole the House accepted the proposal and welcomed Lord Scarman as the best man to conduct the inquiry. Of course there were grumbles from similar sources when his report was published, but I know that it was one of my best decisions, and indeed it became increasingly important as the riots continued to spread in subsequent weeks. By his personality and understanding, Lord Scarman did much to defuse a dangerous situation and I shall always be extremely grateful to him.

Unfortunately the Brixton disturbances were not the last. In July a whole series of utterly disgraceful outbreaks took place. On 3 July hundreds of so-called 'skinheads' clashed with Asian youths in West London. Petrol bombs were used against the police and almost fifty were injured. Between 7 and 9 July there was violent rioting in Moss Side in Manchester. On 10 July there was trouble in London, Birmingham, Preston, Wolverhampton and Hull, as well as other lesser disturbances. There was undoubtedly a 'copycat' element to some of these clashes, which were widely reported in the media. Two-thirds of those arrested were under twenty; two-thirds had criminal records; but the majority, far from being unemployed, held steady jobs.

This July week took me back to my days in Northern Ireland, for there was the same pessimism, the same anxieties and the same need to maintain outward calm and good humour while internally suffering deep depression and self-doubt. It started in earnest in the early hours of Monday morning, 6 July. I was woken up in London by a call from my Private Secretary. The Chief Constable of Merseyside, Ken Oxford, wanted my approval for the use of CS gas as his policemen were under great pressure in a major riot. I took the view then, and I am sure it is right,

Welcoming the Queen to the Home Office in 1982 on the
occasion of its 200th anniversary

With my two sponsors, Viscount Rochdale *(left)* and Viscount Eccles, at my introduction ceremony to the House of Lords in June 1983

" KEEP KICKING, KIDS! I'LL MAKE YOU FAMOUS! "

In full regalia – a portrait by the artist Theo Platt, completed
1988

A Cabinet committee meeting in session, 1985

Giving my *Ad Portas* speech at Winchester College on 12 May 1984

Opening a new auction mart in Carlisle in 1975

The Prime Minister and her Deputy in 1984

In discussion with Mikhail Gorbachev during my visit to the Soviet Union in 1986 as head of an Inter-Parliamentary Union delegation

Christmas 1987 at Ennim with three of our daughters and all but two of our grandchildren

that such decisions can only be taken by those in charge of the operations on the ground. There was no point in putting further questions at that moment. So, amazing as it seems now, I turned over and went to sleep again.

But in the morning I woke up full of doubts about the impossible position I had been in. How could a Home Secretary, in bed in London, or indeed anywhere else, judge what was happening on the streets of Liverpool? And how could he refuse his support to a senior and most experienced Chief Constable? I resolved at once to question, and indeed to get rid of, such a ridiculous requirement. Had I known the full circumstances on the ground in Liverpool, the pressure that the police were under and the inevitable lack of experience in the use of CS gas in a riot situation, I would have been anything but content. I would still have made the same decision but I am sure I would not have gone to sleep again so easily.

In the event, helped by the use of the CS gas, the Merseyside police just succeeded in containing the worst disturbance that night. On the Tuesday I flew up to Merseyside to see the Chief Constable in order to gain a first-hand impression of the situation. There had been further, though less serious, troubles on the Monday night. Ken Oxford is a courageous leader. He fully understood the need for outward calm. Therefore we neither of us betrayed our inner anxieties although I suspect that we understood each other only too well. Nevertheless, he impressed me as a man in complete charge of a dangerous situation.

Once again I was struck by the worrying similarity with Northern Ireland and the disturbances there. Most of the city of Liverpool appeared perfectly normal and outwardly calm until we reached the riot area, Toxteth. Suddenly one drove from a normal city into streets of damaged buses and smouldering fires crowded with hysterical groups of people. Ken Oxford was adamant that we did not stop and particularly that I did not get out of the car. Obviously I obeyed his instructions, much as I wanted to appear publicly. On reflection I realize he was right, not for my personal security but because he and I would only have attracted an angry crowd and therefore further commotion. But this was a serious commentary on the volatile nature of the position at that moment. I then went to see the civic leaders and to visit the policemen and other riot casualties in hospital. I also had a most valuable meeting with the Bishop of Liverpool, David Sheppard, and the Roman Catholic Archbishop Worlock. Both then and subsequently their joint action has been of immense significance to the Merseyside community as a whole. It had been a worrying day, for there was no sign of returning calm in the affected area.

At the airport, before I flew back to London I was met by Douglas Crawford who, although old and ill, had come specially to see me. He was the past Lord Lieutenant of Merseyside and a most loved and respected figure in the city of Liverpool. He was also a great friend of mine, initially in golfing circles. 'Willie,' he said, 'do not worry about us. I know Merseyside. We are difficult people but there is much good in us. Keep calm, trust us and all will be well.' I knew then that he did not have long to live and that it had been a great physical effort for him to come and see me, and after all the emotion of the day I was close to tears. But he had taught me a lesson which I came to appreciate so much. Those words, 'Keep calm, trust us', rang in my ears for the rest of that awful week and governed all my actions. But as I was soon to learn, there were further trials ahead.

On Friday 10 July I visited Manchester, which had suffered from two nights of serious rioting in the Moss Side district. The Chief Constable, Jim Anderton, is an individualist and is well-known for his outspoken and controversial remarks. But he is a first-class leader of his policemen and had succeeded in quelling his troubles. By then the situation in Liverpool had also calmed down and it seemed, as I left Manchester, that perhaps the worst was over. However, as I drove back to London that evening the news on my wireless was most depressing, particularly as we were approaching the dangerous period of the weekend. There were disturbances in several areas and, worst of all, there appeared to be increasing trouble in London. As we came into the Metropolitan area my detective tuned into his police network. It was, as one might say, choked with troubles.

When I got back to the Home Office I sensed exactly that feeling which I had found in Belfast after the major bombing during July nine years earlier. There was a suppressed atmosphere of impending doom, and an unexpressed fear about where it would all end, which stirs individual and family anxieties. I tried to comfort my officials with better news from the trouble spots in the North, but I left for the weekend at Dorneywood with a sense of foreboding which we all shared. When I got there I found my wife doing her best, as always, to appear encouraging and helpful at stressful moments. But I remember sitting out after supper on a beautiful hot summer evening, looking at the fields and trees of Burnham Beeches. It was a perfect, peaceful English scene. Was it really in the same country as the riot towns and cities which I had visited during the week? Was it really in the same vicinity as parts of London a few miles away which at that moment were full of troubles? Surely, I thought, this peaceful countryside represents more accurately the character and mood of the vast majority of the British people. What then does this majority expect from its leaders at a time of trouble such as we have experienced this week? Of course its greatest hope is to live in peace untroubled by such difficulties. Some naturally yearn for tough repressive action, which will somehow rid them of their troublesome fellow citizens But most want, above all, to see determination and firm action calmly taken. Perhaps because it reflects my own instinct, I do not believe that such people respect those who talk far more toughly than they are prepared to act.

On the Saturday as I attended a fête in the Wokingham constituency of my old friend and Minister of State in Northern Ireland, Bill van Straubenzee, these thoughts were in my mind. They were reflected in my speeches and television interviews. Inevitably the 'blood and thunder brigade' in the Press were highly critical of my supposed weakness. They were, of course, exercising the privilege of those who can afford to advocate tough action in others while knowing that they are not in a position to take it themselves. I have never believed that in true leadership it pays to pander to their dramatic headlines, which of course are designed to sell newspapers. Indeed, to do so would be to show the very qualities of weakness which they deride. It is surely wiser, and incidentally requires more courage, to talk calmly and firmly, but then to act with ruthless determination where necessary. That was my approach in reacting to the riots.

Fortunately after the weekend the worst of the disturbances was over, although there were still some minor riots of a copy-cat nature in other towns and cities. At least this meant that the House of Commons debate on the appalling week of riots, scheduled for 16 July, could take place in a calmer atmosphere. I realized that this would be a major occasion for me, when I was called on to review a shameful episode in our nation's life and set out the full nature of the Government's response. I was, above all, determined to give a lead in expressing what I believed to be the basic feeling of many in the country, namely that this was a moment for a comprehensive, calm response. I also wanted to answer those critics who believed in the alternative of a repressive and wholly punitive reaction. I felt that that would only exacerbate tensions and so lead to further troubles. I was confident that if only I could get my message across I would get considerable support in the House of Commons, in much of the Press and indeed in the country as a whole.

I started my speech with a sombre review of the extent of the violence, the arrests for offences committed during the disturbances, the large number of police officers injured and the widespread damage to property and theft from property. I gave the House details of the lessons which I believed we had learnt in police organization, training, tactics and the need for protective equipment. I explained the action which was being taken to profit from them.

I spoke of the measures I was taking as Home Secretary to enable the prisons to play their full part in dealing with the custodial sentences passed by the courts. This part of my speech dealt with the need for a clear, determined response which would deter such criminal violence in future.

'It is the duty of every Government to underline, and act on, their fundamental responsibility to uphold the rule of law. I also have other and wide responsibilities, both as Home Secretary and as a member of the Government. These are simple to state but complex to carry out and achieve. Put briefly, they are to promote the conditions in which violence does not flourish but is rejected, so that a peaceful and harmonious society is a reality and seen to be a reality for all people.'

In this connection I referred to the implications of Lord Scarman's vital inquiry and to Michael Heseltine's proposed visit to Merseyside which subsequently – through his flair and personality – made such an important impression there. I spoke of race relations and the evils of extreme racial activity, because no one could deny that racial feelings and prejudice on all sides had played a major part in the riots. I was utterly determined nevertheless that they should not be used to justify intolerance on grounds of colour. I knew it could only do harm if those who attempted to jump on the racialist bandwagon, from whatever point of view, started campaigns in pursuit of scapegoats.

Finally, I summed up the Government's position as follows. 'I wish to emphasize in conclusion that the immediate task for the Government, backed, I am certain, by the whole House, is to remove the scourge of criminal violence from our streets. To this end, we must give our fullest support to the police and the law enforcement agencies and provide them with all the equipment necessary to carry out their task. But at the same time we must develop policies designed to promote the mutual tolerance and understanding upon which the whole future of a free democratic society depends.'

Roy Hattersley, who followed me for the Opposition, was generous in his comments and I was grateful to him. On the whole I found that, although of course there were critics, my speech had been well received on all sides. It seemed generally that I had struck the right note in dealing with a disgraceful episode in our nation's history. This was certainly the tone of much of the Press comment.

Looking back on that awful experience, I have tried to

analyse my decisions and my reactions. On the police side, I regret that as Home Secretary I did not press for a more thorough and urgent review of police riot training, equipment and tactics after the warning of St Paul's, Bristol, a year earlier. On the other hand, I am convinced that the lessons of those major July disturbances were learnt and that the necessary actions were taken to remedy defects both speedily and correctly. In particular the need for riot helmets and shields was accepted and they were quickly provided. I am certain that this equipment has not only safeguarded the police from unnecessary injuries but has also enabled them to adopt positive and mobile tactics against riot mobs. This in turn has been a major deterrent to rioters, since the consequent effectiveness of a police response has been proved in practice.

In the years since then there have been many different levels of violent disturbance and incidents of football hooliganism, but at least we can claim that there has been no recourse to violent riots on the same scale as those in 1981. While I believe that the improvements in police riot equipment are essential, I am relieved that we have not had to use baton rounds or CS gas again on the British mainland. These are rightly held in reserve, and their use involves risks which can only heighten tension at times when the restoration of calm is a primary consideration.

I have one slight regret. My keenness for water cannon as a riot weapon was never shared by the police service. Indeed, it became the subject of friendly argument and jokes between the Chief Constables, my Home Office officials and myself. They were all convinced that water cannon were too immobile and so provided sitting targets. Further, they argued that they ran out of water too quickly and were therefore out of action when refuelling. Yet I obstinately held to the view that no one likes getting wet, and yet a soaking does not cause lasting damage and is not as likely to provoke a hostile response as baton rounds or the use of CS gas. Nor am I convinced by the argument that German cities are so different from ours that, while water cannon are valuable in Germany, they would not operate successfully in Britain. I was, incidentally, also supported by many representations on this subject from the general public, who strongly favoured the use of water cannon. Despite all that, I feel I must now bow to the greater expertise of the Chief Constables. Anyway, they must be relieved to have me out of the way, for I know that they have convinced my successors of the rightness of their view.

In addition to the introduction of new police techniques, I am convinced that the other decisions taken at the time had a profound influence. In particular, Lord Scarman's report made a major contribution to the improvement of police–community relations. This has been an important development in many of our inner city areas. I know there are critics who contend that efforts to bring the police and the community together only result in less effective policing and more crime. Of course they can produce cases to support their argument, but against that I would contend that some excellent and dedicated work by community policemen has had a major effect in avoiding subsequent damaging riots. Nor can there be any doubt that discussion and co-operation between senior police officers and local community leaders are producing valuable results. Following the Brixton riots, I committed myself to establishing the Lambeth police/community committee, which turned out to be one of the most successful in the country.

There has also been – again thanks to Lord Scarman's proposals – steady progress in the difficult task of improving race relations in the most sensitive areas. Equally, of course, it has to be accepted that many serious tensions remain. Yet whatever the arguments about the past, we have to accept today that the children of Asians and West Indians who came to Britain from their families' homes in the Commonwealth have been born here as full British citizens. Furthermore, they know no other home. Our best hope of building mutual confidence is to assure them of a genuine welcome in what is their own country. This can only be achieved through a patient and under-standing attitude which personally, particularly as Home Secretary, I have always tried to promote.

At the Conservative party conference in 1981 the issue of capital punishment re-surfaced, damaging my standing as Home Secretary and so making it much more difficult for me to make some proposed reforms in sentencing policy. What made it all the more annoying was that I brought the trouble on my own head.

Law and order debates at Conservative party conferences had developed over the years into a kind of ritual. The Press and – as television coverage of party conferences increased – the whole media greatly enjoyed the spectacle of the Home Secretary of the day being roughed up by those who became known as the 'hangers and floggers' in the Tory Party. And of course inevitably the 'hangers and floggers' enjoyed the publicity for their role, as successive Home Secretaries from Rab Butler onwards tried to shrug off their dislike and disdain at the tone of the debate. Nor did it help if the Home Secretary was personally in favour of capital punishment, as Reggie Maudling was. Then the critics simply condemned his weakness at not imposing his will on his colleagues.

I certainly both dreaded and disliked the prospect of the law and order debate, for the atmosphere was so strangely hostile and so different from that accorded to all one's colleagues. It was also infuriating that a debate on the vital issue of protecting our citizens should be dominated and overshadowed by one issue. That was made worse by the certain knowledge that even if capital punishment was restored, it alone could not answer all the major problems of preserving law and order in our society – presupposing that one believed it would actually do more good than harm anyway.

Even more maddening was the undoubted fact that, whatever the supporters of restoration at the Conservative party conference said, Parliament was most unlikely to change its mind. On top of everything else there was no doubt that pressure and even bullying by so-called 'hangers and floggers' served only to force Conservative MPs who were against hanging to stand up for what they believed to be right. It was therefore a diversion from some crucial issues, such as sentencing and prison overcrowding.

However, over the years in Opposition and in Government, I had adopted a technique which seemed to get me through the debate. I tried to make a serious, dull speech on the main issues, making understanding noises about support for capital punishment at the same time as giving no ground. The conference of 1981 certainly required that treatment more than most, for I was already under fire for what the same critics believed was a weak response to the riots in the summer. My advisers and I had therefore prepared a most careful and detailed speech for my reply to the debate.

All seemed to be going quietly and therefore well, from my point of view, until one delegate made a fiery and brilliant speech in favour of capital punishment. He was applauded by Margaret Thatcher herself, who was sitting beside me on the platform. I certainly had no reason to complain about that because, bearing in mind her strong views, she was entirely entitled to do so. But naturally that in itself increased my isolation. Unfortunately I was particularly incensed by this delegate's remark that if Conservative MPs could not go along with a three-line whip and vote for the reintroduction of capital and corporal punishment, they had better not stand at the next election. It seemed to me that such intolerance, on an issue which had always been accepted as a free vote, was not in the best traditions of our Conservative Party. Then a Young Conservative from Brentford, Mike Truman, made a speech against racism and was booed by quite a large section of the audience. My friends all know that I have a tempestuous temper characterized by sudden, short squalls of considerable intensity. This incident stirred me well beyond my normal rages. I felt that I was witnessing scenes of intolerance which I had never expected to see in the Conservative Party. Intolerance is catching in an emotional atmosphere, and my anger did not subside as my friends – who had seen my fury all too obviously portrayed on my face – thought it would. In a temper I decided to tell the Party what I thought of it in an impromptu addition to my speech, as follows.

'After many years of service to this party, I have heard with a good deal of sadness this afternoon the receptions given to Mr Silvester on the one hand and to Mr Truman on the other. Surely in this party, over all these years, we are entitled to different views; we should not be shouted down for them. Why should we be?

'Of course I understand the very strong feelings in the Party about the reintroduction of capital punishment, and the message must be perfectly clear to our Members of Parliament. We had the debate and the motion to restore capital punishment was heavily defeated. The whole conference knows my views, so it is no use going on with that, but what I find distressing is that it should be suggested by Mr Silvester, and partly by the conference, that in some ways our Members of Parliament should be coerced on this issue, which up to now has always been a matter of individual opinion.

'If this party is to go down the road of coercing its Members of Parliament, is it not extraordinary that at the same time it should be saying at every moment of the day how wicked it is for every left-wing member of the Labour Party to do exactly the same? Surely we do not want to go down their road.

'Mr Truman has made a number of criticisms. I do not agree with some of them. You made it very clear that you do not agree with them, either. Very well. But I think that we ought to be careful and to think of what he has said and to understand what he is saying, and not to be so blind to some of his views that we cannot take them on board in considering some of these very difficult and dangerous issues which confront our country. [Cries of 'Rubbish!'] I said that I did not agree with all of his views. But I do not see any reason why it should be rubbish for me to say that there may be some point in what he is saying.'

I had the satisfaction afterwards of many congratulations from supporters in the hall who felt as I did. But I had infuriated the most vocal elements in the audience and the rest of my speech was ruined. Nor did I end by positively requesting support for the harmless resolution before us. I was of course still seeing red. As a result, the resolution was defeated, which appeared to be a vote of no confidence in all our law and order policies, which it certainly was not.

Naturally the occasion became a subject of considerable discussion in the media generally, broadening into comments about relations between the Prime Minister and myself. My supporters thought that she had treated me badly by not publicly showing her confidence in me, for example during her speech at the end of the conference. I did everything that I could to explain why I did not share this view. The mutual understanding between Margaret Thatcher and myself had even by then grown so strong over the years that it was capable of withstanding such strains. Anyway, I was angry with myself and felt that in some ways I had let her down although, in view of the Party's behaviour, I certainly did not feel like apologizing.

In the end we carried on happily as if nothing had happened. Such, I feel, is the value of shared loyalties. After all, I have similarly ignored occasions when I have known that Margaret Thatcher herself was unhappy about something she had done.

Inevitably, the mood of this conference debate made my handling of law and order issues more difficult in the months immediately ahead, for my critics had gained ground. The argument surfaced again in March 1982, with further demands for the return of capital punishment at its centre. The actual triggers were the publication of crime figures and the tragic killing of two policemen. The latter caused the Police Federation, understandably, to demand the return of capital punishment. This was eagerly seized upon by the pro-hanging lobby in Parliament. The crime figures were certainly worrying. Even so, they were not as high as in some previous years. In any event, these figures are not an accurate barometer of the crime situation at any one moment, for a variety of reasons. Suffice it to say that violent crime has remained a serious problem for many years and that many of its causes cannot fairly be laid at the door of the Home Secretary, nor indeed ascribed to his inadequacies or lack of action. Nevertheless, crime figures do provide a useful opportunity for an attack by his critics. The week beginning 22 March provided mine with their chance.

I was due to attend a meeting of the Party Back-bench Committee on the Monday. The Labour Party had understandably jumped on the bandwagon with a Commons debate on the Thursday and I was to speak at the Party's Central Council on the Friday. Ironically, this campaign was mounted soon after we had in fact once again withstood a hijacking crisis through firm action at Stansted Airport. Fortunately, my friends and supporters recognized the pressure for what it was – a determined effort by critics in the Party to get rid of me as Home Secretary. It was the usual story. They wanted a strong man who would introduce violent, repressive measures and who would, as a supporter of capital punishment, campaign actively in Parliament for the restoration of the death penalty.

I understood these feelings only too well but utterly resented the conclusion. I was determined as Home Secretary to maintain my calm but firm response to violence. And I had indeed ample proof that I was neither weak nor inactive in the battle against crime. It is a marvellous feeling when your friends rally to you at moments of difficulty. In a Parliamentary Party particularly their support is crucial to anyone's success in high office. And so on the Monday night I felt immensely reassured by the tone of the Party meeting. My friends turned out in great force. They were pleased with my speech and gave my critics a pretty rough ride. Fortunately, reports of that meeting set the tone for the majority of the Press comments on Tuesday morning. I was then given strong party support during the Commons debate on Thursday, and so I went off to Harrogate, where once more my party friends had rallied in support of me.

I think I made a reasonably good speech in support of what I was doing and what had been achieved. I should have done so, for after all I had had plenty of practice that week. But I was particularly touched by the reception which I was given. Normally I am not a great seeker of standing ovations, perhaps because I have learnt over the years that my speaking style is not one which is likely to provoke them. Obviously on this occasion, however, one would help to round off my week of counter-attack. I felt, as I spoke, that the audience were just waiting to stand up and that, provided I did not actually fall down during the speech, they would do so. At the end I was much relieved to have fought off a particularly unpleasant and, as I believed it, very unfair attack by my 'hanging and flogging' critics. I was also throughout the week greatly encouraged by the support given to me by the Prime Minister which, remembering her views on capital punishment, must have tested her undoubted loyalty to me.

The Falklands War, and Fagan

In April 1982 my preoccupation with all the urgent Home Office problems was, to some extent, interrupted by what became known as the Falklands War. As a member of ODSA (Overseas Defence Committee, South Atlantic), to give it its official name – or the War Cabinet, as it was christened by the Press – I had an inside knowledge of the dramatic events. But I must emphasize that I had no departmental executive responsibilities concerning the war and that I continued with all my Home Office duties. I shall therefore not attempt to give any detailed account of the whole affair. Instead I will concentrate on my reactions to some of the main incidents. I will also attempt a political analysis of the effect of the Falklands War on Margaret Thatcher's position at home and abroad, and on the future of Conservative governments. There can be no doubt that it had a profound influence on all these matters.

From the start the Prime Minister was determined that a small group of Ministers and Service Chiefs should be responsible for the day-to-day running of operations. This was why she set up the committee known as ODSA. Of course this was a sub-committee of the Cabinet itself, which remained ultimately responsible for all major decisions. My membership of this small group quickly persuaded me that its formation was a wise decision. We met under the Prime Minister's chairmanship at No.10 on most weekday mornings for a strictly limited period. This was designed to lead to a brisk, workmanlike meeting. Obviously we had special meetings, to discuss, for example, the detailed plans for the landing on the Falkland Islands themselves. The real success of the committee was ensured by the Prime Minister herself, who was throughout at her clear and commanding best, and by Lord Lewin, Chief of the Defence Staff, who gave us all great confidence. As a result, we worked as a closely knit and harmonious team, in contrast with the stories of dissension between politicians and Service Chiefs in the 1914–18 war.

The dispute between Britain and Argentina was of course long-standing, and it had over the years effectively soured relations between the two countries. We in Britain, for our part, were determined to stand up for the rights of the Falkland Islanders in any decision on their future sovereignty. There could be no doubt that this small body of people passionately clung to their British connection. The Argentines, for their part, held that the Malvinas, as they called the Falklands, really belonged to Argentina and not, as we contended, to Britain. Nor, I suppose, could they understand the real British interest in these islands so close to their own country and so far removed across the oceans from our shores.

For years under successive governments the Foreign Office had been trying to reach an amicable settlement with Argentina. But the Falkland Islanders had passionate supporters in Parliament who were not prepared to contemplate any settlement which affected the British sovereignty of the Islands. Any discussion with Argentina therefore always ended with a parliamentary row at Westminster.

Most unfairly, in my judgement, the Foreign Office and successive Foreign Ministers had been severely criticized by the parliamentary supporters of the Falkland Islanders for their efforts to reach a settlement. Surely some agreement in this vexed dispute must have been in the best interests of all concerned. Certainly its continuation had disadvantages for the inhabitants of the Falkland Islands. But the emotional issue of sovereign rights on both sides produced a stalemate.

Then there are the critics who say that the Foreign Office should have foreseen that in 1982 pent-up feeling in Argentina would explode into a crazy invasion instead of the normal sabre-rattling. It is always easy to be wise after the event and I suppose that General Galtieri would reflect now in disgrace that he never believed in British armed resistance to his invasion gamble. Sadly, both sides misread the real intentions of the other. Such, alas, is the basis of so many conflicts, and in this case Argentina did invade the Falkland Islands on Friday 2 April.

That day I was carrying out my Home Secretary duties on a visit to the Hampshire Fire Brigade in Eastleigh. I was summoned back to London for an emergency Cabinet meeting in the evening. By that time the Governor of the Falkland Islands had surrendered and Argentina was in full control. There was no doubt then about the feelings of shame and disgrace at the humiliation of our country. Already a debate in both Houses of Parliament had been promised for the next day, Saturday – an exceptional move in itself. I think that in the Cabinet that evening we were substantially in agreement that action had to be taken and that there really was no alternative to preparing and sending a Task Force to the South Atlantic.

Saturday was an unhappy day for the Government. The

mood in the House of Commons on all sides was ugly. John Nott, as Defence Secretary, was severely mauled. During the debate I left to report to Peter Carrington in the House of Lords about the House of Commons position. I found him greatly irritated. Because of the calmer atmosphere of the House of Lords they had been having a reasonable debate. No doubt, this owed much to Peter Carrington's own speech and to his complete mastery of the House of Lords, combined with his considerable popularity there. I told him that the mood of our back-benches in the House of Commons was very bad and that they were out for blood. I felt that he must come, together with John Nott, to a Conservative back-bench meeting which had been summoned for that evening. He accepted my advice and I said that I would endeavour to rally vocal support for him at the meeting. It was then that I realized sadly the disadvantage of a senior Minister in the House of Lords at a moment of crisis. It is so much more difficult to muster your own friends and supporters to your aid than it is to canvass them for someone else. This is particularly true when, as in this case, anyone standing up for the Government and its Ministers was going to have a rough ride. I have always felt that if Peter Carrington had been in a better position to exert his outstanding personality at that moment he could have avoided his subsequent resignation, which greatly weakened the Government and indeed the nation as a whole.

In the event, at the meeting both he and John Nott were received with a storm of hostile comment. At Dorneywood on the Sunday I read the Press reports with dismay. In the morning Peter Carrington rang up and said that he would come over to see me. He arrived in the afternoon and we had long discussions, as befits two old friends who had been through many political dramas together. I argued passionately against his proposal to resign, which still today I regard as a loss to the nation of an outstanding statesman and personally a delightful companion. I knew I was losing the argument but at least I persuaded him to go and talk to Alec Home before he finally decided.

I was miserable when he left because I knew that he had decided to go, and indeed for a good reason. He felt that there was so much pent-up emotion against him and the Foreign Office that his successful conduct of Foreign Affairs during the period of a war with the Falklands would be gravely undermined. When I read *The Times* leader on the Monday morning I was even more deeply depressed, for I knew then finally that Peter Carrington would certainly resign. *The Times* had told him to do his duty, by which of course they meant precisely that. It was, in my judgment, a most astonishing leader for *The Times*, of all newspapers, to publish, for Peter Carrington's value to the nation as Foreign Secretary was not something to be written off so glibly. Naturally, the tabloid Press was more dramatic and indeed, in some cases, worse. But they would have been easier to disregard.

Anyway, Peter Carrington and his other Foreign Ministers, Humphrey Atkins and Richard Luce, honourably resigned. Francis Pym was given the unenviable task of taking on the position as Foreign Secretary in these circumstances. He was the obvious choice and admirably performed the task of commanding and calming the House of Commons through the months of the war. I do not believe that anyone else would have been able to make such an important contribution to the success of the Government in the House of Commons.

Those of us who had served in the Second World War should not have been surprised by the remarkable patriotic instinct of the British people. We had experienced the inner determination of those with whom we served and their courage at moments of real danger. Indeed, my whole attitude to life and my deep feelings of trust for the British people rested on my wartime service. Yet I confess that in the early weeks of April 1982 I was amazed by the surge of patriotic spirit. All internal arguments were forgotten as the ships of the Task Force were assembled and equipped with remarkable speed. The cruise liner *Canberra* was prepared and adapted as a troop carrier.

There were emotional scenes as the Task Force sailed. In a strange way the British people had decided that they were not going to be pushed around by Argentina. Few, I suspect, stopped to consider the major logistical problems of maintaining a Task Force in the South Atlantic 8,000 miles away, let alone of landing troops on the Falkland Islands within easy reach of the Argentinian Air Force.

Soon we on the ODSA Committee, as I shall correctly refer to it, were all too well aware of the grave problems and dangers which beset the recapture of the Falkland Islands. We quickly learnt also that we depended on United States help with equipment and, above all, for permission to use the facilities of their base at Ascension Island. Soon I and, I suspect, the others on the Committee were to appreciate at first hand the difficult position in which we had placed our great ally, and in particular President Reagan and his Defence Secretary, Casper Weinberger. No doubt many people in Britain simply took their full support and co-operation for granted.

But the pressures on the Secretary of State, Alexander

Haig, certainly alerted me to the dilemma facing an American nation with close ties and interests in South America. I did not attend the main meetings with Al Haig and his staff as they shuffled between London and Buenos Aires, but I was present at some of the social functions and working dinners during their visits. I have no doubt that Al Haig himself, with his previous NATO experience, was most anxious to help us; but it was equally obvious, when talking to them, that his advisers were divided between the South American lobby in the State Department and those sympathetic to Britain. When one comes to think of it, that was bound to be so. Equally, we began to appreciate the pressures to which the United States administration, from the President downwards, were subjected by powerful figures in Congress and generally in Washington. Naturally in these circumstances the American administration in those early days desperately hoped to find a compromise settlement, and Al Haig directed all his energies to that end.

Against that background we had to persuade the Americans, and of course in particular the President, that we needed more than their benevolent neutrality when it came to vital facilities and equipment. On the other hand, we could not automatically expect such help from them if we were adamantly to reject all proposals for a peaceful settlement. This was, of course, difficult when we knew there was little chance of any such agreement which would meet our aims and indeed the aspirations of public opinion in Britain.

No one who was not closely involved could possibly realize the diplomatic skill and determination with which Margaret Thatcher played this immensely difficult hand.

Certainly she was assisted in her task by the close personal relationship which she had cultivated with President Reagan. But she had also to appreciate that she must not push him too hard, for that could easily be represented as unreasonable pressure and thus be counter-productive.

Fortunately for us, in all the various discussions the Argentines were over-confident and so intransigent. This helped Casper Weinberger to ensure that our Task Force received all the assistance it required, and it thus sailed steadily towards the South Atlantic.

By the end of April, Al Haig's negotiations finished when the Argentines rejected his final package. We had declared that we would await their response which, in the event, brought this diplomatic phase to an end. By then the Task Force had reached the exclusion zone which we had declared round the Falkland Islands. On 30 April President Reagan declared United States support for Britain and the action phase of the war commenced.

On Sunday 2 May I was summoned to an ODSA meeting at Chequers. When I arrived the Prime Minister took me aside and asked me to join a small meeting, as Terry Lewin, the Chief of the Defence Staff, had an important problem to put before us. He told us that one of our submarines, the *Conqueror*, had sighted the *Belgrano* Task Force and was in contact. As the *Belgrano* incident has aroused such controversy, I will simply record my own reaction at this significant meeting.

Terry Lewin told us that, when sighted, the *Belgrano* was not actually in the exclusion zone and she was not at that moment steaming into it, although she had frequently changed course. I remember asking the one question which I felt to be crucial. Could the submarine undertake to remain in contact so that we could know exactly the movements of the *Belgrano* before coming to any final decision about the submarine's action? He replied that with the conditions of the South Atlantic there could not possibly be any such certainty. Personally that was good enough for me. Our first duty was to our sailors and soldiers in the Task Force. If we refused permission for the submarine to endeavour to sink the *Belgrano*, and consequently in her turn the *Belgrano* sank some of our ships in the Task Force, we could never forgive ourselves and certainly – rightly – would never be forgiven by the British people. There was therefore never any doubt in my mind. We had to give permission for the submarine to torpedo the *Belgrano* whenever the opportunity occurred. This was the decision taken at the meeting. The *Belgrano* was torpedoed and sunk that Sunday night. Despite all the furore engendered since, I do not believe that any Ministers in any Government could responsibly have reached any other conclusion in the circumstances.

Nor was it long before the whole nation had to realize that we were fighting a real war. Two days later, on 4 May, the *Sheffield* was sunk by an Exocet with tragic loss of life. As in Northern Ireland, I experienced again that awful feeling of ultimate responsibility for casualties and the consequent family tragedies. I steeled myself and had the opportunity to admire Margaret Thatcher's invariable personal courage at bad moments.

While we were at Chequers on 2 May, Francis Pym, the Foreign Secretary, had been in Washington and at the United Nations in New York. As a result we were told on Monday 3 May that the Peruvians had put forward some peace proposals which had also been backed by the United

States. They offered at this late hour a compromise which we had to consider carefully. If we came out adamantly against it, we risked a hostile reaction from our American allies on whose support we relied. In any event, some of us knew that we were about to embark on an inevitably hazardous landing operation. On the other hand, the proposals represented a compromise which would not satisfy the Falkland Islanders or many people in Britain, who by this time were determined to have no truck with Argentina while she was a belligerent.

It was therefore a very difficult decision that the Cabinet had to take on 5 May. We decided that the proposals should not be turned down out of hand, and so the following day the Prime Minister told the House of Commons that we would make a constructive response to the Peruvian proposals. Before we could do so, the Argentines rejected them completely. With the benefit of hindsight it is clear that we would have had much trouble at home if we had become involved in negotiations on them. Furthermore, in the light of subsequent events we would have sacrificed a great national success and a boost to national morale as a result of outright victory.

Fortunately we were saved from ourselves by complete Argentinian rejection. I confess to a feeling of relief at their reaction. I have, however, to add in all honesty that at the time I believed we would have had to accept these peace proposals, under American pressure, if indeed it had been generally agreed that they did provide a way forward.

It was now clear that the invasion of the Falkland Islands would have to take place as planned. As the date approached, I became increasingly apprehensive about the hazardous nature of the operation. Large troop ships would have to enter San Carlos Bay and remain there for some time while the soldiers disembarked. If the flying weather was good, they would surely provide an easy target for the Argentinian planes within easy range of their bases. Then, even if the landings were successful, there was difficult countryside for the troops to cross before they could reach Port Stanley, the vital and only major objective. It would take time for the troops, and particularly for the equipment, to be transported across such terrain. But this had to be achieved before a successful assault on Port Stanley could be mounted, especially if it turned out to be well defended. If the Argentinian soldiers fought hard, it was obvious that our troops might be engaged for some time in a static battle in worsening weather. Nor was it wise to assume, as some people did all too readily, that the Argentinian soldiers would not resist strongly. On top of that, as the loss of HMS *Sheffield* had shown, our ships in the Task Force were vulnerable to air and, indeed, submarine attacks.

It was therefore a great relief when we heard that the landings at San Carlos on 21 May had been successful and that our troops were firmly established on land. More amazing, certainly to me, was the lack of Argentinian aircraft over the landing area on the next day, 22 May. Actually, the Argentines had suffered considerable aircraft losses. But their pilots had all along shown themselves to be able and brave. Our ships, particularly the larger ones, were able to withdraw quietly as a result of this inactivity and the worst dangers were over.

Our problems and anxieties, however, were certainly not at an end. First, we had the awkward period of waiting while the strength of troops in the bridgehead was built up.

Naturally, far removed from the battlefield, we became anxious for troop advances, because all the time our ships in the Task Force were at risk. Indeed, on 25 May the *Atlantic Conveyor* was sunk. This was a great blow because its cargo included helicopters and much other vital equipment, without which the advance on Port Stanley was likely to be slow and certainly more difficult.

On 28 May came the successful action at Goose Green by the Paras, who overcame tough Argentinian resistance. This was followed in the days immediately afterwards by the tragic loss of life, prominently among the Welsh Guards, when troops were disembarking at Fitzroy on their way to the battle of Port Stanley.

During these difficult days in the actual fighting, we at home were to some extent worried and indeed diverted by various peace plans. They, together with ceasefire calls from the United Nations, made a quick and successful conclusion of the war even more important. I always feared that if our troops became bogged down or stuck in heavy fighting close to Port Stanley, the continual pressures for settlement based on some dubious compromise would have become increasingly difficult to resist.

Fortunately, the attack on Port Stanley was mounted on 11 June and culminated with the triumphant Scots Guards assault on Tumbledown on 13 June. The following day the Argentines surrendered and the war was over. Britain had won an outright victory which represented an immense achievement by our Armed Forces, not only in fighting terms but in the remarkable organization of the logistical support over vast distances. It also provided our country with an amazing boost to national morale. This in turn was reflected in a substantial increase in support for Margaret Thatcher herself and for the Government as a whole.

I have heard some opponents and critics almost complaining about Margaret Thatcher's luck during the Falklands War. This was felt particularly because at the time the Government was going through a difficult period on other issues. I can understand the irritation of the Government's critics. But I would claim that Margaret Thatcher really deserved all her luck. She was faced by a most direct challenge to Britain on the rights of the Falkland Islanders to decide their own future sovereignty. Despite all the troubles and problems, she never wavered in her determination to meet such a challenge and indeed to recapture the Islands. She had the full backing of the British people because she had so correctly judged their mood. She had obtained the essential help and support of the United States of America in difficult circumstances through her diplomacy and strength of purpose. She had clearly impressed many people at home and throughout the world with her outstanding courage. Above all, she had been given an opportunity to prove her capacity as a national leader. No one who worked with her through this time could possibly deny that she emerged from that with flying colours. If, in the process, she suddenly obtained substantial rewards for herself and for her party, surely no one deserved them more. All Prime Ministers need some luck if they are to be successful, but they have to use it to advantage when given the opportunity. Margaret Thatcher certainly did so in the Falklands War.

In political and parliamentary terms, as I have already intimated, I have always dreaded the month of July since so many dramatic political events seem to occur in that period before Parliament rises for the long summer recess. In Harold Macmillan's day there was the 'night of the long knives' reshuffle in 1962. Alec Douglas-Home had resigned as Conservative Party Leader in July 1965. I had had the major Belfast bombing and Operation Motorman in July 1972. In July 1981 there had been the appalling week of the riots. And so, as 1982 came along, I wondered what would happen that July. I did not have long to wait and, alas for me, the incident was one of those totally unpredictable events that plague a Home Secretary's life.

On Friday 9 July a man called Fagan was arrested in Buckingham Palace after entering the Queen's bedroom. Mercifully, the Queen was totally unharmed and indeed showed remarkable courage and calm in dealing with this extraordinary incident.

My first reaction on being told the news was one of intense relief that the Queen was unharmed. Indeed, that feeling so dominated my mind that I did not at first appreciate the full horror of the whole affair. On Saturday 10 July I was due to go to Glenalmond School in Perthshire to attend the annual school prize-giving. I was looking forward to this as a somewhat special occasion, for my father had been in the school and I had never visited it. All my emotional feelings at never having known my father were aroused and so I was preparing my speech with special care. I became so absorbed in this immediate event that I doubt if anyone present on that Saturday afternoon could have realized the other preoccupations on my mind.

Anyway, all the necessary police action had been taken and police inquiries had been set in hand. There was really nothing else immediately to be done. It seemed likely that the story would leak in the Press over the weekend, but it was clear to me that if it did not, then I should have to give the news to Parliament on Monday. Clearly the terms of any such announcement needed discussion between the

Palace and my Home Office officials in the first case.

In fact the story did not break until Monday morning. Over the weekend I began to feel in turn both amazed and furious that such a failure in the security surrounding Her Majesty should have occurred. But it was not until the news broke in the Monday morning papers that the full horror of the incident hit me. Then I felt deeply distressed that I personally, as Home Secretary, should have failed the Queen so dismally. I kept on contemplating the awful possibility that Her Majesty might have been injured in some way. Indeed, my feelings of dismay were such that I felt I must immediately go and see the Prime Minister, and I asked my Private Secretary to arrange the meeting as soon as possible. The Prime Minister's office confirmed that she would see me at once, and so I drove from the Home Office to No. 10, at that time utterly determined to resign at once.

As always on such occasions, the Prime Minister was kind and reassuring. She and all those around her told me that any such action would be absurd. Above all, the Queen was unharmed. And anyway the Home Secretary could not be regarded as directly responsible for the operational action of members in the organizations for which he had overall responsibility. Similar arguments had been put to me earlier by my Ministers and officials at the Home Office. My feelings of utter shame and misery were not assuaged, but I accepted their general advice and resolved to face Parliament and the Press furore which would certainly follow. When it did, I was much comforted by a message from one of my friends. It said, 'Don't be silly and resign. After all, if the Queen and the Prime Minister had wanted a Home Secretary who would be quick and agile in patrolling the Palace grounds and in pursuing and catching intruders, you would have been one of the last people that they would have considered. Thank goodness that is not your job.'

In Parliament I was at least able to tell the House that the Commissioner, David McNee, had immediately on the Friday appointed Deputy Assistant Commissioner Dellow to conduct an urgent inquiry. Furthermore, Mr Dellow had already submitted an interim report and had promised a further one later in the week. I told the House that I would also make a further statement at that time. The reaction in the House was predictably one of relief at the Queen being safe, and at the same time one of complete shock that such an appalling failure of the security arrangements surrounding Her Majesty could have occurred.

The next day there were some demands for my resignation in the Press, particularly of course from those who anyway wanted to get rid of me. Some parliamentary Press writers also stated that they were dissatisfied with my statement in the House, and one said that it had not 'lived up to the level of events'. I met him shortly afterwards and asked him if he would tell me what words in the English language would actually have met his criteria. Of course there was no answer. Sometimes it is quite easy to be a parliamentary critic from the gallery.

It was without doubt the unhappiest moment in my parliamentary career, but my friends in all parts of the House were understanding and their kindness did much to improve my morale. I knew that I would continue to be harshly criticized and derided by some sections of the Press and that I would have to face another important test when I came to make a full report later. Little did I know that before that happened I would have suffered another severe embarrassment.

After the Fagan episode I looked forward to an annual occasion which gave me much pleasure, a weekend visit to the Open Golf Championship, that year at Troon in Ayrshire. I spent a happy weekend and flew back to London on the Sunday night ready to face a week in which I would make a parliamentary statement on Palace security. When I reached the Home Office at about 9 a.m. on the Monday morning, my Permanent Secretary, Brian Cubbon, came in to see me looking very serious. Without more ado he told me that Commander Trestrail, the Queen's police officer, had confessed to having a homosexual relationship over a number of years with a prostitute. He had resigned from the Metropolitan Police. I was so upset that I could hardly believe this unwelcome news. I knew that Commander Trestrail was highly regarded by the Queen, and indeed by all at the Palace. I personally knew him and admired his work. Worse still, the Queen had been in hospital over the weekend having a wisdom tooth taken out. It was all very bad news at a particularly difficult moment and I felt awful that once again the Queen, of all people, had been worried in this way.

I went immediately to see the Prime Minister because I felt strongly that after the Fagan incident I must report this news to Parliament at once. Of course such publicity was bound to be distasteful to the Queen and the Palace, but there would be a far worse reaction if the news leaked out to the Press and the public through rumours – and probably distorted rumours at that. This would clearly have happened if nothing had been said. Everyone agreed and so, exactly a week after the Fagan incident, I was making yet another miserable statement. The House obviously appreciated a statement at the first opportunity and it appeared uneventful at the time.

Two of my answers, though, led to trouble in the Press. I was asked in Parliament when I had been told the news. Perfectly honestly, I replied at 9.15 that morning. When it was discovered that Commander Trestrail had resigned on the Saturday, some Press comment made a story of the fact that I had not been told immediately while I was away in Scotland. But there was no action I could have taken before Monday. Commander Trestrail was the Queen's police officer and Her Majesty clearly had to be told first, even though she was still in hospital.

The trouble over the second answer was caused through a stupid personal mistake on my part. I was asked if Commander Trestrail had been positively vetted. I replied correctly that he had been. No one in Parliament asked me when that vetting had taken place. The fact was that when Commander Trestrail was appointed to his task, Royal Protection Officers were not on the list of those who had to be positively vetted. The procedure had recently been changed. As a result, he had only been vetted some three to four months earlier. This was discovered in Press circles and before 7 a.m. the following morning I was rung up at home. I woke up angry at being disturbed, because I was anyway feeling dispirited and tired. A young reporter asked me why I had not told Parliament that Commander Trestrail had only been positively vetted three to four months ago. Normally I would have told him politely to ring up the Home Office Press Department, which would have been the correct procedure. But in a fury I replied curtly, 'Because nobody asked me', and put down the telephone. That day the *Evening Standard* came out with the headline 'Home Secretary says, "Nobody asked me" '. I realized that such an answer would be damaging in the eyes of the Press, however understandable in parliamentary terms. Quite rightly my valued Press Officer at the Home Office, Donald Grant, was most upset that I had failed to follow our normal procedure, which would have saved a great deal of trouble.

That same Tuesday we had a long meeting in'the Home Office considering the parliamentary statement on Palace security which I had promised for the next day, Wednesday 21 July. As we were in the middle of it there occurred a loud bang, which was obviously an explosion and which appeared to come from the Buckingham Palace area. Within a few minutes we were informed that a bomb had exploded as the mounted squadron of the Queen's Household Cavalry was passing through Hyde Park on its way to taking up guard duty and that a number of soldiers and several horses had been killed.

On top of everything else this really was the last straw. For a moment I felt that I could bear the strain of these continuous blows no longer. Just for a few minutes my usual determination to maintain outwardly good morale at moments of real trial broke, and that must have been obvious to all my Ministers and officials at the meeting. Indeed, I think they felt the same. However, we had to recover quickly and immediately started drafting the statement which I would have to make in Parliament that afternoon.

Subsequently we found that it would also have to include reference to another bomb, which had tragically exploded in the bandstand in Regent's Park and caused more casualties. The unity of the House of Commons at such awful moments of IRA violence can be a source of encouragement, and I sensed that there was in addition a genuine feeling of sympathy for me as I made yet another miserable statement.

The next day, Wednesday 21 July, I made my promised statement on Palace security. I announced that Lord Bridge, Chairman of the Security Commission, would investigate the security aspects of Commander Trestrail's case. On Palace security I expanded on Mr Dellow's report and on his conclusions. I announced the various disciplinary actions which had been taken as far as some of the police officers in the incident were concerned. I told the House that I accepted the Commissioner's proposal that the protection of Her Majesty The Queen, other members of the Royal Family and their residences would in future be the single responsibility of a Deputy Assistant Commissioner reporting directly to the Commissioner. I announced that Deputy Assistant Commissioner Colin Smith was being appointed to this new post. I also informed the House that a permanent group consisting of representatives of the Royal Households, the Police, the Household Division and the Property Services Agency, chaired by a senior Home Office official, would meet regularly to examine the effectiveness of the security arrangements.

The House properly subjected me to detailed and searching questions which reflected the great anxiety at this major security failure. I felt that the statement and the question period went reasonably well. I was, however, most touched and encouraged when I received a generous note of congratulations from the Queen's Private Secretary, Philip Moore. Actually, he had himself been a tower of strength and a great help and support to me throughout the whole awful period.

Looking back, historians may wonder why an event which actually had no immediate effect at all could have created quite so much anguish and furore. I think it must have been due to the feeling of what might have happened, which had hit me so hard at first. In truth, today it all seems too bizarre to have been possible. Indeed, if anyone had written a novel based on the whole story, it would have been ridiculed as too absurd and impossible. Yet it actually happened.

What a fortnight – even in the life of a Home Secretary.

Home Office Affairs

In the meantime, routine Home Office matters went on. My association with broadcasting dated back to my appointment as Opposition Chief Whip in 1964. In that capacity I was directly concerned with the organization of party political broadcasts, plans for party broadcasts at general elections and all the problems of alleged party political bias. As a result I got to know well the leaders of the BBC and the IBA, such as Hugh Carleton Greene at the BBC and Robert Fraser, who was really the architect of the IBA and contributed so much to independent television generally. My dealings with them fired me with an interest in the organization of our broadcasting system in Britain. I developed a great admiration for the way in which our public service broadcasting had been developed. I remain a staunch supporter of it today and know that many people, both in this country and all over the world, share my feelings. Certainly it has grown up as a remarkable British compromise, with public service broadcasting by the BBC facing competition from the growth of independent broadcasting.

The organization of the BBC and the IBA ensures broadcasting standards which are the envy of many other countries. As for political bias I have been, as Chief Whip, at the receiving end of many complaints and involved in numerous arguments. Of course there will always be justified complaints, but there are also a large number which arise from the undoubted truth that there is a measure of bias in the eye of the beholder. There will always be strong political feelings, because television is so potent at influencing opinion, but it is a fact that complaints to the authorities come almost equally from the respective political parties. Nor does the stubborn refusal of some party activists to accept the validity of this argument make it any the less true. Certainly there are justified complaints about the content of programmes from many different points of view. I am, however, not one of those people who believe that these could ever be eradicated by adaptation of the regulatory system. For all these reasons I will always remain sceptical of proposals for change. In a difficult field we should be most careful not to endanger what we have achieved.

Shortly after I became Conservative spokesman on Home Affairs I was delighted when Lord Annan published his historic report on broadcasting in March 1977, expressing confidence in the performances of both the BBC and the IBA. It rejected any idea that they should be broken up and recommended the continuance of the life of the IBA until December 1996.

The Annan Report underlined the importance of the public service responsibilities of broadcasters and the need to secure a balance of programming that responded to minority audiences as well as to a commercially driven mass market. It proposed a new and stronger Broadcasting Complaints Commission to replace the existing machinery which no longer carried public confidence. It also proposed that in bringing into operation the then unused 'fourth channel' we should look to create something different from the existing BBC and IBA structure. Lord Annan's aim was to bring new producers, methods and ideas into programme-making and to provide further services to cater for specialist interests.

I strongly agreed with all these conclusions. I was less happy, however, with the structures that the Annan Committee proposed for putting the ideas into effect. I made this clear very early, on behalf of my colleagues, in a major statement on 24 March 1977. I rejected Lord Annan's view that a new Open Broadcasting Authority be created to manage the fourth channel, and also his proposal that a Local Broadcasting Authority should be set up to manage local radio in place of existing BBC and independent services. It seemed to me from the outset quite unnecessary to create these major new bureaucracies. I also felt that both the BBC and independent local radio services had proved their viability and their diversity. The case was not for their replacement by a new structure but rather for strengthening the existing system and extending it to other areas. It was that which I was determined to achieve.

The Labour Government presented a White Paper in response to Lord Annan in July 1978. It did not legislate upon it. Despite Merlyn Rees's initial doubts, the Labour Party later moved towards support for an Open Broadcasting Authority.

I had a good deal of time to develop my ideas on the best future broadcasting structure, and we were able to enter into office with detailed proposals for reform. Soon after I became Home Secretary I set out our philosophy in a lecture to the Royal Television Society in September 1979. The positive reception it received convinced me that we had been working along the right lines.

Our major broadcasting Bill was presented to Parliament

on 18 February 1980. I was aiming to achieve four main objectives. First, we extended the life of the IBA to 1996 as Lord Annan had recommended, with an option to extend it further by Order. This would provide much-needed stability to television broadcasting, which had been damaged by uncertainty over the future of both major services. I certainly accepted the underlying premise of Lord Annan that there should be a further review of broadcasting structure at the end of that time. However, I was convinced that the quality of product delivered through the IBA structure fully justified the extension of its life.

Our second major step was to revise the financing of local radio. The details of this are not important but our action reflected my personal commitment to maintaining and expanding thriving BBC and commercial local radio services throughout the country. In my time at the Home Office I approved the creation of thirty new local stations, doubling the previous size of the commercial network and increasing the number of BBC stations by 50 per cent.

The Broadcasting Act also created the independent Broadcasting Complaints Commission which Lord Annan had recommended to deal with complaints of unjust or unfair treatment or infringement of privacy in programmes broadcast by both BBC and ITV companies. This was an overdue improvement on the previous system. The Commission came into being in June 1981 and has worked well in practice.

However, the main feature of the Act was the creation of Channel 4. I suppose there is no decision that I made in my political career that has had more of an impact on the daily life of families in Britain. One of my main reasons for rejecting Lord Annan's proposal for an Open Broadcasting Authority was my feeling that such an authority could never be financially viable. There would have been clear risks in creating an authority directly appointed, and funded to a substantial degree, by Government. I wanted to create a channel that would foster greater, rather than lesser, independence and variety in broadcasting. I was determined to avoid the creation of a new bureaucracy. For that reason we decided to vest responsibility for the channel in the IBA.

This was to be created on a new model. The IBA would have to establish a subsidiary for administering Channel 4 with the duty to obtain programmes and to plan schedules. It would emphatically not, however, become a programme-making organization itself. In order to avoid dominance of the new channel by the ITV companies, I also incorporated in the Act strict safeguards to ensure that significant proportions of Channel 4 programmes would come from independent producers; would appeal to tastes and interests not generally catered for by the existing ITV service; would be experimental and innovative; and would be of an educational nature. These guidelines were important, but I did not want to be too prescriptive. I believed that it must be for the IBA itself to meet effectively the objectives we had set out.

There was a particular problem over broadcasting in Wales. Lord Annan had recommended a separate fourth service in Welsh. My colleagues in Wales did not consider that the proportion of Welsh speakers could justify delivering the whole new channel in the Welsh language. I therefore proposed safeguards in the Bill requiring the IBA to ensure that at least twelve hours a week of programmes broadcast in Wales should be in Welsh. Taken in common with BBC broadcasts, that would mean up to twenty hours of air time in Welsh. Our aim was to foster the further development of the Welsh language, while not consuming so many hours of air time that many good commercially produced English programmes might never be scheduled in Wales.

This proposal was violently opposed by Welsh Nationalists and indeed by many people outside their ranks, particularly in Welsh-speaking Wales. The former Welsh Nationalist Leader, Gwynfor Evans, went on hunger strike and had considerable personal support. Eventually Cledwyn Hughes, whom I regarded highly, led an important delegation to see me, consisting of the Archbishop of Wales, Dr G.O. Williams, and Sir Goronwy Daniel, former Permanent Secretary of the Welsh Office and Principal of the University College of Wales. All were highly respected figures in Wales. They persuaded me that it would really cause much bitterness and anger in Wales if we persisted with our plan. I thus persuaded my colleagues that we should abandon it. A Welsh television channel of its own was therefore established offering twenty-two hours of Welsh-language programmes each week. This channel has been a great success and for once I have reason to be glad that I bowed to pressure, not a usual experience.

Channel 4 came into being in November 1982. It soon became evident that producers had taken literally our encouragement of the experimental and the innovative. One of my critics said that I had been responsible for 'letting the loonies on the air'. But all new organizations have to test the bounds of what is open to them and to find their feet in action. In the event, Jeremy Isaacs and his team were seen to have done an outstanding job. The diversity of programmes has, in my view, greatly enriched British broadcasting. Today, there are few who dispute that Channel 4 provides a service of the highest quality and has brought a great deal of new talent into broadcasting.

Initially I kept quiet when I heard voluble criticism of Channel 4, sometimes from my own colleagues. But steadily my confidence in its future success grew, and today I feel very pleased about its achievements. I only hope that in any future changes its distinctive contribution will be preserved.

That leads me to the present time. Of course there are inevitably going to be great changes in broadcasting with the advent of cable and satellite television. I was well aware before I left the Government that my colleagues regarded me as a recalcitrant figure living obstinately in the past as far as broadcasting was concerned. This accusation has some truth in it, but it is not wholly correct. I am fearful of some of the ideas being put forward because I do not want to destroy a much-admired broadcasting system before we are quite certain of what we want to put in its place. I am also disturbed by talk of achieving higher standards in programmes at the same time as proposals are introduced leading to deregulation and greater financial competition, because I cannot believe that they are basically compatible. In any event, I find it hard to understand what is supposed to be so wrong with our present arrangements.

On the other hand, despite these anxieties I am totally prepared to face changes which are made in order to cater for new technological developments in cable and satellite. I just do not believe that we know enough about these yet to be certain as to what we ought to do.

Immigration policy was another headache during my term as Home Secretary. It had already presented us with problems of party management in Opposition. In this way the issue was similar to our previous internal difficulties over Rhodesia in the late 1960s.

The basic division of opinion in the country on the emotional issues of colour also divided our own Conservative Party. There was unanimous agreement on the need for firm control of future immigration. Indeed, it was extraordinary in 1979 to look back to the introduction of the Commonwealth Immigrants Act in 1962. Then the Labour Party had been totally united in passionate opposition to its passage and pledged itself to repeal it. Many in our own party had grave reservations about the Act, so much so that the Conservative Government at that time was anxious about its ability to get the legislation through Parliament. The Labour Government after 1964 not only did not attempt to redeem its pledge to repeal the Act, but in 1968 introduced further strict controls on East African Asians in Jim Callaghan's Bill. By 1979 opposition to the Commonwealth Immigrants Act had been conveniently forgotten. Few, certainly in the Conservative Party, would readily admit that they had ever been opposed to it seventeen years earlier. But difficulties arose when it came to balancing the extent of the restrictions with the promises given to immigrants' families by previous Conservative Governments. We had produced a policy in Opposition which was included in our 1979 election manifesto. This was broadly acceptable to our party as a balanced compromise. But I knew that putting it into operation through legislation would certainly cause us emotional difficulties and divisions of opinion. These would be hard to resolve and so time for careful consideration was necessary.

We did, however, have to hand one potential area where legislation was urgent and would attract substantial support. Edward Gardner had chaired the committee which produced a report on a future Nationality Act. He was a respected figure in the Party and was subsequently a great help to me as Chairman of our party's Home Affairs Committee. We concluded that we should introduce a new Nationality Bill as soon as possible. It was bound to be a major and complicated measure and was therefore suitable for introduction as early in a new Parliament as possible.

No Government had attempted to tackle the difficult question of what should constitute British nationality since the 1940s. The Attlee Government had adopted criteria which were wildly optimistic, both in terms of the breadth of citizenship envisaged and in the expectation that there would be no major movement in world population from continent to continent. By the 1950s and 1960s the advent of the jet airliner and the consequent expansion of intercontinental travel totally changed the whole scene. Many thousands of families came to Britain from what had been the Empire. They settled in this country and established themselves as full citizens.

Soon successive Governments of both major parties recognized that an island as densely populated as Britain simply could not sustain the levels of settlement that we were experiencing. The new Nationality Act acknowledged that circumstances had changed, and it redefined rights in a way which reinforced the position of those who had settled in Britain. At the same time it avoided the absurd position under the Attlee legislation whereby new rights to citizenship were acquired generation after generation by millions of people living thousands of miles from British shores. The British Nationality Act was therefore a much-needed and valuable measure which I believe will stand the test of time. Timothy Raison eventually guided it through Parliament in 1981 with skill and patience.

We had set up a new citizenship with consequent rights, but the Nationality Bill was not in itself an immigration measure. Therefore during the passage of the Bill we made it clear that we would look again at the particular provisions in the immigration rules which referred to citizenship of the United Kingdom and its colonies.

We consequently published a White Paper in October 1982 setting out our proposed new rules. They were debated in the House of Commons thereafter and caused me considerable difficulty. The White Paper itself was debated on 11 November 1982, and the particular rules were debated on a prayer – a parliamentary procedure whereby the Opposition can challenge action taken by the Government under delegated powers – on 15 December, when the Government was defeated. Finally, after some slight amendments, new rules were brought forward and accepted on 15 February 1983.

The main argument concerned the position of husbands and male fiancés coming into Britain. This had long been a vexed question, because of the arranged marriage system widely practised in the Indian subcontinent. There was clear evidence that this procedure had been used extensively as a means for men to obtain settlement in this country by marriage, thus evading immigration control, and so enter our jobs market by the back door. The right of men to marry and to bring in wives had been established in the 1971 Act and was not contested.

It had become clear by this time that the serious discrimination in the rules between the absolute right of British male citizens automatically to introduce their wives and confer citizenship on them, purely by token of marriage, and the limits on the rights of female citizens to introduce husbands was causing distress. We therefore took the opportunity of an enforced change in the rules in order to bring the language into line with the British Nationality

Act. We proposed to allow British citizen wives to introduce husbands to citizenship, but at the same time insisted on certain safeguards to prevent bogus arranged marriages being used as a means to evade entry controls.

I realized that the Opposition parties did not share our concern, because they took a much more relaxed view about the entry of husbands and male fiancés than did those of us in the Government. The critics on our own back-benches, however, suspected and disliked the proposed new rules, objecting to what they saw as the relaxation of the tough line against the abuse of arranged marriages. We in the Government, and indeed many on our own back-benches, considered that the safeguards written into the rules for marriage candidates were adequate. And so we concluded that it was right to make the change and to extend the rights of female British citizens.

During the general debate on the rules, the Government was therefore criticized by two absolutely opposing factions – on the one hand, by the Opposition parties who were prepared to see an increased entry of husbands and male fiancés and, on the other, by our critics on the back-benches who feared that the new rules would allow in too many husbands and male fiancés. By the time we came to debate the rules on the prayer a few weeks later, these diametrically opposed factions had made common ground. In the event, this remarkable coalition succeeded in defeating the Government for the only time in the Commons that Parliament. New rules had then to be introduced after the forthcoming Christmas recess. I made some minor changes and, with some forceful help from my ministerial colleagues, our back-bench critics in the main decided this time to support the rules and they were passed. They justified this action by the need to avoid continuing party controversy as a general election approached.

It was an unhappy episode from my point of view. But on reflection I do believe that the change we made was right and that the new rules have not, in the event, produced the trouble that was predicted. As Home Secretary I also had to accept that in making a decision I was likely to face a split either way. Failure to adapt the rules in line with the British Nationality Act would have caused even greater trouble from a large section of the Party.

Once again emotional arguments over immigration, with all its racial implications, had been an inevitable part of the Home Secretary's life. Moreover, it was one that had to be faced. But I do resent the speeches and comments of those who consistently pretend that all these problems could have been avoided. They know perfectly well that our difficulties in a small, overcrowded island stem from our imperial past. They also know that we have had consequent responsibility to people in many parts of the world who were suffering from oppression and bitter conflict in their home countries. Previous Governments and Parliaments had in fact fulfilled their duty to people in this awful position and had allowed them to enter Britain. Therefore our predecessors had willed the end and thereafter successive Governments and Parliaments had to will the means.

We have also to face the fact that on occasions we as a nation have recruited people from the British Commonwealth to carry out unpopular jobs here at a time of job shortages. In doing so we welcomed them to our shores. Such people have settled here and brought up families in due course. Their children now know no other home. Surely they are entitled to be full British citizens and to be treated as such. Talk of an alternative of repatriation is as impractical as it is insulting and divisive. The answer has to be strict rules on immigration fairly enforced. It is only against this background that any efforts at improving race relations can succeed. All the fury of the critics has never convinced me that there is any other sensible course of action for Britain to follow.

I shall now refer as a matter of history to my short and wholly unsuccessful effort to reform Section 2 of the Official Secrets Act. I do so in the hope that the account of such an unhappy personal experience might have some relevance to current discussions on this vexed issue. It still remains one of those tiresome problems which is so difficult to face and yet which will not go away.

In 1979 there seemed to me to be a good opportunity for action. The issue was carefully studied under Ted Heath's Government by the prestigious Franks Committee. Lord Franks reported in 1972 and recommended a reduction in the scope of the criminal law in relation to official secrets. However, the Labour Government of 1974–9 failed to reform the law in this area. Yet the Franks Committee recommendation was a basic agreement which it ought to have been possible to use as a starting point. On the one hand, few would question that it is essential for matters prejudicial to national security to remain confidential. At the other extreme, few would argue in favour of the existing terms of Section 2 of the Official Secrets Act 1911, which implies that everything a Crown servant learns in the course of his duty is official and subject to secrecy, whatever its nature and whatever its source. Furthermore, we had made it clear in Opposition that we believed that an overhaul of the law was long overdue. More important, the outgoing Labour Government had recently published a White Paper in July 1978.

All this seemed to provide some possibility for the

development of a consensus if a Bill was introduced. Of course I should have remembered from my own experience that the members of an outgoing Government beaten at an election are unlikely to feel committed to some of the difficult proposals made when they were still in Government. Frankly, there is no good reason why they should feel so committed. Nor should I have forgotten the obvious ambivalent attitude of the Press. They dislike the ineffective Section 2 of the Officials Secrets Act in principle, but actually they are even more basically hostile to an effective replacement provision which might be used more frequently for prosecution. Nor can any approach to the subject disregard the fundamental conflict between a Government, which inevitably believes that some secrets have to be protected in the national interest, and the ever-increasing demands of a media hungry for freedom of information.

I soon learnt these lessons in 1979 and another important one in addition. Whatever agreement there may be in principle, the real conflict and difficulties arise as soon as the details are discussed. This was clearly evident on the second reading on the Protection of Official Information Bill in the House of Lords on 5 November 1979.

Quintin Hailsham, then Lord Chancellor, and my Home Office Minister, John Belstead, did their powerful best as Government speakers. But the critics abounded and the second reading debate, which ended in accordance with House of Lords custom with an unopposed second reading, served only to prove that the committee stage would be an extremely difficult and even painful process for the Government. It also proved that the Bill had been introduced without sufficient consultation either within Parliament or with major media interests outside. Personally I plead guilty, as I was clearly responsible for this failure.

At this moment what became known as the Blunt Affair blew up. Inevitably it created a furore and set off a bout of secrets mania. In the hectic atmosphere of the time the Government rightly decided that it was not possible to proceed constructively with discussion of the Protection of Official Information Bill as it stood. It was therefore withdrawn on 20 November both unwanted and unsung.

The whole issue of official secrets has also to be seen against the background of the 1988 *Spycatcher* issue which, in my opinion, occupied far too much time and attention. I hold strongly to the view that those who work in our intelligence service owe a lifelong duty of secrecy to the nation. Otherwise they have it in their power to damage our country's interests and also, on occasions, to undermine the position of those who are continuing to work in the service. For this reason I remain convinced that the Government was right to pursue Peter Wright in the Australian courts and to continue its legal proceedings right up to the House of Lords. In the final event there can be no doubt that the House of Lords judgment upheld the basic position which the Government took throughout. I did, however, regret some of the comments about Robert Armstrong's visit to Australia. No one could deny that he was an absolutely outstanding civil servant and that no better representative or witness could possibly have gone to Australia. But as head of the Civil Service he was placed in an invidious position which inevitably enabled the Australians to indulge themselves in their favourite pastime of 'Pommy-bashing'. In my view Robert Armstrong only enhanced his high reputation by the stoic and good-humoured way in which he weathered the storm of critical comment.

These unfortunate experiences have convinced me of the need to compromise as the proposed new Bill proceeds through Parliament. The Government must have the right to protect some secrets in the national interest, but it must limit its requirements to what is strictly necessary. This commitment must be backed by a drive throughout the entire Government against any action to cover up errors with pleas of secrecy. As a result of a long ministerial career, I have come to the conclusion that accusations of such bogus secrecy are wildly exaggerated. But I suppose it is the essence of such activity that it may be conducted without ministerial knowledge.

On the other side, the very success of investigative journalism has whetted the insatiable appetite of the media generally. I recognize that journalists generally believe that, unless the battle against Government secrecy is constantly waged, the freedom of the Press would be endangered. I wish I could convince them in return that a sensible relationship over political stories, combined with less harrying of public figures in their private lives, could – and should – be achieved. In the meantime, the first requirement is that a Bill on official secrecy should be taken through Parliament in a spirit of compromise. Those who are out of Government at the moment should remember that if they achieve their aim of returning to power they in turn will need to preserve some secrets in the national interest.

As the years have passed I have had the chance to reflect on my four years as Home Secretary. My main reaction is one of gratitude. I feel that it was a great honour to preside over this historic department of State with its long-standing traditions.

In particular, it was a real privilege for me to welcome Her Majesty The Queen on her visit to the Home Office on 25 March 1982 to mark the department's 200th anniversary.

Such a visit is a great moment for a Government department and, as always, the Queen's presence was an inspiration to all who shared in it. Her Majesty unveiled a commemorative plaque and talked to many of those who worked in the department. I suppose the Queen's remarkable and detailed knowledge of any subject should not be surprising, in view of her experience over the years, but her understanding of places, people and their problems has never ceased to amaze me. Personally, I soon learnt that it is extremely unwise to attempt a bluff of any sort with Her Majesty. The wise course of action is never to pretend that you know an answer unless you are totally sure of it. If you do not know, admit it quickly, otherwise you will certainly be caught out in the most charming manner.

Despite the inevitable trials and tribulations I was extremely happy at the Home Office and greatly appreciated the support and friendship of my Ministers and of many dedicated civil servants. The names of some of those most closely associated with me are referred to by name in various accounts, but I feel I must record a special debt of gratitude to my Principal Private Secretaries, John Chilcot, John Halliday and Tony Rawsthorne, throughout these years. Many others worked in my Private Office and many senior officials gave me invaluable help and advice. I shall always be indebted to them all.

Naturally I have mixed feelings about the overall effect of my time at the Home Office. Perhaps inevitably, all Home Secretaries feel frustrated when they are remembered for the troubles they faced, which have overshadowed their positive achievements. For example, I suppose I am bound to be associated with the 1981 riots, with difficult Tory party conference debates and perhaps, more absurdly, with Fagan getting into Buckingham Palace.

But I assess my time in terms of some real achievements, much unfinished business with hopes unfulfilled, as well as cases where hopes were dashed through errors on my part. I would claim as my most fundamental achievement the increase in police strength and the improvements in police morale following the decision to implement immediately in full the Edmund-Davies police pay award in 1979. I believe that following the riots in 1981, fundamental and lasting improvements were made in police organization, equipment, training and tactics in relation to civil disturbances. On the other hand, I regret in general that the increase in police numbers and the improved status of police officers in the community has not led to a consequent increase in police effectiveness and efficiency in the eyes of the general public. Certainly strenuous efforts have been made by many senior police officers, but I do not think that any of them can be wholly satisfied with the results.

I personally am particularly disappointed with the effects of the Police and Criminal Evidence Act. Perhaps it is much too early to form a judgment on the achievements of such a recent Act. My doubts probably arise because I was so sure that it was right at the time of its introduction. It was based on the outstanding report of the Philips Royal Commission on Criminal Procedure. The Bill was brilliantly conducted through Parliament by my Minister of State, Patrick Mayhew. Indeed, because of the general election in 1983, it had two careful scrutinies. Many of its provisions were widely accepted and in theory they should have contributed to better relations between police and public. So far this does not seem to have happened. Indeed, the Act tends to be blamed in police circles for increased bureaucracy, wasting valuable police time on the streets in pursuit of criminals. I do hope that it will not develop in this way, and that police procedures can be sensibly adapted to meet its requirements more swiftly and with less bureaucracy.

Second, I am convinced that I was right in my early decisions on prison building, prison maintenance and the working of the prison system. At least I can claim to have reversed the years of neglect in these areas. It is all too true, however, that Rome was not built in a day, and much remains to be done.

There is, however, another side to the prisons where noticeable success has eluded everyone. This relates to the serious overcrowding which continues to threaten, and indeed to nullify, measures for prison improvement and reform. Of course it is difficult to keep numbers sent to prison in check at a time of rising crime. Inevitably public reaction is to keep all criminals off the streets and out of the way. However, as always, the issue of sentencing is more complex than it might at first appear. I am a firm believer in the principle that each individual should be treated on his or her merits. That is as true for the criminal as for any other member of society. Punishment should not only fit the crime, it must also be effective in dealing with the individual criminal. That is why we promised in our 1979 manifesto that the basis of our policy would be a search for 'more flexible, more effective sentencing'.

Any politician, particularly a Home Secretary, strays into this territory at some risk. Quite rightly, the judiciary is highly sensitive to any suggestion that its sentencing practice should be dictated by the Government. I believe that I never remotely put myself in such a position. But there was a time when Judge Pickles did accuse me of wielding a 'big stick' and of viewing the judiciary as 'a minor branch of the executive'. As, in the same speech, he also described me as 'kind, well-meaning and busy' I should probably not complain too much. Not all my critics have been so generous.

This judicial outburst came in October 1981 in the most delicate stage of development of our policy on sentencing. As I have described, one of my first priorities had been to rebuild morale in the prison service and begin a major prison building programme. I was prepared to this extent to agree with another comment from the same judge: 'It goes for us to decide who goes inside and for him to make the room.' But I did not feel we could stop there. I also wanted my officials to study how effective different sentences were and to try new ways of dealing with offenders. All the main measures in my criminal justice legislation were designed to extend the range of penalties available to the courts.

Britain puts far more petty offenders into prison than other comparable countries. I found that far too many people were going into prison who might have been better treated outside; far too many were also staying inside longer than was needed. In some cases our overcrowded prisons were becoming breeding grounds for crime. My aim was a sentencing structure which, while recognizing that custody may be essential, ensured that it should be used only where necessary. In adopting that policy I was looking for a double benefit – punishment that fitted the offender as well as the crime, and fewer people in our overcrowded prisons.

My basic philosophy – that serious crime should merit long sentences, while for lesser criminals we should seek short sentences or alternatives to prison – was shared by senior members of the judiciary. Lord Chief Justice Lane gave clear guidance to this effect. In February 1981 I outlined my views in a speech to the Magistrates' Association. Prison overcrowding was very much in my mind at the time – and I said so. One of my difficulties in the course of the year was to be the confusion that arose in some people's minds between a policy that was genuinely designed to get out, or keep out, of prison those who need not be there, and the misguided view that we were somehow intent on opening the gates and reducing the number of prisoners at all costs.

Under the rules which were then operating it was not possible for parole to be extended to prisoners serving less than eighteen months. I thought it reasonable to float the idea of release under supervision for offenders in this category. This was at first reasonably well received, although Hugo Young in the *Sunday Times* came out with the rather depressing headline 'How will the judges defeat Mr Whitelaw?' This seemed at the time to be exaggeratedly pessimistic. None the less, it was in this area that as consultation continued I was to come up against the reaction from judges and magistrates that a policy of automatic supervised release would undermine the power of the courts to determine a sentence, and represented unacceptable interference by Government in sentencing policy. I was told that, far from reducing the prison population, we would find that the courts imposed longer sentences, taking the expectation of supervised release into account. I also faced criticism from the Conservative Party, where the false idea that we were about to let out prisoners indiscriminately had gained ground; this concern was undoubtedly one of the many underlying factors in the rough reception I received at the party conference in October 1981.

Whereas a Home Office report published that May had looked favourably on supervised release, I was forced to the conclusion by the autumn that the policy, though right in my view, was not feasible in the present climate. I therefore decided to adopt an alternative approach and to activate an unused part of the Criminal Justice Act 1977. This would allow the courts, when determining a sentence, to say that part of it only should be served inside, while part should be in the form of a suspended sentence. Up to this point courts could only suspend the *whole* of a prison sentence, a policy which unnecessarily denied them flexibility. The partially suspended sentence was different from supervised release in that no one could argue that the Government was intervening on sentencing policy; the decision would be entirely that of the court. I was confident that I could carry both magistrates and judiciary with me on this decision. On the other hand, no one could predict with certainty that it would have any substantial effect on the prison population.

It was in the light of this complicated, but important, debate that our Criminal Justice Act in 1982 extended even further the scope of the 1977 Act and enabled broad use of partially suspended sentences. It also brought in a range of other new options for the courts and abolished the outdated sentence of borstal training. For the first time we allowed the use of custodial sentences of less than three years, but more than six months, for young offenders, but insisted that these sentences should relate to detention centres or to youth custody rather than imprisonment. We also allowed sentences of as little as three weeks in detention centres, rather than the three months which was then the minimum. Finally, we introduced the concept of a residential care order for repeat offenders already in care, and extended the use of the highly successful community service orders. I ensured that Clause 1 of the Act contained the basic principle of my policy. No court should impose any custodial sentence on a young offender unless it was satisfied that no other method of dealing with him was appropriate. I am certain that in this, and in other items of legislation, we made considerable steps forward in making available to the courts a better range of sentencing. My policies were fiercely criticized by some at the time, but few now would want to reverse them.

Nevertheless, I still feel frustrated by my failure to get across the value of supervised release. I still wish that some variant of it might yet find favour. I appreciate that I must have mishandled the issue, for I united against it many people who were at the same time genuinely concerned with the problems of prison overcrowding. My disappointment with myself is all the greater since Douglas Hurd is today faced with an even higher prison population and hence a greater problem.

I cannot help ending consideration of this issue with the sad reflection that all too many people in positions of authority have turned their backs on the prison problems and prefer to look the other way. They appear to neglect the important contribution of a sensible sentencing and prison policy. If we persist in sending to prison large numbers of petty offenders, and indeed of non-violent offenders, we risk using our prisons for the wrong purpose. It has to be faced that sending some people to prison, particularly for the first time, can in fact recruit them to the ranks of criminals because of the associations that they have there. This is particularly true of prisons which are so overcrowded that there is little chance of using them as places for reform. No one is suggesting that violent criminals should not be sent to prison and kept there as long as is felt necessary. The public are owed such action and in general terms are increasingly receiving it. I cannot, at the same time, accept the simple demands for locking everyone up without any consideration of the type of offence they have committed. Yet that is the danger inherent in our present public attitude to our prisons.

Moving on to immigration, I believe that the Nationality Act has provided a sound and sensible basis for British citizenship in the future. I also believe that my immigration policies, which were at one time so hotly contested, have not turned out as the critics predicted, and that immigration numbers have steadily declined. That in itself seems to have led to a gradual improvement in race relations which is much to be welcomed. At least it seems hopeful that some of the emotion has gone out of both subjects.

Finally, on broadcasting, I take pleasure in the success of Channel 4 and the Welsh channel which I introduced. I hope that they will continue to be allowed to play their distinctive part in any future broadcasting arrangements. I appreciate that the introduction of satellite and cable broadcasting will necessitate changes. My only plea is that we do not rush into destroying our present system until we are certain that we can put something better and more in tune with modern developments in its place. For all its faults our system has many supporters both at home and abroad. Before we act, we want above everything else to be sure that change is our ally.

Leader of the Lords

At the beginning of 1983 the inevitable speculation about the date of the next general election started. It was then that I fully realized that I had spent nearly four years as Home Secretary. I knew all Prime Ministers rightly feel that changes in some of the major jobs in the Government are necessary, particularly at the start of a new Parliament.

I hated the idea of leaving the Home Office, despite all its trials and tribulations. I had been very happy there. I had a great regard for my officials. But in my heart I knew that a change would be right one way or another. I was somewhat battle-scarred and probably more tired than I knew. I was also just about to be sixty-five. I considered resigning from the House of Commons or staying there while sitting on the back-benches. There really were no other ministerial jobs which made sense for me. No one, including myself, could ever contemplate the possibility of making me Chancellor of the Exchequer. I would have hated being Foreign Secretary, because I dislike travel and much prefer this country to any other. I had been Leader of the House of Commons as far back as 1970 and so to return to that job would have been absurd.

During this time the Prime Minister and I had some general discussions about the election and indeed about the possibilities for the next Parliament. From these I discovered that she was considering asking me to be Leader of the House of Lords. I made it clear that of course I would do anything she wanted, but if I was not going to stand at the forthcoming election I ought to tell my constituency as soon as possible, since I had been MP there for twenty-eight years. But nothing was settled and so, when a general election looked imminent in the spring, I told the Prime Minister that I felt in the circumstances that I must stand.

However, I remained worried as far as my position in the constituency was concerned. At the recent redistribution a considerable area of Westmorland, north of Shap, had been added to my already vast constituency. This change was in some ways consequential on local government reorganization, as Cumberland and Westmorland had been amalgamated into Cumbria. My constituency, Penrith and the Border, was all in Cumberland, and the Westmorland area was in Michael Jopling's constituency. He was Government Chief Whip at the time. Both of us were totally opposed to the change, because the Westmorland area hated any idea of joining what had been a Cumberland constituency. The people there were extremely jealous of their Westmorland identity, and rightly so. Furthermore, they could not understand why the Home Secretary and the Government Chief Whip could not stop the Boundary Commissioner's report from going through if they really wanted to. They simply were not prepared to accept that it was part of the whole procedure that the Boundary Commission reports were not interfered with in such a way. They therefore blamed us both, and probably me in particular, for the change. I knew that I would receive a rather hostile reception from the Appleby area as a result. Furthermore, the Liberal candidate, Michael Young, had started to make mischief out of the inevitable rumours that I might be retiring after the election or indeed going to the House of Lords. Neither the Prime Minister nor I was in a position to deny such suggestions categorically, even if they were in fact no more than intelligent speculation.

I decided that I had to fight a hard election campaign and be in the vicinity far more than in previous elections. I therefore spent a great deal of time touring the area. Soon I discovered that my fears were justified. My reception in the Westmorland area was not as good as it should have been at a time when the Conservative Party was obviously doing well. Nor was it as good, perhaps naturally, as in my old constituency in Cumberland.

Our Penrith and Border count was once again held on the morning after the election. And so on Friday 10 June I learnt that my majority was well over 15,000. On the face of it this was a good result and my supporters were well pleased. Personally I was less happy. I knew that in the larger constituency my majority should have been higher, and that the largely increased Liberal vote meant that the Westmorland area had not supported me as strongly as they might have. I certainly did not bear any grudge against them for this. I fully understood the position, but of course it was one that I had hoped to avoid by my work during the election campaign.

I kept these private thoughts to myself as I set off that Friday afternoon for London and Downing Street. I turned my mind to my discussions with the Prime Minister on the future composition of the Cabinet. I realized that this time it would be different, because my own personal future would be a central factor.

It was clear that we had gained an overwhelming majority, even greater than we had expected in our most optimistic assessments. I knew that in these circumstances the Prime Minister would want me to become Leader of the Lords, because we both appreciated the increased importance of the Lords and the consequent difficulties of management which would arise from a large Commons majority.

When she asked me at our meeting if I was prepared to go to the Lords as Leader, I repeated my previous undertaking to do whatever she thought best, but I immediately warned her of my anxieties. Janet Young, the existing Leader of the Lords, was very popular and able, and I therefore feared that the peers might resent the imposition of a senior Cabinet Minister to take over from her. I appreciated that she would be very disappointed, and as I liked and admired her, I was unhappy about her position. Second, on my own personal grounds, I was not sure that I, who had spent twenty-eight years in the Commons, would necessarily adapt easily to the House of Lords, nor that I would be acceptable to the peers.

In the event Janet Young, who was naturally sad to give up the leadership, was appointed Minister of State at the Foreign Office. She would obviously have liked to remain in the Cabinet but at least Foreign Office work attracted her. She took her disappointment with characteristic understanding and became a tower of strength to me in her new position. I remain most grateful to her for her unfailing kindness in what could have been a difficult situation for us both.

Third, I remained anxious about a by-election in my constituency of Penrith and the Border when I was leaving the seat immediately after I had been elected. It would obviously be a difficult situation and I warned the Prime Minister of my anxieties about the result. Fortunately, the constituency chose an excellent person in David Maclean, who has already made a considerable mark in the House of Commons. He just managed to hold the seat at the by-election, when there was inevitably considerable dissatisfaction at my having left so soon after a general election and at having to fight the seat all over again. However, all was well – even if only just – in the end.

The Prime Minister appreciated all these problems but nevertheless felt that she wished to go ahead. She also indicated that she intended to revive hereditary peerages, which had last been given in 1964. She recommended to the Queen a viscountcy for George Thomas, the retiring Speaker of the Commons, as had been the tradition, and one for me – making us both Viscounts. I said that I greatly appreciated this kind gesture and the offer of such a particular honour in the circumstances. But I added that I would be perfectly happy to go to the Lords, as requested, with a life peerage as had all the others recently. I also reminded the Prime Minister that I had four daughters and no sons. However, she was in no way diverted by this. Subsequently I was asked by the Press why I had not pressed for a remainder which would allow my peerage to be passed down the female line. I replied firmly that I regarded such a suggestion as entirely inappropriate in the circumstances. Remainders had been granted recently only to outstanding war leaders, such as Lord Mountbatten, and I was certainly not in that position.

The next few days were spent in dealing with Garter, Principal King of Arms, the appropriate authority on the details of my peerage. Fortunately, there was no complication in my simply keeping the name Whitelaw. Penrith, as the main town in my constituency and the town closest to my home, seemed the obvious choice for what is known as the territorial designation that has to form part of any title.

These formalities normally take some time, but in my case speed was essential as I had to be introduced and take my seat before the opening of Parliament only a week later. By that time I had to be in place as Leader of the Lords. Thanks to much hard work by Colin Cole and his staff, I was able to be introduced in the House of Lords as Viscount Whitelaw of Penrith on Thursday 16 June.

For the introduction ceremony I had to have two sponsors of the same rank as myself. I was lucky to obtain the services of Viscount Rochdale, a distinguished Cumbrian and industrialist who was a close neighbour of ours, and of Viscount Eccles, a distinguished Conservative Cabinet Minister during my early parliamentary days. The introduction ceremony is colourful, formal and frightening, particularly if you are coming in as the Leader, as I was. The connoisseurs of the drill are highly critical of the performance of the new peer and his sponsors, and I certainly admit to having felt very much the new boy. It is strange that at every stage in one's life a new step brings with it its own apprehensions – school, university, Army, House of Commons and House of Lords all produced the same feelings for me.

I knew that first impressions in the House of Lords were important, because I appreciated that many of the peers would be suspicious of me. They would obviously fear that I would remain a House of Commons man and so seek to introduce into the House of Lords what could be described as Commons ways. I was determined to prove to them that I wanted to serve the House of Lords' interests first and foremost, and that I wished to learn my job from the beginning.

I found that this was doubly important because the Leader of the House of Lords occupies a very particular position. He is, of course, the Leader of the Government there and is responsible for getting the Government business through the House. But he has much wider responsibilities to the whole House. In particular, as there is no Speaker, he is ultimately responsible for the effective control of the business. I deliberately say 'ultimately' responsible, for the House of Lords rightly prides itself on its system of self-regulation.

Those who have been in the House of Commons are at first amazed that the system works, but they soon discover that it does. Certainly the business takes rather longer than it would if there were a Speaker but, so long as the peers as a whole want self-regulation and determine to work the system, it has many advantages for a revising chamber which is not the central battleground of party politics.

Even self-regulation, though, occasionally requires the use of authority and this is when the Leader of the House comes in. If his interventions are well timed and most politely phrased, they will be instantly accepted. But experience soon taught me that it was best to keep in tune with the mood of the House, and only to act when the speaker or the discussion was clearly wearying the House as a whole. Then, suitable phrases such as 'Your Lordships may feel that it is time to pass on to other business' or 'I hope that the noble Lord will feel that he has made his point' will be well received. I always erred on the side of caution and did not mind when I heard comments such as, 'I wish Willie would knock that old fool down.' After all I relied on the old fool's good will and the critics did not. At first I was extremely nervous and probably erred too much on the side of caution, but gradually I became both more courageous and perhaps a trifle more authoritarian as my confidence grew. Above all, the system works because it is an assembly which by nature is generous and kind. I soon learnt to my amazement that, unlike the House of Commons, most peers, including those on the Opposition benches, wished me well and wanted me to succeed as Leader. Furthermore, the corporate spirit of the House of Lords extends far beyond the members to the officials and staff. It is a friendly, and so basically a happy, establishment. In some ways I believe this is due to its sense of continuity which an elected chamber by its nature cannot possess.

I was very lucky in my colleagues and those who advised me. The Government Chief Whip is a crucially important figure in the House of Lords system. Lord Denham, the present Government Chief Whip, must have been specially made for the job. He has been a Lords Whip for over twenty-five years and has an unrivalled knowledge of the House of Lords and its procedures. He is particularly jealous of its rights and privileges. He has an unerring instinct for the moods of the House and for the likely attitude of its members from day to day. What is more, he hides all these qualities and an extremely acute brain under the cloak of natural charm and a splendid sense of humour. He was exactly the Chief Whip that I needed, for I trusted him implicitly and whenever I appeared to be in danger of reverting to type, as a House of Commons man, he applied a powerful rebuke in favour of the House of Lords traditions. He taught me that sometimes the Government would lose divisions in the House of Lords, usually when it deserved to do so. This lesson is difficult to learn for an ex-Commons Chief Whip. But as time went on it helped me in my dealings with my ministerial colleagues in the House of Commons. In all these ways Bertie Denham certainly ensured my great enjoyment of the job as Leader of the Lords.

He and I were well served in turn by two first-class young

officials as Secretary and Business Manager: David Beamish, incidentally BBC Mastermind victor in 1987, and Rhodri Walters respectively. We owed them a great deal. The Leader of the House also relies on the clerks and in particular the Clerk of Parliaments. When I became Leader, Peter Henderson, an outstanding Clerk of Parliaments over many years, was just about to retire. He was succeeded by John Sainty. Both of them gave me much wise advice.

I was lucky, also, that Lord Hailsham, a very old friend and ministerial colleague, was Lord Chancellor. He had been Leader of the House of Lords in his time and was greatly experienced in every field of Government. Additionally, Quintin Hailsham is always stimulating as a colleague – brilliant, mischievous, charming and infuriating in turns. But always he is there as a staunch friend and ally when required. No one could ask for more.

I was most fortunate to have John Belstead, a long-time friend and colleague in Ireland and at the Home Office, as my Deputy Leader. I am so pleased that he has now succeeded me as Leader and is in the Cabinet.

Such help is badly needed by a Leader in the Lords, for together with his overall responsibilities, he is largely judged by his ability to pilot the Government business through the House. He is the leader of a ministerial team which faces a major and often underestimated task.

There is usually only one Cabinet Minister, in addition to the Lord Chancellor and the Leader of the House, in the Lords. He is generally particularly busy in his department, as David Young is at present in the Department of Trade and Industry, and so is inevitably limited in the amount of time he can hope to give to the Lords' business. The main burden has to fall on the Ministers of State, Parliamentary Secretaries and the Whips. Most of them are likely to be young hereditary peers, for older members have business commitments or have come up from the House of Commons on at least semi political retirement. These Ministers have to face very experienced peers, many of whom have considerable knowledge in their own fields. Furthermore, most of the young Ministers have only limited political experience behind them. I have the highest admiration for those who served me, particularly for their mastery of many technical legislative measures. They work very long hours and no one could suggest that in financial terms they are well rewarded. But their work is crucial to the successful handling of the Government's business. Bertie Denham and I tried to bring on some new Ministers and both of us today are proud of their success.

Against this background I had to assess my prospects of carrying through the job that the Prime Minister required of me in the setting of a large Commons majority. There is no doubt that a Government which is dominant in the House of Commons tends to get its business through too easily. As a result, inevitably they seek to push through too much legislation too quickly. Frequently Bills come to the House of Lords ill-digested and certainly in need of amendment.

The House of Lords is well equipped to carry out this task provided it is given enough time, but it is part of the House of Lords' strength that its procedures cannot be unduly rushed. This soon means that House of Commons Ministers in charge of Bills get irritated and petulant with the House of Lords. Worse still, they find that their Bills are sometimes amended against their will by a defeat in the House of Lords.

I soon realized that I had one great advantage in dealing with the resulting strained relations between the two Houses. First of all, none of the House of Commons Ministers could claim that I was ignorant of the Commons procedures. After all I had been a Whip, Chief Whip, junior Minister and senior Minister there for nearly twenty-five years. Second, I was a sufficiently senior Minister in the Government at least to ensure that my House of Lords point of view was heard loud and clear. Few of my colleagues will deny that I certainly used that opportunity. But I hope they would agree that I recognized my side of the bargain. If I was to be credible in saying what I could not achieve, I had to make sure that once I accepted an assignment I would deliver.

It quickly became clear to me that we were bound to lose some divisions in the House of Lords. In fact, the Government suffered more defeats in my time than in that of my predecessors, although I think I can claim that this had something to do with the controversial nature of some of the legislation and indeed with the background of the large Commons majority. I tried to make use of defeats to obtain compromises and concessions from my colleagues in the Commons which would improve the Bills. I think in general that worked well, although I have lived to regret some of the results of my pressurizing.

I recognized above all that throughout this work I had to preserve the good will and understanding of my Cabinet colleagues in the House of Commons. If I could do that, then I would be ensuring not only that the Bills concerned might be improved but also that the House of Lords was fulfilling its role as a revising chamber.

The job of the House of Lords in its amendments to Bills is to ask the Commons to think again. If that spirit of compromise between the two Houses works properly, the Government in the House of Commons, when considering the Lords' amendments, will try to make some concessions. If it does so, then I maintain that the House of Lords, even if it is not fully satisfied, should accept the position when the measure returns to it. If it gains no such concession, I would hope that even then the House of Lords would exercise considerable care before throwing the particular amendment back to the House of Commons with a further defeat. Of course the House of Lords would be within its constitutional rights in doing so, but I believe that the system can only work in the spirit of mutual compromise. I am glad to say that it always did so during my period of leadership.

So far I have concentrated on the House of Lords' legislative work, upon which most attention is focused. There is another side to which all too little publicity is given. These are the general debates on important issues of the day. The House of Lords by its nature and composition is an excellent forum for well-informed discussion. The debates are conducted in a calm atmosphere and individual speeches are seldom interrupted. Those taking part in them are, in the main, people who are experienced and knowledgeable on the subject, particularly since the introduction of life peers. There are in truth few topics on which such qualities are not exhibited. The members include, in no order of priority, ex-Governors of the Bank of England, ex-Chiefs of the Defence Staff, leaders of many industries, ex-trade union leaders, ex-Chairmen of nationalized industries and broadcasting organizations, leaders of the legal profession at all levels, leaders in university life, those with considerable interests and knowledge in agriculture and forestry. Taken together, such people represent a most formidable group and a remarkable fund of knowledge of our nation's affairs. Nor is this list in any way exclusive. Alas, these debates are seldom fully reported in the newspapers because they are overshadowed by matters of current political controversy which have more news value.

It was for this reason, among others, that soon after I became Leader my old friend, Christopher Soames, a former Leader of the House, came to talk to me about televising debates in the chamber. He was a great enthusiast and had already raised the subject. His remarks fell on extremely fertile ground, for I had long been a strong supporter of televising Parliament in general. I had never succeeded in converting Margaret Thatcher or my parliamentary colleagues as a whole to television for the House of Commons. But the House of Lords seemed different, in that surely we could not lose by an experiment. After all, the arguments about encouraging uproar and bad behaviour which held force in the House of Commons clearly did not apply in the House of Lords. Anyway, more publicity could only do us good, particularly as far as the serious debates and the most valuable work of the Lords' Select Committees were concerned.

I therefore encouraged him to go ahead and promised my active support. Accordingly, Christopher Soames introduced a debate on the subject on 8 December 1983, when the House voted by seventy-four to twenty-four in favour of the principle of televising its proceedings. A committee was set up composed of supporters and opponents of the project under that most valuable House of Lords figure, the Chairman of Committees, Lord Aberdare. As a result of their report, the details for an experimental period of approximately six months were authorized on 27 November 1984. The experiment began on 23 January 1985 and on 12 May 1986 the House voted to continue to allow television in.

It is said that the programmes are watched by up to 300,000 viewers. Of course these figures are modest, but I feel they show that the programmes are valuable. Certainly they have increased knowledge of the House of Lords' work and thus an appreciation of it. All in all, I would claim that the televising of its proceedings has given the House of Lords some extra popularity with no adverse effect.

It is this practical experience which makes me sceptical of changing the composition of the House of Lords as it is today. I believe that the introduction of life peers gave the House a new look. No one starting afresh could ever devise a House of Lords with its present membership. But in its strange way it works. I understand the feelings expressed by Peter Carrington and others on the merits of an elected chamber, but I believe their reason is faulty for one major consideration. Surely experience with all assemblies – of which the most recent is the European Parliament – shows that the moment their members are elected they demand more powers. That, of course, is exactly what worries many Members in the House of Commons and I believe what basically caused the failure of the House of Lords Bill in 1967. They do not wish to concede more powers to a second chamber. If, once elected, the second chamber does not get those powers, it becomes a pale shadow of the main elected chamber and its members become disgruntled. In any event, I believe that such an elected chamber would always remain a poor relation if it competed with the House of Commons. The present House of Lords, as it is not elected, cannot compete and certainly does not seek to do so. It has a different role and therein lies its strength.

I would be prepared to consider the possibility of an election among the hereditary peers to choose a limited number of their colleagues to serve in the House of Lords. This has been done in the past by Scottish peers. I am certain that even such a measure would raise considerable difficulties, particularly as far as party balance is concerned.

However, if such an arrangement could be sensibly worked out, the result would be a House of Lords membership probably close to the existing number of peers who are active in its proceedings. Personally, I would not go even as far as that, but I certainly would go no further for the reasons I have given.

Government at the Centre

Leadership of the House of Lords is not an official Government position on its own. It is normally combined with one of the great offices of State. In 1983 I once again became Lord President of the Council, eleven years after I had given up that office on going to Ireland. I found the work with the Privy Council Office as agreeable as ever.

My immediate predecessors had also undertaken the job of Minister for the Civil Service. I was quite certain that this was not the job for me if I was going to lead the Lords effectively in the difficult circumstances of a large Commons majority and also help the Prime Minister, as was her wish. Accordingly, I set up a small office in the Cabinet Office and became known as Deputy Prime Minister, although there is no provision for such an appointment in our constitution. Whatever I was called, I knew well what was required of me now that I had been relieved of the immensely detailed work at the Home Office. I had to work closely with the Prime Minister and her office and, with her authority, to play a major role in the Cabinet side of Government. In this way I could take some of the detailed work off her shoulders, particularly in the chairing of various Cabinet committees.

Over the years this role developed and, as it did so, it put a considerable administrative strain on my small Private Office of four officials. Since I retired there has been much comment on the amount of responsibility I took on. It was only through those in this office and the excellent Cabinet Secretariat that such a role was possible. If therefore I did perform a valuable function, then this was greatly due to my staff and in particular to my three Principal Private Secretaries during this period, Janet Lewis-Jones, Joan MacNaughton from the Home Office, and Mike Eland from the Customs and Excise Department.

During my ministerial career I had never appeared particularly willing to be served by a woman as a Principal Private Secretary. Perhaps this was because I had a fairly formidable female surrounding at home, with a wife and four daughters. There was therefore much amusement in Whitehall about the collapse of my male chauvinism with two female Principal Private Secretaries. But I soon learnt what a wise surrender (if that is the right word) it was. Janet Lewis-Jones and Joan MacNaughton were absolutely first-class in every way. Finally, Mike Eland had the task of reconverting me to male society. No one could have done it with more efficiency, charm and skill. He saw me right through my illness and up to my resignation. I am deeply grateful to them all, as well as to all those who served in my office with such devotion. They even learnt to read my handwriting!

During these years I also had the remarkable and rewarding experience of working with the organization at the centre of Government. This consists of the Prime Minister's own office at No.10 Downing Street and the Cabinet Office under the Secretary to the Cabinet. This whole area of Government has been brilliantly satirized in the *Yes, Minister* series on television. If any such portrayal is as greatly enjoyed by those who are being laughed at as it is by everyone else – and this series certainly is – it must be based on an element of truth. And up to a point it is. But naturally there is another and serious side to this story.

The whole structure of Government depends on the smooth working of this central organization. Clearly I cannot speak personally about the Downing Street staff's direct work for the Prime Minister, for the best of all possible reasons – I have never been Prime Minister. I do not therefore, for example, have a definite view on any changes in organization which might have the advantage of providing more back-up for a Prime Minister. But I have worked closely with a series of Private Secretaries in Downing Street at all levels. As a result, I am amazed at their skill in dealing with an enormous workload while at the same time showing great courtesy and understanding in their contacts with tiresome ministerial personalities, of whom no doubt I was on occasions one.

My role in Press handling, crudely referred to as 'Minister for banana skins', brought me into particularly close contact with Bernard Ingham, the Prime Minister's Chief Press Officer. He has an especially challenging task. Constant contact with Press correspondents means that he has to provide answers to all manner of difficult questions, often at very short notice. I found that he carried out these duties for the Prime Minister with skill and distinction.

There is, then, an important distinction to be drawn between the No.10 staff and the Cabinet Office. The former work directly for the Prime Minister, whereas the latter, under the Secretary to the Cabinet, serve the entire Cabinet. Of course, successive Secretaries to the Cabinet have naturally become close advisers and friends of the Prime Minister of the day. But the outstanding characters with whom I have been associated as Secretary to the Cabinet – Burke Trend, John Hunt, Robert Armstrong and Robin Butler – have always followed the tradition that they serve the whole Cabinet. I would be much surprised if any Cabinet Minister had ever sought their help or advice in vain. Of course, they may not have liked the advice when they got it, but it would certainly have been as disinterested as possible.

The officials in the Cabinet Office are seconded from Government departments at various levels and serve there for limited periods. They gain a wide experience of Government which must be advantageous to them in their subsequent careers, for many have reached senior positions in their departments.

I have mentioned this organization in some detail because I regard a knowledge and appreciation of it as important in any successful ministerial career. I have always taken the view that if a Minister is to get the best value out of his Civil Service back-up, he must seek a mutual understanding with the officials concerned. For example, I have never made any secret of the fact that I like to work through personal contact and discussion rather than through the detailed study of briefs, however brilliantly written. Many civil servants find this way of working difficult at first, for they are by nature and training writers rather than talkers. I hardly need add that politicians are usually formed in the exact opposite mould.

Civil servants perhaps need to be reminded sometimes that they normally write their briefs during their working day and that the Ministers have to read them late at night or early in the morning. But of one thing I am quite clear: efficiency in Cabinet committees depends on Ministers mastering their briefs. All those who have sat with me on such committees have witnessed my mounting irritation as some Minister carefully reads out a dreary departmental brief which he obviously only partially understands. Little did they know that the efficient Cabinet Secretariat had already briefed me on the views of the department concerned.

It was during these same years that my own mastery of briefs was put severely to the test. I became directly involved in the economic field, for which I have little natural aptitude. That did not mean that I was not a careful student of the running of the economy from a political standpoint. However, essentially pragmatic by nature, I had never been greatly interested in economic doctrines. I had always minded far more about the effect of any particular economic policies on the lives of ordinary people. I suppose this would classify me as a 'Wet' in modern parlance. On the other hand, I know that I constantly disappointed the so-called 'Wets' for not standing against some economic decisions, particularly in the early 1980s. They believed that I was sacrificing my convictions out of excessive loyalty to the Prime Minister. There may have been some truth in that accusation, because I had made up my mind that, having set out on a course of firm monetary discipline under Geoffrey Howe as Chancellor of the Exchequer, it would be folly not to follow it through. The fact that Nigel Lawson has after all so successfully built on the foundations that Geoffrey Howe laid, makes me feel that on balance I was right. I certainly believe that the country and our party owe much to Geoffrey Howe for his courage in taking some painful economic decisions during his time. If I have a regret it is that I did not press for a more co-ordinated strategy backed by more money for inner cities immediately after the riots in 1981. Perhaps I was too easily put off by the fear of appearing to reward riots and by the risk of wasting money through lack of sufficient advanced planning. But as the original careful policies began to show results in increased prosperity, I became a strong supporter of Nigel Lawson as Chancellor of the Exchequer. He has certainly not disappointed me.

As the economy improved and prosperity increased, the pressures for more public expenditure grew. As a result, I became involved more closely with the economy as Chairman of what has become known as the Star Chamber. Basically this was instituted as a means of settling arguments between the Treasury and the spending departments on their targets without involving the entire Cabinet. There can be no doubt that such arguments are best settled in small groups, but in the event of continuing disagreement the Cabinet as a whole has to take the final decision, particularly as it is the Cabinet which sets the overall target.

The system as developed has some disadvantages, in that the group is not in a position to judge priorities between departments. Nevertheless, I think it does provide a useful function which saves time and tedious argument in the Cabinet itself.

The first step has to be individual negotiations between the departments and the Chief Secretary to the Treasury. Normally most of the departments settle at this stage, and it is only the most difficult problems that are left to the Star Chamber. Indeed, in the last two years the Star Chamber itself has not been required at all, and that is as it should be. But if the Chief Secretary and the department concerned cannot resolve an argument, then the Chairman of the Star Chamber is assisted by other Ministers, particularly those without a department or those who have settled their claims already.

Detailed dispute on the figures then takes place. Naturally, on occasions, these can lead to strong differences of opinion. It was the job of the Chairman, as I saw it, to preserve good will and hopefully some sense of humour. After all, it was important for us all to remember that we were on the same side and in the same Government. On the whole I hope my colleagues feel in retrospect that the meetings were conducted in such a spirit.

There was also another requirement, one that was both more important and much harder to meet. This was the need for complete confidentiality. It was one thing for the conflicting arguments to be conducted between colleagues in private, but it was quite another, and highly damaging, for the rival claims to be set out in the Press. Alas, this did happen on occasions, to the detriment of sensible compromise solutions. Even the most passionate supporters of open Government must surely appreciate that any organization is entitled to some confidential opportunities to settle detailed financial priorities, without the assistance of the mobilized pressure groups that are inseparable from public discussions.

For these reasons I disliked publicity for the Star Chamber and, as Chairman, shunned it completely. Indeed, it was a strange feature of my work inside the Government at this time that my success depended not upon good publicity but on trying to keep my name out of the Press, and certainly off the television screens.

Fortunately, publicity for another of my tasks was unlikely, since the subject matter was totally incomprehensible to the general public and only dimly understood by most of those concerned with it. That was the annual settlement of details affecting the Rate Support Grant. Each year that I was involved I felt sorry for the officials at the Department of the Environment, and indeed for those in the local authorities, who had to understand and work it. I was once complimented on my grasp of the details. No greater tribute could possibly have been given to the officials in the Cabinet Office who briefed me.

Paradoxically, another of my assignments which received much publicity was greeted with amusement and cartoons, because of my assumed total innocence of the subject. That was my chairmanship of the Government committee on AIDS. My friends pulled my leg mercilessly. My daughters recounted with glee my early lectures to them as children on the facts of life, and these stories undoubtedly gained in the telling. On top of that, whenever I went to a party or reception, people came up and talked to me about nothing else. But I bore all this stoically because for once any publicity was good publicity, for public appreciation of this most serious problem is crucial. Even if my chairmanship created amusement among my friends, there is certainly nothing amusing about the dangers of AIDS as an epidemic.

And so these were interesting years for me, as I spent my time between detailed Cabinet work and the House of Lords management. Of course, as a senior Cabinet Minister, I was also involved in some of the more publicized events of the period, even if I was not a direct participant. The first of these was the prolonged miners' strike which, after all the past confrontations, had such a profound effect on the miners' union and its relations with the Coal Board and the Government. No doubt it also contributed to a shift in the balance of power inside the trade union movement.

Those of us who were close to events can have had no doubt about the skill with which Peter Walker, as Secretary of State for Energy, and Ian MacGregor, as Chairman of the Coal Board, played their particular roles. Arthur Scargill, on the other hand, made numerous mistakes, particularly in the handling of his own members. In this way, he split his own union and forfeited the support of many of his colleagues in the trade union movement. From his point of view these were fatal errors.

Like all such confrontations, success for the nation in surviving this deliberate challenge was not achieved without unhappy strife and bitterness within communities and between families. No one can have enjoyed the scenes on television of pitched battles between the police and the miners on the picket lines. Nevertheless, in view of my time as Home Secretary, I had particular reason to feel admiration, as did so many others in the country, for the conduct of the police. Thank goodness we had enough policemen available. Thank goodness they were well trained and organized for civil disturbances. It is sad for the nation when police have to be used in such circumstances, but nothing can detract from their great individual courage. The confrontation of the miners' strike had to be met by the Government and successfully overcome.

The next incident to which I refer was, on the other hand, a totally unnecessary diversion. That was what became known as the Westland crisis at the end of 1985 and the beginning of 1986. The issue was the future of the Westland Aircraft Company, which was in a serious financial position.

Much has been written about the Westland incident, which developed into a damaging row from the Government's point of view. It also occupied, in my opinion, an absurd amount of parliamentary time and Press comment. I am, however, a bad judge of the whole affair, because for once in my life I was in no way a conciliator but an absolutely committed supporter of one side of the argument. As a result I hated the row and took little part in it. The incident has been so extensively described that I will not seek to dwell on the background details.

Suffice it to say that the Westland Aircraft Company was a most important supplier of helicopters to the Ministry of Defence. It was also a major employer of labour in the South-West of England. It had been in increasing financial trouble, mainly due to a worldwide slide in the market for civil helicopters. Its problems increased in 1985, partly due to Indian unwillingness to confirm an order for twenty-one helicopters. There were also management problems in the company, which were being tackled by a powerful new Chairman in Sir John Cuckney.

There was general acceptance that some rescue plan was necessary if the company was to survive and the jobs of its workforce to be saved. The argument centred on the best plan to adopt. Having examined the position, Sir John Cuckney concluded that the best option was a merger with the giant American helicopter company, Sikorski. The other option was a European consortium of helicopter manufacturers who would bid for the company.

As 1985 drew to a close, I could never understand why the Government should dispute the Westland Board's judgment under Sir John Cuckney. Nor do I believe for a moment that the European consortium would ever really have got its act together and made a bid for the company. Of course I understand Michael Heseltine's cherished vision of a European defence policy, and thus his advocacy of the European consortium. But I did not myself believe in its feasibility in practice.

I became increasingly bored by the argument and irritated

by what I regarded as an unnecessary and potentially damaging controversy. Since then I have blamed myself for not helping the Prime Minister more by stressing the vital doctrine of Cabinet collective responsibility, in which I am a passionate believer. I should have realized earlier that Michael Heseltine was labouring under what he regarded as a genuine grievance, at a time when I thought he had merely become obsessed with his own proposals and arguments.

I was thus surprised and amazed when he decided to walk out of the Cabinet. I regretted his departure, because it takes all sorts to make a Cabinet and his flair and personality were bound to be a loss. Yet he had to accept the consequences of his own action, which at various stages in the controversy he must have contemplated.

I minded far more about the subsequent resignation of Leon Brittan. He had been my Minister of State at the Home Office and my successor as Home Secretary. I knew him to be not only an exceptionally clever man but a wholly honourable and intensely loyal person. No one could ever have accused him in the Westland crisis, or at any other time, of failing to honour the principle of Cabinet responsibility. But in a tragic way he became a victim as the consequence of its failure. I regard the whole affair as a salutary lesson to all Cabinets of the dangers they face if they allow themselves to conduct internal arguments in public. Otherwise it was one of those incidents which, despite the furore of the time, had no lasting impact.

In the early summer of 1986 there came a fascinating diversion from my normal Government work. I was invited to lead an Inter-Parliamentary Union delegation on a visit to the Soviet Union. This delegation was to return the visit to Britain of a similar party from Russia, led by Mikhail

Gorbachev in December 1984, shortly before he took over power.

Our party consisted of seven Tories, six Labour members and one Liberal, together with a first-class interpreter in Richard Pollock, senior House of Commons Clerk Clifford Boulton, Donald Pike from the IPU and my Principal Private Secretary, Joan MacNaughton. Denis Healey was my Deputy Leader and Alan Beith was the Liberal representative. I think it could fairly be said that as a group we represented a wide spectrum of political opinion, but as it happened we all seemed to get on well together, which added to the enjoyment of an important visit.

We were in the Soviet Union from 23 May to 2 June and visited Moscow, Leningrad and Tbilisi in Georgia. From the beginning it was clear that Mikhail Gorbachev was personally determined that our visit should be a success, because he had clearly appreciated his reception when he came to Britain on what was one of his earliest foreign trips. This made a great deal of difference to our stay, as any difficulties arising in the Soviet Union are quickly solved at the top. We were assured that many bureaucratic roadblocks lie in your route otherwise. I shall refer to some of the highlights of our tour, not in any chronological order.

Naturally, the most important occasion was our meeting with Mikhail Gorbachev. I was to see him first, on my own, and give him a personal message from the Prime Minister. My meeting, and the subsequent one with the whole delegation, took place in a huge gilded hall in the Kremlin. I reflected that it had probably looked much the same in the days of the Tzar. Our excellent Ambassador, Brian Cartledge, and I waited outside two heavy ornate doors. Just before Mikhail Gorbachev was due to arrive these were swung open, and we waited at one end of the hall while he and his staff entered at the other, at least some hundred yards away. I was immediately struck by the presence of this comparatively short figure as he walked, with considerable poise and dignity, towards us. There was no doubt in my mind at that moment that Mikhail Gorbachev was a powerful personality. When he reached us he proved to be both friendly and charming, yet I was aware of a steely determination in the background. He was obviously a tough character, but on reflection I realized that he would have to be so, in order to reach the position he now occupied.

In our short discussion he was outgoing and forceful, but became immediately defensive if any sensitive issue arose. This was particularly true of the Chernobyl disaster, which had recently occurred. He was obviously pleased when I offered, as instructed, any technical help from Britain that might be of value.

When the whole delegation gathered for talks with him, we united on the subject of human rights and David Crouch, Chairman of the IPU, put forward the representations which we had promised for the release of certain political prisoners. Mikhail Gorbachev's mood changed abruptly to one of petulant irritation but, largely because of the quiet way in which David Crouch handled the issue, the Soviet leader did not take offence, as we had feared.

We spent about three hours with him and he clearly enjoyed the discussion. At that stage he was giving little away about his own future disarmament proposals and, as he knew that he had a British delegation in front of him which comprised several different shades of opinion on defence, he was more interested in probing our own views and exposing our divisions. Above all, he showed that he was a formidable advocate of his own position and that,

337

unlike previous Russian leaders, he thoroughly relished an argument. We came away with the knowledge that he was an immensely forceful and outgoing politician who would continue to fascinate and attract Western observers, in marked contrast with many of the aged, inflexible Russian leaders of the recent past. On the other hand, none of us was left in any doubt about his underlying determination and toughness – features which have been publicly demonstrated on many different occasions since – and it was fascinating to witness them in action.

While we were in Moscow we paid two interesting visits. On the Sunday we went to Zagorsk, over thirty miles away and a centre of the Russian Orthodox Church. We found large numbers of Russians at prayer in well-maintained, highly decorated chapels. We also met there by chance the members of a British Council of Churches delegation led by the Archbishop of York. Closer to Moscow, we visited Star City, and the Yuri Gagarin Cosmonaut Training Centre, and met some Soviet cosmonauts. The training establishment was well equipped and the living accommodation for those working there, in a large wooded area, looked much better than those we had passed elsewhere. Clearly there was no shortage of funds for this privileged enterprise.

While in Moscow we had talks with various Ministers, did some sightseeing and were given the opportunity to see the ballet from the President's box at the Bolshoi Theatre. The members of the delegation convinced themselves that I was sitting in the Tzar's chair and Denis Healey in Rasputin's, which caused great amusement.

From Moscow we travelled to Leningrad by the night sleeper train. There are only double sleepers on this train, but I was privileged to be given one of them to myself, while the rest of the delegation had to share. It was therefore somewhat ironic that our rather dull and uncomfortable journey, for everyone except me, should have been described at home by the *Daily Mail* under the headline 'Whitelaw Rides Red Love Train'.

Apart from the Kremlin and Red Square, Moscow is not an attractive or exciting city. It has the appearance of having grown up as a sprawling village. The Kremlin, though, is a magnificent Tzar's palace which has been beautifully preserved in its original state.

By contrast Leningrad is a really beautiful city with lovely buildings full of great treasures. It is also steeped in history from the time of Peter the Great, who built it, right through the October Revolution to the appalling privations experienced during the siege of the city in the 1939–45 war. It is a moving experience to visit the great memorial to all those who died in the 900-day siege – some 640,000. As a delegation, we walked the long distance up to the memorial itself, where I laid a wreath. When one hears at first hand the experiences of family suffering during this siege and the courage with which they were borne, one realizes that the ordinary Russians' dread of war and longing for peace is totally genuine. No doubt this makes them easily susceptible to propaganda about war-mongers in other countries, but I am sure that the feelings in themselves are utterly authentic.

We spent some time looking round the Hermitage and the beautiful palaces outside Leningrad, which originally belonged to the Tzars and their relations. All the buildings are beautifully maintained and indeed, in many cases, are being exceptionally well restored. Equally the treasures in the Hermitage are displayed with great care and taste. It is astonishing to see the pride which a Communist regime today so obviously finds in its history and, indeed, in the possessions of the Tzarist regime. I look forward to returning to Leningrad some time.

Our departure from Leningrad to the airport for our flight to Tbilisi seemed likely to ensure that, far from returning to Leningrad, our days would end there. Our usual motorcade dashed madly from one end of Leningrad to the other at over eighty miles an hour, our cars leaping into the air as we hit canal bridges. It was, moreover, a busy afternoon in the city, and sitting in the front car I simply could not see on many occasions how we could possibly miss old people on the road as we swept past them. My companion, a Leningrad leader, appeared totally unmoved and his confidence was justified in the end. He must have regarded me as a highly nervous passenger.

That night we arrived in Tbilisi for the really enjoyable stay which traditional Georgian hospitality ensures. Up till then we had suffered in one way, and perhaps gained in another, from Mikhail Gorbachev's determined campaign against alcohol. The days of endless vodka toasts at lunches and dinners had gone and had been replaced by sips of fruit juice. We wondered what would happen in Georgia, with its fine wines and renowned hospitality. We did not have long to wait. On arrival we were given an official dinner. At the end I turned politely to our splendid host and thanked him for an excellent meal (at which fruit juice was still the order of the day). Quick as a flash came the reply – equally speedily interpreted – 'No good without wine'. He added that this was an official dinner, at which drink was prohibited, but assured me that our subsequent meals would be unofficial and that we would drink wine. And he ended, 'We in Georgia have very good wine.' He was as good as his word.

We spent our time in Georgia seeing the lovely countryside and many of the traditional and historic old buildings.

We visited museums and, for a modern equivalent, the Palace of Solemnities, where elaborate weddings and anniversaries are celebrated, strictly without any spiritual content. The effect was somewhat unnerving. We were also taken to a wine company, where we had a splendid tasting session.

Lastly, on the Sunday before we left for the airport, we were scheduled to visit the works of a noted Georgian sculptor. He had a beautiful house high up on a hill overlooking Tbilisi. Some of us were not particularly enthusiastic about this visit, as our interest in sculpture was limited, but we soon found that a study of sculpture was not the real purpose. We were given a sumptuous lunch with many different wines. I explained to our host that my home in England was close to a fine hilly area, the Lake District. 'Oh,' he said, 'you and I are men of the hills. We will share the best wine of the hills which I can produce.' Much to his fury, Denis Healey was unable to claim this distinction and had to be content with a greatly inferior wine. Refreshed by the wine of the hills I found that the return flight to Moscow was a short one indeed.

Back in Moscow we had further talks, including a meeting with Andrei Gromyko, who was nostalgic about Britain and asked me to give his good wishes to the Queen, which on my return I naturally did. We expected that in his new role as President he would want to concentrate on Home Affairs, but in fact he was only too ready to be drawn back into his old Foreign Affairs role. Here he showed that even if Mikhail Gorbachev was changing Russian attitudes, he was living firmly in the old days of the Cold War between East and West. He was careful not to appear at odds with Gorbachev, but it was pretty obvious that their approaches contrasted greatly. In view of their respective ages and experience this was probably not surprising. Subsequent events may perhaps indicate that the differences were indeed more fundamental than they appeared at the time.

And so we returned home after an enjoyable and, I think, most valuable visit. My main task was to ensure that our delegation helped to continue the process of building increased understanding and co-operation between the Soviet Union and Great Britain. Modestly, I believe that our delegation as a whole felt that we had made some steady progress. Personally I had been in Russia only once before, in 1964, and then as a very junior Minister. I found that this visit twenty-two years later, at a very different level, reinforced my impression of the genuine warmth and feeling of the Russian people. Despite all our major differences as nations and our contrasting ways of life, I believe we can cautiously increase our mutual exchanges to the benefit of both nations.

My final reflection on this period – and indeed, to some extent, on my whole time spent working with Margaret Thatcher – is to consider how two such different people managed to get on so well together. Of course, as Prime Minister and Party Leader, it was in her hands to decide how she treated me and used me. I must therefore say at the start that it was her personal kindness and constant understanding which gave me the opportunity to help her. For my part, I hope I always remembered that she was the Leader, who had to face all the ultimate pressures and take the final decisions. Life at the top is very lonely and extremely demanding. Anyone in an immediately subordinate position should never forget the exceptional pressures which a Leader faces, and the personal reactions which they provoke. I believe we both started from these particular positions, and understood them.

Second, we both had a passionate belief in our party and so in its Government. We probably had somewhat different perceptions of how we would like to see it react in particular circumstances. On such occasions I would certainly have the chance to argue my case, but of course I had to accept that in the final event Margaret Thatcher was the Leader and had the ultimate right to decide. I do not think I ever left her in any doubt that I understood that relationship.

Third, we both knew that we were very different people with varying backgrounds, interests and thus reactions. As a result we had never been close personal friends before we were brought together in this particular political relationship.

I am often asked what it is like serving a woman Leader. In general I would say it is no different from serving a man, except that it would be futile not to appreciate that women are always ready to use their feminine charms, and indeed their feminine qualities, to get their way. Margaret Thatcher is no exception, nor could anyone fail to recognize her great personal charm. Perhaps it was easy for me to work with a woman as I had been brought up by my mother and spent much time alone with her. No one who knew her could deny that my mother was a powerful character.

I was reminded the other day by the hostess who brought my mother and Margaret Thatcher together of their only meeting not long before my mother died. No one knew how it would turn out, since my mother was immensely protective of me and, naturally perhaps, proud of my performance. She was therefore very suspicious of this woman Margaret Thatcher, who had been preferred to her son as

Leader of the Conservative Party. In the event, I am told, for I certainly was not present, that they got on famously together. My mother subsequently became an immense fan of Margaret Thatcher, even to the extent of upbraiding me for failing to support her more effectively. Alas, she died before she could see Margaret Thatcher as Prime Minister and her son as Home Secretary. I know she would have been far more critical of the latter than the former.

On another topic, I am asked if Margaret Thatcher ever listens to points of view other than her own. This question, with its perception of her, angers me, for it is grossly unfair. I think she probably enjoys an argument more than most people, and the more vigorous it is, the better, as far as she is concerned. She is by nature a conviction politician and so has very strong views, yet she can certainly be swayed and influenced by good arguments in the final event. I wish the critics would realize that no one could have presided over such a successful team as Leader unless they had been prepared to take account of internal discussions. Of course it is not easy to convert her, but that should surely be the case with a powerful Leader. She is certainly the type of chairman who leads from the front and from the start of a discussion makes no secret of her own feelings and views. But all chairmen have their different methods, even if most successful ones like to get their way in the end. I know that I am totally different from Margaret Thatcher in the way that I handle meetings, and that some people regard me as too conciliatory. But I have to acknowledge the truth of the remark which Norman Tebbit alleges that I made to him: 'My image is emollient – and so I am, but only when I am getting my own way.'

I suspect too that Margaret Thatcher did not always find me easy to deal with. She had to experience – which I must say she did stoically on occasions – my sudden and unexpected outbursts of rage when crossed in argument. She often accepted, although I imagine she sometimes found it irritating, my cautious approach to parliamentary difficulties and tendency towards compromise. She seldom interfered with my conduct of sensitive Home Office issues, although she must have disliked some of my decisions on the treatment of offenders, and perhaps particularly on broadcasting matters where we have never quite seen eye to eye.

In particular we tended to have different views on the bias of BBC programmes. Naturally, Prime Ministers feel particularly sensitive to criticism which they consider unfair, since they are constantly in the firing line. My feelings about the BBC, on the other hand, were conditioned by my experience in dealing with broadcasting matters as Opposition Chief Whip during the 1960s. When I argued our party's case at that time I felt that I was treated most fairly by the BBC, sometimes to the intense irritation of Harold Wilson and the then Labour Government. As a result, I could never agree with those, certainly a majority in my own party, who consistently believed that the BBC was wholly biased against Conservative Governments. After all, I had heard the same arguments from Labour Ministers when they were in Government. I came to feel that there was something more important than constant arguments about bias, which were inevitable as the immense power of television increased, and that was the maximum possible independence of the BBC from Government and party political interference. Upon such independence the BBC's national and, indeed, worldwide reputation is based.

My experience and so perhaps inevitably my views were

very different from those of the Prime Minister and the overwhelming majority of my colleagues. And so when there were controversies over different television or radio programmes, I tended to come out as a defender of the BBC. In addition to my natural instincts, I also felt that as Home Secretary it was my duty to stand up for their point of view. This led to spirited discussions on occasions. As is well known, the Prime Minister is a regular listener to the BBC's *Today* programme and, waking early as she does, is extremely well informed of every detail in the news each morning. So she naturally came to some meetings with that day's programme in the forefront of her mind. I have to say that on occasions I wished I had stronger grounds on which to stand up for a BBC programme. I recognize that I had some bad mornings when I abandoned defence of the indefensible. But generally I stood my ground for I felt it was good for me and for my other colleagues, including the Prime Minister, to test our views against each other. Anyway, we probably all rather enjoyed the arguments and perhaps sometimes they did affect subsequent Government reactions.

I suppose the Prime Minister listened to me most on parliamentary and party matters, where I obviously had a great deal of experience, and least on economic and foreign policy, where I did not claim any special knowledge and where other senior Ministers bore the responsibility.

She was always very. generous with her time in giving me opportunities privately to express my feelings on any subject. She also consulted me frequently and kept me fully informed on major issues. I therefore seldom had any reason to argue with her in wider ministerial meetings and usually intervened only if I felt I could be of general assistance.

I can only conclude with a general observation. Margaret

Thatcher is a remarkable and powerful Leader in every way. Of course, like everyone in her position, she has her critics and detractors. No doubt she has made mistakes, but no one can deny her incredible achievements, nor should anyone neglect the great contribution that Denis Thatcher has made to them, as the country as a whole has increasingly recognized.

An Unexpected Finale

In the early months of 1987, as is inevitable in the fourth year of any Parliament, speculation started about the date of the next general election. The Government was in a strong position, thanks largely to Nigel Lawson's excellent handling of the economy. The broad mass of the population was better off and knew it. Furthermore, the Prime Minister had just come back from a visit to Moscow which was highly successful and greatly enhanced her already dominant position as a world leader. She had established a good relationship with Mikhail Gorbachev. Discussions between the great powers, the United States and the Soviet Union, on arms control were proceeding hopefully. As a result, prospects for world peace were more encouraging. Peace and prosperity form a sound basis for any Government at a general election.

In the event the decision to hold a June election, thus ending uncertainty and speculation, was an easy one. Suddenly I realized that this would be the first general election since 1950 at which I would not be standing – a bizarre feeling. Margaret Thatcher asked me to help at Central Office, and indeed to chair a committee which provided answers for all our candidates on difficult questions of policy. We generated, as always, an enormous quantity of paper and I am assured that at any rate some of our answers were valuable and appreciated by the candidates. In addition, I spoke in quite a large number of constituencies. But, compared with previous general elections, I had an easy time and even managed to watch the British–USA Amateur Walker Cup golf match at Sunningdale.

My reflections on the campaign are therefore more like those of a spectator, even if a very involved spectator, than ever they had been in the past. We Conservatives made a slow start, perhaps because we were not as sure as usual about the real nature of the opposition. I suspect we imagined that the idea of the Alliance with two Leaders would be more dangerous than it in fact turned out to be, and that it might replace Labour as our main opponent, particularly in the south and west of England. We ought not to have been so deluded, for we now know as a result of subsequent events that the two Leaders – and, indeed, the two parties – were basically unhappy bedfellows. I think we feared that they might make a show of unity for the limited period of an election. There was also no doubt that we were surprised by the power of the media approach from the Labour Party, and indeed by their packaging of Neil Kinnock.

However, once we settled down to standing on the strong ground of peace and prosperity, and the risk of losing all through Labour's economic – and particularly its hopeless defence – policies, the result was not in doubt. Success in getting this message across, with Margaret Thatcher at her considerable best, no doubt gained us extra seats during the concluding stages of the election and provided a very large majority in the final event. I thus have little time for all the arguments about the details of the organization during our campaign. When a team has won, the leaders are entitled to the credit. This certainly goes for Margaret Thatcher herself and for Norman Tebbit, as Chairman of the Party.

In the autumn, after the general election, I began to think about my own future. I was going to be seventy the following June and had always felt that this was the moment to go. Curiously, some time in October I said to my excellent London doctor, John Gayner, that I wanted him to tell me the instant he felt that the time had come. He promised to do so. And so I forgot about it and left the matter to him.

Even more strangely, a nagging doubt kept on coming back to me. I was genuinely in two minds about my future. I was very happy in the House of Lords and greatly enjoyed being its Leader. I did not find my Government work too arduous because I was well served and, I suppose, experienced in the job.

I do not remember experiencing any particular stress during November and early December, apart from the increasing number of social engagements inseparable from the approach of Christmas. Indeed, I recall only one occasion when I showed any indication of pressure.

For some time I had been worried about the size of the Government's legislative programme and the consequent strain that was being placed on both Houses of Parliament. This is an occupational disease as far as Governments with large majorities in the Commons are concerned. But as Chairman of the Cabinet Committee which planned the programme, I felt that my colleagues were pressing me too hard on this occasion, when we faced the highly contentious Community Charge, Education and Housing Bills. Looking back now that the programme has been completed, not without stress and strains, I think that perhaps I allowed myself to worry too much.

My feelings boiled over, as is so often the case, on a

completely unimportant occasion. Bertie Denham was arguing the case for some later sittings in the House of Lords in the weeks immediately ahead. I remember exploding quite unreasonably with the words, 'I simply can't stand these late sittings any longer. I am getting too old for it.' I do not suppose anybody at the meeting thought much of it, but I know at the time that I felt I was coming to the end of my tether. However I cursed myself inwardly for giving vent to such trivial feelings.

With the benefit of hindsight, I realize that my outburst must have been a sign of increasing strain. Yet in the days before my collapse I felt quite relaxed. My wife and I spent a quiet, and as always very happy, shooting weekend with Rory and Elizabeth More O'Ferrall at Elveden in Suffolk. We came quietly home to London on the Sunday evening.

On Monday 14 December I actually had some free time in the morning and went shopping with my wife to choose her Christmas present. I had lunch with Trevor Kavanagh of the *Sun* and, as he described it subsequently, had a quiet and frugal meal. In the afternoon I attended the House of Lords' sitting at the start, and then had a meeting with the party Leaders in the Lords. We had a friendly and relaxed discussion, departing in something of a pre-Christmas atmosphere.

I left soon afterwards and walked over to St Margaret's Church, Westminster, where I was to read one of the lessons at a carol service in aid of Westminster Hospital. This had been organized by the Wives of Westminster Committee, of which my wife is Chairman. I read the lesson feeling perfectly normal and returned to my seat.

Suddenly I started to cough. Alec Home, who was sitting beside me, said afterwards that it was a strange sort of cough. I sat down for the Speaker to read the next lesson and started to yawn compulsively. I remember thinking how rude this was when the Speaker was reading a lesson, but I could not stop and only hoped that nobody noticed. When the moment came to rise for the next carol I simply could not move.

Dr Richard Staughton, a leading consultant at Westminster Hospital, who had read a previous lesson, was sitting just across the aisle from me, as were two senior sisters from the Intensive Care Department. They knew what had happened, which I did not, and were beside me in a flash. Mercifully the service was just ending and I remember watching people leaving and staring at me in surprise. On the whole no one could have collapsed in more convenient circumstances. I was in an ambulance in what seemed to be a few minutes and was almost at once surrounded by doctors and nurses at Westminster Hospital, including – to my delight – my own doctor, John Gayner, whose presence was a great encouragement. Dr Gibberd, the leading neurologist at Westminster Hospital, looked after me with calm firmness and a total control which were most impressive and comforting. I shall always feel greatly indebted to him.

The feeling in my right hand came back, as did my speech. I was soon peacefully installed in bed surrounded by some delightful nurses, who were my faithful companions and friends through the next few days in hospital.

As I tried to sleep, which was naturally pretty impossible at that moment, I realized how lucky I had been to have all my faculties completely restored so soon. At the same time I began to consider what John Gayner would say to me in the morning. I thought I knew, and when he came early on he proved me right. 'You remember,' he said, 'what you mentioned to me in October?'

'Yes,' I replied.

'Then I am telling you now you have been very lucky to get away with a warning. You must retire as soon as possible.'

When he left I felt sad at the idea of leaving the Government, and grateful for all my luck in a career, and indeed in a life, which in so many ways had exceeded my wildest dreams.

I was roused from my reverie by a familiar voice in the corridor outside my room. 'Here comes the person who has made all that possible,' I said to myself. It was, of course, my wife.

Index

More Autobiography from Headline:

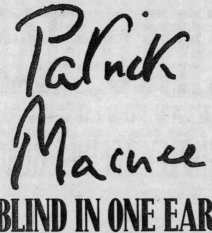

BLIND IN ONE EAR
AUTOBIOGRAPHY OF AN AVENGER
'Amusing and often painfully honest' *Daily Express*

The bowler hat. The rolled umbrella.
The bespoke suit. Patrick Macnee is known
to millions for his portrayal of that epitome of
the English gentleman, John Steed, in the
internationally successful television series *The
Avengers*. Born of aristocratic parents, he went
to prep school and Eton. But the conventions of
upper-class English life end there. Pa was a
drunkard and a gambler; Mama was a lesbian,
who moved in with her formidable lover Evelyn,
bringing her bemused, be-kilted son with her.
Expelled from Eton for running the school
'book', Patrick made his first tentative steps into
the footlights. The limelight took a little longer;
he did not achieve overnight cult status as
John Steed until he was nearly forty. The rest,
as they say, is history . . .

Witty, inventive, bizarre and eccentric, *Blind in
One Ear* is the extraordinary autobiography of
an extraordinary man.

'Rich in anecdotes . . . but what sets aside this
book is the quality of Patrick Macnee's writing
about his crazy childhood.'
Mail on Sunday

NON-FICTION/AUTOBIOGRAPHY   0 7472 3305 5   £3.99

CHILD STAR

AN AUTOBIOGRAPHY

SHIRLEY TEMPLE BLACK

'An extraordinary piece of work' *Daily Mail*

For the first time, Shirley Temple Black – the quintessential child star of the 30s and 40s – tells in her own words the extraordinary story of her life as an actress.

Starting her career at the tender age of three, she was soon performing alongside such stars as Gary Cooper, Cary Grant, Ginger Rogers and (her favourite) Bill 'Bojangles' Robinson. However, all was not always sugar-sweet aboard the Good Ship Lollipop: she was made to perform in exploitative movies by unscrupulous studio bosses; there were numerous kidnap threats and even a murder attempt against her; she made a disastrous teenage marriage to an incorrigible womaniser. Eventually, though, she found lasting love and happiness with ex-naval officer Charles Black, and waved goodbye to Hollywood for ever. Filled with revelations and personal anecdotes, CHILD STAR is at once candid, funny and poignant – and an inspiration to all.

'An awesome book, far richer than the average Hollywood apologia' *Sunday Times*

'Temple tells it like it was, with great good humour, more charity than is frequently warranted and healthy dollops of cynicism' *The Times*

NON-FICTION/AUTOBIOGRAPHY   0 7472 3303 9   £4.99

RICHARD
BRANSON

THE INSIDE STORY

MICK BROWN

"An excellent biography – engaging but far from idolatory" *Guardian*

ADVENTURE CAPITALIST

Unorthodox entrepreneur and City businessman, philanthropist and intrepid transatlantic yachtsman and balloonist: not yet forty, Richard Branson is all these and more. How did he achieve so much so quickly? What is the key to his success?

In his bestselling biography, Mick Brown examines Branson's life and analyses his highly idiosyncratic business techniques in dissecting the many elements that make up 'the Branson phenomenon'.

"Well researched and attractively written" *Observer*

"An important biography" *Daily Telegraph*

"That rarest of all things, a biography which meets its own claims to be both authorised and critical" *Sunday Times*

"Mick Brown has a good ear for choice anecdotes and an entertaining way of passing them on" *Guardian*

NON-FICTION/BIOGRAPHY   0 7472 3469 8   £4.99

A selection of bestsellers from Headline

FICTION		
TALENT	Nigel Rees	£3.99 ☐
A BLOODY FIELD BY SHREWSBURY	Edith Pargeter	£3.99 ☐
GUESTS OF THE EMPEROR	Janice Young Brooks	£3.99 ☐
THE LAND IS BRIGHT	Elizabeth Murphy	£3.99 ☐
THE FACE OF FEAR	Dean R Koontz	£3.50 ☐
NON-FICTION		
CHILD STAR	Shirley Temple Black	£4.99 ☐
BLIND IN ONE EAR	Patrick Macnee and Marie Cameron	£3.99 ☐
TWICE LUCKY	John Francome	£4.99 ☐
HEARTS AND SHOWERS	Su Pollard	£2.99 ☐
SCIENCE FICTION AND FANTASY		
WITH FATE CONSPIRE The Destiny Makers 1	Mike Shupp	£3.99 ☐
A DISAGREEMENT WITH DEATH	Craig Shaw Gardner	£2.99 ☐
SWORD & SORCERESS 4	Marion Zimmer Bradley	£3.50 ☐

All Headline books are available at your local bookshop or newsagent, or can be ordered direct from the publisher. Just tick the titles you want and fill in the form below. Prices and availability subject to change without notice.

Headline Book Publishing PLC, Cash Sales Department, PO Box 11, Falmouth, Cornwall TR10 9EN, England.

Please enclose a cheque or postal order to the value of the cover price and allow the following for postage and packing:
UK: 60p for the first book, 25p for the second book and 15p for each additional book ordered up to a maximum charge of £1.90
BFPO: 60p for the first book, 25p for the second book and 15p per copy for the next seven books, thereafter 9p per book
OVERSEAS & EIRE: £1.25 for the first book, 75p for the second book and 28p for each subsequent book.

Name ....

Address ....

....

....